Max Hafler

Max Hafler trained and worked as a professional actor for many years. He now works as a director, deviser, writer and lecturer. He was a resident voice teacher at Galway Youth Theatre for twelve years and taught voice in youth theatres all over Ireland for Youth Theatre Ireland (formerly the National Association of Youth Drama). He has taught ensemble and directed productions including many notable young people's Shakespeare productions. A successful playwright and adapter, he has written several plays for young people, including *Alien Nation*, *Battle Stations* and *This Means War!*

When the National University of Ireland, Galway, established drama courses in 2000, Max was invited to teach Voice and Chekhov Technique on their BA and MA programmes – and is still doing so. He runs Chekhov Training and Performance Ireland (www.chekhovtrainingandperformanceireland.com), and is the author of *Teaching Voice: Workshops for Young Performers*, also published by Nick Hern Books.

Max has worked in many applied drama areas with disability groups, with medical students, business students, schoolteachers and lecturers, giving him a full understanding of the issues that are faced by a facilitator when working within a particular group. He discusses his work extensively in his blog: www.maxhafler.wordpress.com

Max Hafler

WHAT COUNTRY, FRIENDS, IS THIS?

Directing Shakespeare with Young Performers

Max Hafler

NICK HERN BOOKS
London
www.nickhernbooks.co.uk

A Nick Hern Book

What Country, Friends, Is This?:
Directing Shakespeare with Young Performers
first published in Great Britain in 2021
by Nick Hern Books Limited,
The Glasshouse, 49a Goldhawk Road, London W12 8QP

Cover image: Gavin Alcorn Friel (Captain) and Fiona
Buckley (Viola) in *Twelfth Night*, photo by Max Hafler

Designed and typeset by Nick Hern Books
Printed and bound in Great Britain by Severn, Gloucester

A CIP catalogue record for this book is available
from the British Library

ISBN 978 1 84842 803 4

Contents

PART THREE
Moving Towards Performance:
Devising, Short Scenes and Soliloquies

Preface

You will find that, when it comes to acting and directing, I am a curious mixture of freedom and discipline. It is not always the discipline that should come first either. Sometimes spontaneity, imagination, openness and instinct need to predominate before you start learning about dealing with all the other technical attributes that enable good performance. It took me many years to realise that discipline and spontaneity need to be symbiotic. Acting is a strange thing; one of the things that attracted me to it as a child was that you didn't need to learn how to do *anything* before you could try it out, unlike the painstaking discipline of playing a musical instrument for instance. However, without *some* discipline and skill, performing Shakespeare is very challenging.

Working with young people on Shakespeare can produce incredible results, which is often, in many respects, better than work from professional companies. Too often for me, professional actors performing Shakespeare carry the great weight of history on their backs, a kind of cynical exhaustion which says, 'Yes, I know you have seen and heard this a thousand times.' They often do not play with freshness nor remember that their audience may not have seen the play. This problem is often compounded by conceptual directing where actors are manoeuvred into a concept rather than encouraged to respond creatively.

Of course, in some areas your young actors will not be as strong as a trained professional group, you will not have the same budget, the same talent pool, the same skills, the same amount of rehearsal time nor the same level of life experience. However, what you *will* have is an incredible energy waiting to be tapped, a strong sense of ensemble often totally lacking within some professional productions and an incredible joy and commitment to performing. If you can guide and support your group and expand these positive areas, at the same time as giving technical support along the way, then you and your group are going to have a great experience whether you're devising a project around a Shakespeare play, looking at some scenes, or mounting a full production.

I sincerely hope that this book will help you guide your young people, in whatever context you approach Shakespeare, whether in class, at youth theatre or at college, into this amazing material from centuries ago, which in many respects is as relevant now as it was then.

The idea that Shakespeare is not for the faint-hearted or only for a privileged few is a myth which still exists today. At the very least there are still many people who consider there are 'ways' of saying and performing it. When I was first introduced to Puck's 'My mistress with a monster is in love' at ten years old, I noticed that it was a lot easier than I thought it would be. Yes, there were some tricky words but the rattling rhythm and excitement of the piece thrilled me. As a young man who played Puck for me decades later in a youth theatre production remarked, 'I was scared of doing Shakespeare and now I'm not'. In fact, in many ways, once you get past understanding the language, Shakespeare is *easier* for young people because it is poetic and out of their immediate reality. It can really free the imagination and take them into new areas of experience.

I have worked as an actor, director, teacher of voice and acting, playwright and writer. Right now, I am working at the National University of Ireland Galway as a teacher in Voice and the Michael Chekhov Technique, in addition to my several varied teaching commitments and directing projects. I also run Chekhov Training and Performance Ireland (www.chekhovtrainingandperformanceireland.com), dedicated to promoting the Chekhov work . Much of my directing work has been on classical productions and many of those have been with young people in youth theatres and colleges. My main influence and approach to acting is Michael Chekhov, whose psycho-physical approach I use not only as an acting and directing tool but also to invigorate the imagery of dramatic language which, for me, is absolutely key to success in Shakespeare. Chekhov Technique is physical and visceral. A strong aspect of this work is to actually physicalise the psychology of the characters. Its effect on the text and actor can be very immediate. This physical approach generally works well with young people and can be quite transformational in terms of their capabilities.

Directing young people in Shakespeare requires a holistic approach so this book is not a 'voice book' per se but there are two voice sessions within its pages because without an approach to voice you are going to have problems with Shakespeare. It is not purely a book about directing either, though there are several chapters about that. Nor is this a book solely about Chekhov Technique, as we will be looking at all sorts of methods to bring out the best from your young people.

It is an amalgam of all the above and more.

Acknowledgements

I would like to express my gratitude to:

Matt Applewhite, and all at Nick Hern Books.

To Tony Hegarty, who did the first read-through and edit and whose suggestions, patience, love, support and deep knowledge of teaching has strengthened this book immensely.

To David Zinder, Lenard Petit, Sarah Kane, Sharon Cromwell, Dawn Arnold, Bruce Myers and Jonathan Gunning, for showing me some exercises which I have developed or used in this book.

To Ted Pugh, Joanna Merlin, Fern Sloan, and the other extraordinary teachers of the Michael Chekhov Association and Michael Chekhov Europe.

To Rebecca Bartlett, Niamh Dillon and Andrew Flynn for their encouragement and support of my work at Galway Youth Theatre.

To all at Youth Theatre Ireland for giving me the opportunity to explore voice work with generations of young people all over Ireland.

To Professor Patrick Lonergan and all at the Centre for Drama, Theatre and Performance at the National University of Ireland, Galway, Ireland.

To all the young people who have given permission for their images to be in this book. Participants: Ciara Brady, Fiona Buckley, Patrick Fogarty, Katherine Wheatley, Daniel Murray, Kate O'Mahony, John Pinel, Nathan Mannion, Ethan Jordan, William Loughnane, Eamon Doran, Mairead Noonan, Pimapsorn Fern Thavornnart, Conor Gormley, Gavin Alcorn Friel.

To Florence Robinson, who taught me voice and acting long before I went to drama school, and to Joyce Morris for her encouragement and support.

To my mother, father and grandmother, who always believed in me.

To Nicole Gervais, Aranos and Jane Talbot who took some of the pictures in this book.

And last but not least, to all the students with whom I have worked, both young and older, particularly on Shakespeare.

Max Hafler

Part One

Our Journey and How to Get There

Introduction
Our Journey

What country, friends, is this?
Twelfth Night: Act One, Scene Two

It has been one of the great joys of exploring Shakespeare with young people to help them discover that it is indeed, for *them*, even though they can be initially daunted by it.

Young people are often nervous of Shakespeare: bad classroom experiences, a feeling that the language is a barrier and that the plays are too high-brow, boring and so far removed from life's everyday experience that they seem irrelevant. For directors and facilitators of young actors, it is hard to challenge these assumptions, but it is worth it. In our harshly materialistic environment, you will be opening doors for them into poetic drama and new theatrical worlds. If you are working in school, in addition to assisting with their intellectual understanding of the work and enabling them for exams, you will be giving them a more holistic and deeper understanding of the work.

By the end of this book I hope you will have gained an understanding of my approach, and will hopefully apply aspects of it to your interactions, projects and productions of Shakespeare that you might undertake with your own young people. Whilst there is some theory and discussion at the beginning, as in my book *Teaching Voice* (Nick Hern Books, 2016) this is primarily a hands-on book, giving *practical* support.

Of course, you will dip in and out, looking for the areas of support you need. In this book, I hope to take you on a journey from basic skills, through intermediate explorations, to short scenes and devising, and finally give you support towards mounting a full production.

Who This Book is For

This book is for anyone who wants to direct or explore Shakespeare with young people in a practical way, be they youth theatre leaders, teachers of secondary or undergraduate courses, or new directors working on Shakespeare with young actors.

I do not assume you are necessarily going to do a production; you might only go as far as the end of Part Three, where you devise a short Shakespeare project with your group, look at very short scenes or soliloquies, because that is as far as your group either can or wants to go. However, to follow this book from the beginning to the end is to chart a journey towards doing a production with your group. I would suggest that, before embarking on a more complete production, you do a good deal of preparation with your group, and explore much of the earlier part of this book in practical workshop with them.

Overview

Part One, **Our Journey and How to Get There**, is an introduction to the work, laying out the principles and ideas we are going to develop through the rest of the book. If you want to get a deeper understanding of the exercises and approach, try not to be tempted to miss it out and move on to the practical work.

Part Two, **Skills Workshops: Background, Voice and Acting**, looks at the reasons for working on Shakespeare with young people and provides the basic tools to work with your group practically in workshop. We look at Shakespeare's original theatre in order to help young people understand *why* the plays were written as they were. We explore through improvisation and exercises some of the dynamics present in the Elizabethan theatre space, particularly the actors' relationship to the audience. There are two workshop plans for voice work (an absolute priority if you are going to look at Shakespeare in a holistic and effective manner) and two acting workshop plans utilising the Michael Chekhov Technique, which offers many accessible acting tools for young people to explore and use. We use a variety of Shakespearean extracts for exploration in these workshops. While you don't need to use the pieces I suggest, I have picked them to correspond to the broad subject matter of each workshop.

Part Three, **Moving Towards Performance: Devising, Short Scenes and Soliloquies**, looks at the practicality of working with the text and getting the students to really inhabit the language and themes of *Macbeth*, the play we are using *most* in this section of the book. It includes a chapter on creating devised drama projects with text, movement and original writing. There is also a chapter working with short, manageable scenes from the play which will be helpful for less experienced directors and performers. This section also gives some assistance in directing soliloquies from a number of Shakespeare plays, expanding on the techniques and exercises explained in earlier pages. The work in this section can be an absolute end in itself, or is ideal as a stepping stone towards a full production.

Part Four, **Making the Play with Young Actors**, explores making a Shakespeare production. Primarily, we will be using *Twelfth Night* in this section. We further develop some of the general techniques and pathways, though now at a deeper level. We also explore general directing issues, how to build bridges to the material, and issues of engagement. We explore intelligent editing (as opposed to the idea of putting the text into modern language), and transposing of scenes and speeches. Most importantly, we develop through exercise and discussion what the young actors bring to the play and the production, so they are at the very core of our interpretation, rather than having some arbitrary concept concocted by the director imposed upon them. We then move on in the following chapter to a fundamental Foundation Week Plan, the purpose of which is to up-skill the actors, look for responses to the story, and encourage the importance of the text, whilst at the same time exploring the energy and conflicts in the play, both physically and theatrically. Finally, rather than a journey through the rehearsal period, I have chosen specific areas to highlight that I feel are important. These chapters will offer the reader further potential pathways to work with young actors, particularly in ensemble, which can easily transfer to other plays.

Chapter One
Tools and Pathways

A rose by any other name…
    Romeo and Juliet: Act Two, Scene Two

Why Do Shakespeare?

If you have bought this book, you are probably surprised I am asking this question. I feel it's important to give you some understanding of my perspective of working with Shakespeare before we embark on exercises, workshops and productions. That way, you will get the most out of them.

I think you have to decide when your group is ready to tackle Shakespeare. For some people – teachers, for example – you may not have a choice.

What is amazing about Shakespeare is that, despite the poetry, despite the manners and mores of another time, despite the archetypes of kings, queens, fairies and peasants, he and his collaborators speak to us now. Let's focus for a moment on the issues of family, ageing, cruelty and redemption which course through *King Lear*; those of romantic love, identity and gender in *Twelfth Night*; tyranny, revolution, personal responsibility and 'doing the right thing' in *Julius Caesar*. And despite any obfuscation created because it was written long ago, I feel the *directness* of Shakespeare really speaks to young people; characters asking questions and challenging audiences to help them decide on a course of action is involving and can be intoxicating.

However, there are several Shakespeare plays I would be wary of putting before a group of young people, because their overview seems, quite simply, at least questionable. *The Merchant of Venice* and *The Taming of the Shrew* are obvious examples, due to their inescapable assumptions about Jews in the one and the role of women in the other. Many productions have found ingenious ways to soften the prejudices inherent within these texts; to make *The Merchant of Venice*'s anti-Semitic world the critical target of the play or to make Katerina in *The Taming of the Shrew* ultimately wily rather than obedient. Of course, both these plays can be a great starting point for devising and discussion, and there are wonderful scenes within them. However, when it comes to exploring the whole play in depth, I for one, would steer clear of them in their original forms, unless you are going to challenge what appear to be their premises.

I hope to lead you and your young people through our work together in voice and acting towards a deeper shared understanding of Shakespeare, but I feel it is worth briefly describing a rather negative theatrical moment in order to draw something positive from it, build our own ethos as to how to proceed, and get a handle on the challenges involved.

I remember an event where young people were the audience. It was a particularly atrocious production for schools of *Macbeth*. In the interval I listened to a group of young people talking angrily about how bored they felt and how they longed to escape. One of them complained he was sitting next to a teacher and therefore could not escape and *had* to sit through it. Luckily for me, I was an adult and fled.

And what is worse is that the young person, having witnessed such a production, would probably never imagine that Shakespeare had anything to offer them. They would hate it, probably for the rest of their lives. If you are an adult and have had the misfortune to attend one of these kind of experiences, you might well ask the question at the top of this chapter, 'Why do Shakespeare?' Your next question might be, 'How can I make it relevant?'

So what could possibly be the answer? Perhaps if the production were in modern dress, with some current music, or if it were given a setting like a TV crime series, it might make the young person more engaged? Perhaps if we added a good soundtrack? Or maybe if we threw in some film and multimedia?

Updating

Well, we can do all those things, but it doesn't mean it is going to work. It might get you through the performance but will it encourage the young person into believing that this is amazing and profound material? Updating can simply make it more bearable, rather than truly *accessible*.

Films like *Romeo + Juliet* (Baz Luhrmann, 1996) with Leonardo DiCaprio and Claire Danes, can only be partially successful in engagement because they try so hard to be 'cool'. Updating *can* mean that the play gets forgotten; that its success is measured not by emotional intensity or truth but by style alone.

Let's look at the obvious problems in an updated production: immediately we notice characters talk about objects that are not in evidence, like daggers, swords or cross-gartered stockings. There is no immediate correlation. In fact, putting the play in our own time period immediately intensifies our distance from the time in which it is set. It is something to have a giggle about, to see as cleverness; it is distancing rather than engaging.

Of course, Shakespeare's plays were full of anachronisms in his own time. Look at the mechanicals of Athens in *A Midsummer Night's Dream*. They ooze the character of rural Tudor workmen rather than Athenians. These anachronisms were made, I am certain, to provide what *our* updating tries to do, to connect the material to the audience. For instance, Marullus, at the start of *Julius Caesar*, describes 'chimney-tops' when he speaks of the mob cheering at a victory march, not because they were part of the landscape of Ancient Rome, but of Elizabethan London. All Shakespeare wants to do here is unite his audience, encouraging them to remember the triumphs or parades they had seen through the streets of London, or spark their imaginations to create it in their minds. In other words, the 'updating' is built into the text. It was not layered on afterwards, and this is an important distinction with the updating that happens now.

As Peter Brook says in his book *Evoking* (*and Forgetting!*) *Shakespeare* (Nick Hern Books, 2002), 'one must recognise the crude modernising of a text and the potential within it that is being ignored'. On the other hand, if we look at a more traditional take on *Romeo and Juliet* in Franco Zeffirelli's film version (1968), in which the beautiful cast play out the story in fifteenth-century costume and Italian period surroundings, we might be equally alienated, and feel it has nothing to do with us. However, the fifteenth-century option does give us the possibility to get more emotionally involved with the story because we are not having to allow for the fact that when the character says 'sword' he is actually holding a gun. Setting aside the slightly stilted delivery of some of the actors and the occasionally intrusive soundtrack, much of this film still moves me.

So where does that take us? I agree with theatre academic and playwright Oliver Taplin, when he states in *Greek Tragedy in Action* (Methuen, 1985): 'It seems pointless to pretend that one can become an Elizabethan. It is not just that the exercise is doomed to failure; it is to turn our backs upon ourselves.' We want to find common ground with the past and the present, both for our young actors and, if they have one, their audience.

Peter Brook again: 'The "present" and "contemporary" are not the same thing.' We will return to this later through practical exercises, but I believe that as soon as we become over-specific as to setting, we are dooming and narrowing the expansive and emotional aspects of Shakespeare's work; that establishing contemporary references is fine and effective (changing the gender of a character to reflect a more modern contemporary feel, for instance) but it needs to be done cleverly, or it will become the sole focus of a production. On the other hand, making *some* contemporary references is essential, otherwise why on earth do we bother to perform and study the plays at all? What are they teaching us about life and experience right now? A production or course of study to my mind has to be *relevant*. This is as much an issue for you as the teacher/facilitator/director as it is for anyone else.

For instance, in a modern-dress production I did of *Measure for Measure* in 2014, Escalus was a female judge and Mistress Overdone a man in drag. This made many references to our modern world with regard to sexual repression and exploitation, particularly when Overdone was carted to prison hounded by a prejudiced mob. The play, costumed in modern dress, only *referenced* it (no mobile phones, motorbikes or anything that would fix the play too manifestly in the present). The costume was there for the audience to make connections. This meant that the updating did not become the *reason* for doing the play, but it made some strong connections to our contemporary modern life.

Translation

Another way of 'updating' is to examine the possibility of 'translating' the text into modern English. To me this has to be an absolute last resort, because so much of the power of Shakespeare comes from the imagery within the text. If you denude the play of that language, you take away character, psychological journey and atmosphere. The play becomes *only* the story, when it is so much more. It is like going on the internet for a precis of *Macbeth*, reading it and then imagining you have experienced the play. To convince students, it can be useful to ask them to describe their favourite song to a friend without singing it, then ask them if the listener got a feeling they had experienced the song from the description alone. The answer, of course, is *not really*. Poetry is the language of *feeling* and one of the principal ways we need to connect our young people with the text.

Of course, you might consider your group would not be able to deal with the language as it is and that what I am saying is impractical. In that case, you have to make sure that you encourage them to explore as much of the language as you feel they might be able to experience. This is often where devising around certain scenes or characters can be especially useful, when you can use other entry points but still retain some of the original language. I believe that without using/exploring *some* of the original text you are depriving the student actors of a complete experience.

When doing a production, I think it useful to have an assistant, a designated person, to work with the understanding of the text alone before the actors come to rehearsal. If you are working in a workshop or classroom, that person, of course, is going to be you.

The Language

Shakespeare's language, especially the imagery, carries and holds almost everything. It gives us the psychology, energy and rhythm of the character. It creates atmosphere and environment. I feel it is the very magic of the language that can initially draw students towards the profundity of the plays and engage them. I use the word 'magic' in its truly transformative sense. It can involve them on a deep level, provided they can be given some tools to understand and experience the way it was used, to find a route to its immense power, and then explore that complexity for themselves. If we can encourage the young people to do this, even in short pieces of text, we will be making the language, the character and the story live.

I am going to explain this further and then fully explore it later on, practically with exercises. I will offer suggestions as to how to approach language with physicality in a way that might really help young people get into the text. But first, some theory.

Images

The idea of the images being the essence of the play is explored by G. Wilson Knight, the celebrated Shakespeare scholar and practitioner. In his book *The Imperial Theme* he states: 'The action is not decorated with images: the images *are* the action' (my emphasis). Images are complex and multilayered, and unlock and explore complexity of character and situation. There is a popularly voiced belief that Shakespeare is without subtext. There *is* subtext, but it comes directly from the *image*. Poetry integrates both the conscious and unconscious, it is an ideal way of exploring the full complexity of intention.

Let's look at one example of this depth of imagery, from *Macbeth* (Act One, Scene Seven), as Macbeth struggles with the idea of murdering the King, Duncan:

> But here, upon this bank and shoal of time,
> We'd jump the life to come.

Macbeth is looking for certainty in the future, certainty of success. However, the very use of the shifting image, 'this bank and shoal of time', tells us, the audience, that Macbeth knows subconsciously *already* that certainty is not a possibility. Through the image we discover that Macbeth knows something of the ensuing voyage of chaos to come, and the young actor may choose to use this in the way the speech is delivered, imagining a quality of drowning perhaps or impending darkness engulfing him.

To show how such a use of metaphor expounds feeling and character in an even more concrete way, let's take Oberon's speech from *A Midsummer Night's Dream* (Act Two, Scene One). After receiving the magic flower with which he is going to ensnare Titania, Oberon, the Fairy King, begins with the famous, lyrical:

> I know a bank whereon the wild thyme blows,
> Where oxlips and the nodding violet grows,
> Quite over-canopied with luscious woodbine,
> With sweet musk-roses and with eglantine.

On one level this opening creates a magical picture and atmosphere; at the same time it is almost as if Oberon is completely intoxicated by the imagery for a second, and we, the audience, experience the picture sensually too; then later there follows:

> And there the snake sheds her enamelled skin,
> Weed wide enough to wrap a fairy in.

This image of the shiny dry skin of the serpent is hard and dragon-like; it is ugly. It is an image of something discarded, unwanted, something which has outgrown its usefulness, rather the way Oberon might feel about Titania herself. The coiling nature of the image, emphasised by the use of the repeated '*w*' sounds, implies strong physical sexuality and dark feelings turning in on themselves. Oberon abandons his pastoral idyll for the image of the snake and uses it to launch into the next, literally venomous, statement:

> And with the juice of this I'll streak her eyes,
> And make her full of hateful fantasies.

The imagery powers the workings of the actor's imagination, and charts the character's emotional journey. The poetry gives us all these layers. Once the young actor realises this, the poetry becomes much more than archaic words on a page. They become a magic tool, a musical score, to take the actor into the very soul of the character. How you make this happen, without poring over the script for far too long and drying up this *essence* we are looking for, is the challenge.

How do we achieve this, with our young people? We do it by approaching language through the imagination and the body, with practical exercises.

The Michael Chekhov Technique

Of all the different training methods I have explored, Michael Chekhov Technique has been the most thorough, expansive and freeing, and I use it as the bedrock for all my work. His technique works exceptionally well with young people, especially when working on Shakespeare because it is an *active* technique and immediately engages them in a way that 'table work', much allied to study and schoolwork, can alienate. I do not neglect the language but use Chekhov to enliven it: understanding intellectually alone is not the core of acting. Chekhov Technique is about experience.

I am going to share a lot of this work with you as the book progresses, both in the acting workshop chapters and through my suggestions for workshops, rehearsal and devising. Chekhov Technique infuses all of my work with whatever level of performer I am working. I think you will find it helpful.

Michael Chekhov (1891–1955) was one of the most innovative actor/director/teachers of the twentieth century. A nephew of the great playwright Anton Chekhov, he acted in the Moscow Art Theatre with extraordinary success, occasionally coming into conflict with Stanislavsky and others who worked there. As a teacher, he has influenced generations of actors, teachers and directors. His belief in the creative imagination and use of the body to find sensations and feelings for the character makes acting a truly magical art of extraordinary potential.

Within the body lies so much of who we are at any moment. It is quite literally a channel through which all our energies and experiences come. It is the manifestation of our history and even though so many of the cells in our bodies are replaced and replenished through our lifetime, there is something that is manifestly *us*. It is alchemical, impossible to define and so much more than 'body memory'. When you align this psycho-physical work with the use of a vibrant imagination, you open up new and exciting pathways to acting.

The technique makes the connection between voice, imagination, body and feelings. This is important because it makes us into whole people, as well as whole performers. It offers an *awareness* both of ourselves and the world. This should be one of our prime aims when working with young people, who may not necessarily make performing their career but can hugely benefit from this enhanced awareness.

The body should be our friend, and it can be, if we loosen it up and make it porous to all the sensitive influences of which it is capable. Young people tend to have very polarised views about their bodies, from free and elastic, to tense, uneasy and closed. This can be a challenge for them and for us, but using the body to free breath, feelings and language is healthy and positive.

I am going to recommend a series of books on and by Chekhov you might like to read and will go on to explain more. There is also a glossary of terms of the Chekhov Technique elements used in this book in the Appendix. Now I am just going to highlight a few of the elements I shall be using in the early acting workshop plans and give you a taster with a few exercises.

Radiating and Receiving Energy

'Radiating' is allowing your natural energy to flow out into the space and to your fellow human beings. Chekhov is very concerned with energy and there are many exercises to develop it within his books. Notice how easy it is to communicate with people you like, the energy pours out of your eyes and face quite naturally. With someone you know less well or don't like, you either pull your energy back or create a mask so the interplay between you is guarded, even when it *appears* open. Chekhov believed that we should always be radiating our energy strongly onstage, even when the character is negative or depressed. We have all seen even professional actors let go of their energy onstage and wondered why we lose interest in them. The process of 'radiating' is offering our performance to the audience. It is an act of generosity. And everyone can do it. Also, when working with a scene partner, you are often 'receiving' their energy. This is so much more than merely listening. It is responding to your scene partner with your whole being. It can be developed easily because we often share with each other this way in our daily lives.

Try a little experiment.

- Very slowly open your arms and imagine you have a light in the centre of your chest. Imagine a *sun*, if it is helpful.

- Imagine you are sending that energy out into the whole room and, if you are standing before one, out through the window. Get a sense of how that feels.

- Try saying a line like, 'Give me your hands if we be friends' (*A Midsummer Night's Dream*, Act Five, Scene One). Feel it flowing outwards.

- Now let your energy drop. No longer imagine the light and your energy streaming out, but keep your arms open. Notice how that feels different. Say the line again: notice how it takes more energy. You feel cooler, more detached, you start thinking of something else. Your body is not matching your mood, your face becomes harder and colder.

- *Without moving your arms*, reconnect that light/centre with your imagination and you will immediately notice a difference. Try the line again.

- Now, maintaining that sense of radiating from your centre, let your arms fall and say the line again. Radiate your energy outwards. Notice how this feels. Radiating your energy is as much part of that oft-expressed quality, *projection*, as breath and clarity.

Psychological Gesture

In Michael Chekhov Technique, a 'Psychological Gesture' is an inner gesture made *externally* to provoke sensation and, ultimately, feeling. It's one of the most useful tools and the one you are most likely to know something about.

It is a physical manifestation of the character's inner intention, what they are *doing*. Are they *pushing away*? *Tearing*? *Embracing*? Once decided on and practised, the gesture can then be imagined and internalised, so that it will provoke the feeling as the person speaks.

Let's explore this a little.

- Let's take Juliet's line, 'O Romeo, Romeo, wherefore art thou Romeo?' (Act Two, Scene Two). What is Juliet *doing*? For instance, is she *reaching* for love? Let's say she is.

- Try a reach, stretching your arms out, sending your energy out into the space and far into the room in which you are. Bend your knees. Try not to *think*, but *listen* to your body. Send your energy out beyond your fingers. You might start to feel a sense of desperation and longing. Try the gesture a few times.

- Now try and make a sound. A moan or a sigh might come out.

- Now say the line, still with arms outstretched. Notice how the words are filled more strongly with purpose and feeling.

- Trying to keep this feeling in your body, bring your arms down and say the line again. You will find you have retained a lot of the specificity and intensity. If not, go back to the gesture, say the line again, then bring your arms down again and try speaking again. Initially it can be tricky to retain the intention when you bring your arms down.

- This movement or 'Psychological Gesture' provokes very authentic feelings without the danger of the young actor associating them directly with a real (and possibly traumatic) event from the actor's life.

- Try the same procedure but this time imagine you are *grabbing* or *pulling*. Notice how that feels in your body. Try the gesture a few times.

- Keep the gesture going and make a sound. Try and keep that sound *open*. What I mean by that is: don't growl or grunt. Then say the same line as you pull. You will notice a big difference in the way you feel and how you say it.

I hope this example will convince you, if you need convincing, that this activation of the body to find an authentic voice for the young actor, and then the character, can be potent, fast and effective.

In addition, rather than using this physical gesture to explore psychological character intention, it can also be used to explore the emotional content and dynamic of a word or phrase. In other words, instead of taking the character's *action* as the impulse for the gesture, you take the *word* as the root of it. More of that later.

General Atmosphere

The final principal element I will mention here is 'General Atmosphere'. Chekhov says, 'atmosphere is the oxygen of performance'. He goes on to say that performances without atmosphere can never be satisfying to either actor or audience; that in life, atmospheres exist independently of our own experience and that there is something specific in the air, even when there is no one present. Just accept this for now, whether you acknowledge it or not.

As audience members, we have all had the feeling that despite an amazing set and fabulous lighting, and even what feels like truthful acting, there is still something wrong. It is hard to pin down what it is, but you can bet that it has something to do with a lack of atmosphere. Atmosphere must be generated by the actors, as well as by the lighting and design.

Let's say we walk into a church, a library, a classroom or our own front room. In each of these places there is an atmosphere that exists. This atmosphere might be there because of the purpose of the building, the energy in the room, what colour it is, how much open space there is, or what's happened there. Of course, how we *react* to it is personal to us. The atmosphere does not undermine our ability to respond; in fact, it always provokes a response in us because it is so powerful.

An analogy I often use is as follows. You are going to a party that for some reason you do not want to attend, but you have steeled yourself to go. You reach the front door and ring the bell. Let's say it is a noisy party. The music is blaring out. The door opens and a friend greets you. As the door opens you get a blast of the atmosphere. You smile, and there is a little struggle you have with yourself as to whether to accept the atmosphere and jump in, whether to try and remain in your bubble, or whether to just change your mind and go home! Once in the house, you may continue to struggle or the atmosphere may just overwhelm you and you will enter into the spirit of it.

These atmospheres need not be literal (library, hospital, cosy pub); this is just the tip of the iceberg. They can also be abstract things like embarrassment or laughter, or concrete images like broken glass or feathers. Often these less literal atmospheres can be even more effective at expressing the 'invisible'. These powerful atmospheres can be generated by the young actor using the power of...

Imagination

As I say in my book, *Teaching Voice* (*2016*):

> Words and images react with you when you read a book and you create your own world prompted by them. It is an alchemical reaction. When you see the movie of the same book it is frequently disappointing because the images presented are not *your* images. The film is simply not the way you imagined it. What's worse is that those movie images can never change, whereas when you read a book the images can change when you read it again. Your own images can help you speak with more feeling and power.

Going back to what I was saying about images with regard to language, try reading this image aloud to yourself:

> And with the juice of this I'll streak her eyes,
> And make her full of hateful fantasies.

What do you imagine? I imagine a wet, sticky hand squeezing juice on Titania's face. She is lying in a golden nest. The juice smells like vinegar. It almost burns her skin and, though she sleeps, I see her crying out in her sleep before settling back into a deep slumber as the spell does its work. I see Oberon's face, looking for a moment at his queen and for one second regretting he has done it, then his face hardening, before he melts into the darkness. All this and more, happens between my reading of the words and my imagination. Try speaking it now quite slowly; consciously reimagine these images (or, better still, your own) and you will really feel the text achieves a stronger reality. Notice that it makes the text feel more rooted and truthful. This connection – this formula, if you like – between words and imagination is at the very heart of what the Elizabethan theatre was all about.

What we see often in professional productions of Shakespeare is a lack of connection to language and imagery. It is a denial of the imagination's power. When people try to reproduce a flat, 'modern' delivery in Shakespeare it is often alienating, because when they do it they are denying a simple realistic truth: that how we speak and what we say are, to some extent, who we are. The flat delivery of intricate, exquisite lines dislocates us and our young actors from the play.

Again from *Teaching Voice*:

Exploring through imagination sometimes involves a risk, especially for teenagers who often consider themselves above it and for whom taking that risk might expose them to looking or feeling foolish. Work with the imagination demands they let go of this fear. Reminding them that acting has its roots in *let's pretend* can often be reassuring.

It is your job to take them there.

Part Two

Skills Workshops: Background, Voice and Acting

Chapter Two
Warming Up

Let him be prepared.
Measure for Measure: Act Three, Scene One

It is my firmly held belief that you cannot really perform and explore effectively without a warm-up of some description. For me, having a warm-up at the start of a session is vital at whatever level you are working. In addition to awakening the tools of the body, it creates focus and unity, enabling your group to let go of the pressures of their day and concentrate on the work.

So I am putting down a *minimal* warm-up here for those people for whom time constraints are severe, or for those who feel their group might not be ready for a slower more in-depth one.

I have called this warm-up...

Connecting Up

The next few exercises are to warm up the body and voice a bit. They are not a full preparation, but their job is to focus. More importantly, they are to connect voice, movement, feelings and imagination together. A few of these exercises can also be found in *Teaching Voice*, but I have adapted some of them here to save the facilitator time.

Beach Ball

The purpose of this exercise is to connect the breath to the movement and improve focus.

- Ask them to stand in a circle. Ask everybody to stand feet parallel to shoulders, knees slightly bent, spine straight but not stiff, shoulders easy, head aligned with spine, looking ahead. Ask them to notice the base of their spine relaxing, as if they are sitting down on the air.

- Ask them to slowly lift their arms as if they are holding a large beach ball (about a metre across) to their chest. Watch for tension in their bodies. The most likely place is the neck and shoulders. Suggest they consider that part of their body and say to themselves, 'Let go'.

- Next, ask them to *breathe down*: to imagine they are breathing right into the soles of their feet. If they have a lot of chest and shoulder movement they should not be concerned but simply notice it. If the mind wanders, bring the focus back to the breathing.

- Then ask them to breathe in and very gently, at the same time, to open up the arms. Then ask them to breathe out, bringing their arms back in to the beach-ball position. Suggest they imagine a connection between the breath and the movement of the arms. (Repeat three times.)

- Next, ask them to bring their arms to their sides, then, as they breathe in, to slowly raise them as if they are drawing an arc with their fingers over their heads. Their hands should be palms up. Ask them, in the space between the in- and out-breath, to turn their hands so that the palms are down, then to breathe out and bring their arms in the same arc back to their sides. (Repeat three times.)

Teaching Tip: Notice if you do this exercise regularly, whether anyone in the group gets distracted as it goes on, and for any disconnect between the gentle opening and closing of arms, any flighty eye movements or what I call 'deadeye' (eyes with no energy in them). Bring this to everyone's attention when you finish. People should focus out, sending their energy into the room as they open their arms, and contain their energy as they bring their arms back in. This is a reference to the *Radiating and Receiving Your Energy* exercise I pointed out to you in Chapter One, when I opened up the possibility of working with Chekhov Technique.

Breath Dance 1

This exercise can be developed into a piece of instant choreography, but here we are simply trying to get each group member to warm up the body, stretch and connect to the breath. You may need to demonstrate this first.

- Tell each person, at the same time as they breathe in, to make any large movement they like. The movement and the breath have to be connected. They cannot move unless they are breathing in or out.

- On the out-breath, make another movement. The idea is that the breath and movement are one, always.

- Tell them to note the pause where your breath changes from an 'in' to an 'out', and your body is still. There is a kind of suspension or sustaining, a moment that has all sorts of possibility within it.

- Once they get proficient in this, you might ask them to change the tempo of the breath, which means, of course, that they have to move quickly; a gasp, for instance, makes for a fast movement.

- Let this go on for a minute or so and then bring it to a close.

Head Rolls and Yawn

- Ask them to drop the head to the chest and then *very slowly* roll the head to the right, to the back, to the left and back to the front in a circle. (Four times each way.)

- As they drop the head back, suggest they let the jaw go.

- Ask them to take a breath and let out a sound from the pit of the tummy as their mouths open. It should sound like a yawn.

Puppet with Lines

- Ask them to stand in a circle and reach up as if they are being pulled up on a string. When you clap or say 'go', let them release and hang from the waist.

- Whilst in their hanging-down position, ask them to let go, releasing the knees, so they release the back further. They should go floppy and loose like a puppet, bending over from their waists.

- Ask them to shake their head and shoulders *only*, and let out a moaning sound. Do it with them so they are not embarrassed. Ask them to feel like they are breathing from their bellies, that they might feel the tummy moving against the thighs.

- Then, *very slowly*, ask them to bring themselves to standing, curling up the spine vertebra by vertebra. The head and neck should be the last to go into place.

- Now ask them to repeat the exercise, but this time to bring that moan up with them as they bring themselves to standing, trying to keep the breath coming from the belly. They can breathe as often as they need to. Once standing straight, ask them to open their arms and send the sound out into the room. Imagine the whole room is being filled with their sound. You will need to demonstrate this first.

- Now ask them to repeat the exercise one more time, this time speaking a short line. Let's use 'O for a muse of fire!' (*Henry V*, Act One Chorus). Ask them to keep repeating the line until they are standing straight and with arms open, sending the sound out into the room. Suggest they look at others in the circle as they speak, and that they notice they are sharing their energy with each other.

Hand-Throwing

- The group stands in a circle. Ask everyone to turn to the left and find someone to look at on the other side of the circle.

- Ask them to put their weight on the left foot and change their weight to the right foot as they throw their right hand towards their partner and at the same time shouting '1'; they throw again, shouting '2' and so on, up to '8'. They do this vigorously, radiating the voice and energy towards their respective partner.

- Now ask everyone to turn to the right, and throw with their left hand, counting the numbers vigorously as before. This is a good releasing exercise. Now ask them to do exactly the same but this time not as loudly, but still to feel that their voices are going to their partner.

I use this exercise as an introduction to Radiating/Receiving, the Michael Chekhov term discussed in Chapter One, which encourages this generous sharing of energy, fully communicating across a space and for projection. It emphasises the voice as something that you use to reach others with your emotions and ideas. Ask them to notice how, when they 'throw', they make that connection with the person across from them. It is also one of the exercises in which we are encouraging them to use their *whole body*.

Stretch, Yawn, Shake Out

- Ask the group to stretch and yawn. Ask them to notice how the throat relaxes and opens at the back when they do it. It is good to yawn if they are nervous before performing.

- Now get them to shake out the body vigorously with a groaning sound. Because we are working a lot with the body through all our work, it is important to remember this 'shaking out'. A lot of feelings are stored in the body. These can be stirred, especially when you work psycho-physically.

Consonant Characters: Voice and Body

This exercise can achieve very successful results and emphasises the connection between body and voice.

- Ask the group to find their own space and tell them you are going to say a consonant: let's start with '*sssss*'. Everyone is going to say '*sssss*' and keep saying it. Ask them to let the body go with the sound; in other words, they start to be the character of '*sssss*' with their whole voice and body, and move around the room. This is quite easy and nowhere near as 'out there' as it sounds. Get them all to do this at the same time, working on their own, and when they feel more comfortable, they can relate to each other.

- Let them play with this sound for about half a minute at least, before shaking out. Then change the sound to '*guh*', '*vuh*', '*buh*'. Try a vowel sound like '*ah*' or '*eee*'. Get them to let the body and the sound work together. Say that this will happen naturally if they don't think about it too much.

Teaching Tip: Try and get them to forget about *thinking* when they are exercising. This is very hard because our whole education is programmed primarily towards thinking. However, if they listen to their bodies with a 'Feeling of Ease' (a Michael Chekhov term which encourages us to move with an easy motion) then the sound will likely come out clear and true. They can think about it afterwards!

Radiating and Receiving (*Throwing the Ball*)

This is a Chekhov exercise and, though not primarily a vocal one, we are going to add the text from the Act One Chorus in *Henry V*.

- In a circle, the group is going to mime throwing and catching a ball to each other. I always explain we are miming it so we do not have to worry about 'dropping it' and can be perfect 'catchers and throwers'. This exercise is about radiating and receiving energy, from both voice and body, not a sports lesson.

- The *way* we throw is important. The student must have one foot behind the other and be able to throw underarm with an easy swing.

- The person who 'catches' must receive the 'ball' looking at the thrower, so a connection is made between the two. Then the thrower can return to their regular stance once the catcher throws to someone else.

- Now, one person has the 'ball'. They pick someone and 'throw' to them. The other 'catches' and then 'throws' to someone else, and so on. Do not initially go fast. Keep it smooth and steady.

- When people 'throw', it is important they stay with their throwing arm extended, looking at the person they are throwing to and sending their energy towards them. They are *sustaining* the movement. This is important so the young actor can feel both that the movement is finished and that they have sent energy to the catcher; that there is an exchange between them.

- Stop the exercise for a minute and just do a few corrections on the form of throwing. Are they throwing underarm? Are they reaching out and sustaining? People are often very reluctant to stay with their arm outstretched for a second. They 'throw' their energy out quickly and weakly. Point out how onstage it is terribly important to share and communicate with the other actors, as well as the audience.

- Now ask them to add a sound when they throw. Let them use their own name or just a 'hey'. Get them to notice when they feel their voices do not reach their 'catcher'. Explore for a second the *why* of that. Could it be they need more breath to project effectively?

- Eventually, start to add short lines from the *Henry V* text we will use in the next chapter (or if you are using this warm-up for another play, use whatever text you are working on). Use 'O for a muse of fire!', 'A kingdom for a stage!', 'Princes to act!', and 'monarchs to behold the swelling scene!'

- Help them by getting them to speak *as* they throw. That way, the breath will be more free. They are literally 'throwing the voice'. Indeed, one of the reasons they may not reach their 'catcher' with the words is because they simply have not enough breath, or are tense. We will address this a little more in later chapters, but it is tackled in a lot more detail in *Teaching Voice*.

And now, let's begin.

Chapter Three
Shakespeare's Theatre:
A Discussion and a Workshop Plan

Think, when we talk of horses, that you see them...
Henry V: Act One, Chorus

As an introduction, I want us to look at the *idea* of Shakespeare's theatre, through a series of games and exercises. When I say *idea*, I mean to consider the structure of that theatre, its practical limitations, the mores and the audiences (different at court from the public playhouses and different again once some of his plays were staged indoors).

Why might this be a useful place to start? Because I think if your young actors understand why the plays were written as they were, they may not find it so easy to dismiss the language as too complicated, or as a student wrote to me recently, 'I chose this short speech because it had a typical long-winded Shakespearean sentence in it.'

This does not mean I want them to perform a Shakespeare play in period costume or ignore the fact that this is the twenty-first century, but knowing something of how and why the play was written gives the young actor a great springboard from which to jump.

Below is the first workshop. It should last about 45 to 60 minutes. You will need a large room.

The Workshop: 'The Great Globe Itself'

Unusually for me, I would like to start with a discussion! The goal here is to draw people into the world of the Shakespearean theatre. If you have read *Teaching Voice* you may be familiar with this already.

Shakespeare's theatre was a 'wooden O', a circular space with a thrust stage into the audience. You might like to show the 'performance' section of the film *Shakespeare in Love* (1998), directed by John Madden. Other than that, you might be able to take a look online at some extracts from productions at the modern replica of Shakespeare's Globe, or bring in pictures.

Throw the subject open for discussion: 'How is the Elizabethan theatre different from the theatre of today?' Here are a few things we might like them to notice:

- The plays were performed in the open air, so despite the excellent acoustics in the theatre, the playing had to be expansive.

- There was little or no scenery. There was no desire to be 'realistic', either because it could not be achieved, or because, literally, *it did not matter.*

- There was no stage lighting, which is often one of the main tools used to create atmosphere in our modern theatre. This meant that it was almost impossible for anyone to be *discovered* onstage at the start of a scene. There was no 'lights up!' and no curtain. This meant the characters had to come on speaking in the middle of a discussion to grab people's attention. This happens many times in Shakespeare's plays. It gives the plays incredible momentum. It is as if the very words drive the characters onto the stage.

- However, costume was very important and there was a 'tiring-house' (literally a space for dressing, or 'attiring' and for storing costumes and props). I am convinced that in a play like *Antony and Cleopatra*, where we have the creation of two diametrically different worlds, Rome and Egypt, the minor characters who populate these worlds create location and atmosphere by their very presence, in their exotic and contrasting costumes.

- The audience was very near the stage, so audience and actors could see each other very clearly. This enhanced their very intimate relationship, rather than there being any feeling of separation between performers and audience. Sometimes the audience was directly addressed, often within a scene. They could be confidantes, co-conspirators with the characters; they could also be 'the crowd' addressed as Citizens of Rome, Soldiers of Agincourt, etc. The relationship between audience and actor is, in a sense, like bardic storytelling; something we might even equate with modern rap and performance poetry.

- Audiences could contain the fact they were being consulted, be massively invested in the story, use the spoken images to create the physical world in which the characters lived, and at the same time understand that they were attending an artificial theatrical performance.

- The Elizabethan audience had to respond more imaginatively through the magic created for them by the spoken language, imagery and the story. The language had to carry the bulk of the responsibility for creating atmosphere and location, to support the story, character and psychological development.

- The audience came from *all* social classes. This meant that the plays had to have something to appeal to everyone, from elite witticism to broad humour. There is an amazing communal feel to much of Shakespeare's work: the feeling that it speaks to everyone, even when there are few working-class characters on view. *A Midsummer Night's Dream* or *The Tempest* show this sharing of stage time between the working-class characters and the nobility very clearly. In general, the poorer characters speak in prose and the 'nobler' characters speak through poetry.

Three Things to Consider about the Elizabethan World

1. There was no social media, no internet, no movies. I think people do not realise how their imaginations, outlooks and lives would be different without this technology. For the Elizabethans, the imagination was one of the main ways they created fantasy.

2. Society was very stratified, especially for women. There was no way a woman could be seen performing on a public stage. This is, to some extent, explored in the movie *Shakespeare in Love.* This fact had a big impact on the structure of the plays. Though there were large important female roles (played by teenage boys), they generally did not share the same amount of stage time as the male lead. However, Shakespeare frequently uses this restriction to his advantage by having his heroines disguise themselves as boys, which creates an ambivalent (and very modern) frisson between characters like Rosalind and Orlando (*As You Like It*) and Orsino, Olivia and Viola (*Twelfth Night*).

3. The theatre was considered, in some respects, subversive and powerful. Elizabethans lived in a difficult time with shifting religious allegiances. There were some things you simply could not talk about onstage without putting playwright and company into serious danger.

Warm-up

Now it's time to get everyone on their feet. Use the *Connecting Up* warm-up (page 25), focusing on loosening and connecting the voice to the body.

Imagine

The purpose of this exercise is to get the group to start imagining and realising, if they didn't before, the power of the imagination to create the Elizabethan world for themselves.

- Tell them we are going to try and imagine what it might be like to be an Elizabethan actor onstage at the Globe. Warn them that you are going to feed them some lines from the opening of Shakespeare's *Henry V* by the Chorus later on in the exercise. The Chorus is encouraging the audience to create the story with their imaginations. Tell them not to worry if they get the text wrong but just keep going and say what they think you said.

- Now ask them to find their own space and tell them they are going to work alone. Ask them to close their eyes. Ask them to imagine they are on a stage in Elizabethan times. Ask them what they notice. What does it feel like under their feet? What can they see in front of them? What colours can they see?

- Ask them to imagine they are an actor on that stage. What are they wearing?

- What type of character are they playing? A hero? A villain? A clown? A servant? A queen? A lover? A soldier? A prince? Ask them to breathe the character in, as if it is filling them up inside.

- Now ask them to imagine they are standing like that character. Ask them to create a 'statue' of that character. Tell them to try not to think about it too much.

- Now ask them to open their eyes and walk around the space as if they were that character. Ask them to work on their own, really moving around the 'stage'. Now ask them to imagine that the whole theatre is full of people waiting for you, the actor, to speak.

- Now ask them to listen to your line and to repeat it altogether, to the 'audience' afterwards. You say, 'O for a muse of fire!' They say, 'O for a muse of fire!' You say, 'A kingdom for a stage!' They say, 'A kingdom for a stage!' You say, 'Princes to act!' They say, 'Princes to act!' You say, 'And monarchs to behold the swelling scene!' They say, 'And monarchs to behold the swelling scene!'

- If their response is too quiet, repeat the text with them and encourage that openness by getting them to throw open their arms as they say the lines. You will notice a marked difference.

- Ask them to stand still, close their eyes and let their imagination come back into the studio.

- Ask them to shake out thoroughly and open their eyes.

- *Flyback* on the experience (a Chekhov term for the space to review what happened during the exercise). Ask them how it felt to imagine the scene. Can they remember any detail they became aware of? You might find that someone has created a whole story for the Elizabethan actor. Perhaps this is their first performance and they are nervous.

- Ask them if anybody had trouble speaking loudly. Someone will definitely say yes. Explain that in order to radiate their voices they need plenty of breath and to feel like their voice is filling the space.

Teaching Tip: It is a tricky note to give, but try and give them *time* to imagine. Don't just rush on.

Some young people love using their imaginations and others are afraid of doing so. This exercise might not work for everyone but will for some. If you have had the backup discussion, those afraid of 'going there' will have material to use and *will* have something to say.

Please Note: It's important that you understand I am not trying to make young actors speak over-loudly, but usually they need to *start* loudly because it is often the only way they can find their voices expressively at the beginning. The more you work with the voice, the more flexible you can be with volume, pitch and tone. Working with the body in tandem is a huge help.

Imagining the Audience: 'Have you heard the one about...?'

The radiating and receiving we started to consider in a few of the early exercises in Chapter Two now has its first practical application.

How many times have we seen professional actors fake a 'connection' with the audience when they speak soliloquies? This is not a genuine connection, but a kind of glazed generality in the eyes; a 'looking into space'. If you watch a comedian, you will never see this deadness in the eyes; their energy is always streaming out even when they have to take in a big crowd. In this exercise you are going to ask your group to walk around and tell everyone a joke or a story and really communicate it to us.

- Tell the group to walk around the space. Ask everyone to stand still. Now pick a person to tell a joke to everyone else. Give them all the same joke to tell: 'How am I like a broken plane? Because I'm always being grounded.' (I know, an excruciating joke!) You might mention that Shakespeare was full of puns like this. Tell them that what we are looking for is a real connection with your 'audience', to share and radiate it.

- Alternatively (for those deeply embarrassed by jokes) they can tell a *brief* story of something that happened on their way to workshop today. Ask them to tell it to us all as if it is terribly important.

- After one person has spoken, get them all to walk about and then tell them to stop.

- Choose someone else to speak then get everyone to move again and stop, and so on.

- Make sure the jokers really connect with the others, sending their energy out into the space. If they don't, then get them to open their arms as they speak, or point as they speak to people in the group. This will only work well for those who are connected to their bodies but it will improve everyone.

- Shake out.

- *Flyback.* Ask them what they found out. Some people will say that they couldn't speak loudly enough. Explain that this is probably because they are not using enough breath. Some people will add things to the joke or, if they have a natural comedic feel, they might take pauses. Tell them that sometimes it's effective to look at the audience first before they speak. Note that everyone told the joke differently. If someone does the story option, you might find it useful to be positive about the people who really shared their information with us, the audience.

Word Power

The purpose of this game is to start to make the connection between what we imagine when we hear a word and how, in turn, this affects how we say it.

- Ask them to stand in a circle. Tell them to close their eyes and that you are going to say a word: 'forest', for instance. Ask them to consider what happens when you say the word to them.

- Try another: 'battlefield'.

- Try another: 'ocean'.

- Try another: 'nightclub'.

- Try another: 'cave'.

- Ask them to open their eyes and talk about what happened when you said the word. They will talk about seeing a picture, or perhaps remembering something, or seeing a colour. Remind them that in Shakespeare's time, people were very sensitive to language.

- Get them to close their eyes.

- Now, this time you say a word, they imagine it, then they say it into the space. Ask them to let what they imagine affect how they say it.

- Try 'wounded': they imagine, then they speak.

- Try 'love': they imagine, then they speak.

- Try 'aggression': they imagine, then they speak.

- Try 'feather': they imagine, then they speak.

- Try 'palace': they imagine, then they speak.
- Repeat this process and this time, with their eyes closed, tell them to make a *gesture* when they speak. For instance, with 'wounded', they might close their body. Ask them how it feels when they engage their body. Did they notice any difference with the way they spoke the word? They will hopefully say, 'It was better.'

Teaching Tip: Stress how they are trying to link up the image/sensation they get with the feeling in the word, which is also to do with the *sounds* in the word.

Creating Atmospheres: Location

Peter Brook, in his book *Evoking (and Forgetting!) Shakespeare*, has this to say about the Shakespearean theatre:

> As there was no scenery, if someone said 'we are in a forest', we were in a forest, and the next second someone said 'we are not in the forest', the forest had vanished. This is faster than any cut in the cinema.

Without the assistance of lighting or set, the actors and audience had to do a lot more work to create atmosphere. Whether it was, as Brook states above, that people were just incredibly imaginative and were able to create the world of 'the forest' or 'the battle' in their minds without effort, it is essential that we are sensitive to the atmosphere in each scene.

Michael Chekhov believed that we could *create* atmosphere, and that atmosphere was 'the oxygen of performance'. In other words, the atmosphere influences the way we speak and feel. If you consider it, it is obvious; you might say the same thing in a few different places: a library, a church, a museum or a bus station. But where you *are* means it will come out differently in intention, volume and feeling. Creating location is a very basic power of atmosphere and is essential in the Shakespearean theatre. If you want to explain it to them, I might suggest you use my 'going to a party' analogy above (page 19).

When I ask in the exercise 'Is the atmosphere heavy or light?', you might consider this first with the group: we know what a heavy atmosphere is like, a thick atmosphere or a buzzing atmosphere. We know we say things like, 'I feel up', 'I feel down' or 'I feel spaced out'. Atmosphere is energy and energy *moves*.

- Get them to work on their own. Tell them: 'Imagine you are in a library. Take a deep breath and breathe in the atmosphere. What does it *feel* like to be in a library? What's the atmosphere like? Is there movement in the energy in the library or is it still? Does it feel heavy or light on your skin? What can you smell? Is there a lot of movement in it? Start to walk around the room as if it is a library. You might start to make up a story for yourself and that's okay, but try and focus on the atmosphere.'

- Suggest they stay in the atmosphere and say: 'To whom should I complain? Did I tell this, who would believe me?' (*Measure for Measure*: Act Two, Scene Four). I chose this line because the words are easy to understand and questions are even more likely to be affected by the location. Ask them to say it a few times, allowing the atmosphere to affect them. Tell them to focus on the atmosphere and nothing else.

- After they have done this for a minute or two, tell them to shake it off, but stay focused. Get them to close their eyes and imagine they are in the atmosphere of a prison, whatever that may mean to them. Say something like: 'Take a deep breath and breathe in the atmosphere. What does it *feel* like to be in a prison? What's the atmosphere like? Do you see a colour? Are there windows? Does it feel heavy or light? Is there a colour or a sound, maybe an echo?

- Ask them to open their eyes and start to walk in the prison atmosphere. Now ask them to say the same line a few times: 'To whom shall I complain? Did I tell this, who would believe me?' They will find the line sounds and feels different.

- Tell them to shake it off, but stay focused. Get them to close their eyes and imagine they are in the atmosphere of a place of worship. Say something like: 'Take a deep breath and breathe in the atmosphere. What does it *feel* like to be in a place of worship? What's the atmosphere like? How does it make you feel? What's the temperature like? Is there a lot of movement in the atmosphere? Open your eyes and start to walk in this place's atmosphere.' Then tell them to say the same line a few times.

- Tell them to shake it off but stay focused. Get them to imagine they are walking in fog. Try the line again.

- *Flyback.* Ask them what happened. The most obvious and important thing is that where we are and the *atmosphere* of where we are affects how we speak and feel. It even affects the meaning of the line.

Location is only the start of this atmosphere work, as we shall explore in Chapter Seven.

Sharing with the Audience: In On It

This is an exercise from *Teaching Voice*, which I feel explores the actor's relationship with the audience in the Elizabethan playhouse. I have quoted it here in its entirety as it is totally relevant to our exploration. I might suggest you use this exercise or alternatively the 'Starting the Show' exercises that follow it.

- Ask them to get into pairs.

- Tell them they need to make up a short improvisation between two people who are not necessarily telling the truth to each other. Ask them to consider times in their everyday lives when they are thinking something different to what they are actually revealing: job interviews, attempts to lie to keep out of trouble, meeting a demanding friend who is telling them some personal secret, etc.

- Each pair performs their improvisation to the group, acting both with their partners and also giving 'asides' to their 'other partner' (the audience) about what is happening onstage. In Shakespeare's plays the audience is frequently treated as a co-conspirator or friend. (To my mind, this is a much more enjoyable starting point than saying that soliloquies and/or asides are about people talking to themselves.)

- If you are going to give everyone a turn it will be quite a long exercise, but it is a great way to get them to play with the audience/actor relationship, have fun and perform! Be selective if you do not have the time.

Here is a funny idea as an example. A mum with a school-age child who is misbehaving has been asked in to see the principal.

PRINCIPAL. Ah, Mrs Harrison, come in.

MRS H (*to audience*). I've had to miss my lunch hour for this. (*To* PRINCIPAL.) Thanks a lot. What do you need to see me for?

PRINCIPAL (*to* MRS H). Mind if I have my lunch?

MRS H (*to* PRINCIPAL). Noooo. (*To audience.*) There is nothing wrong with Charlie. He's just a bit... lively. Whatever you hear in the next few minutes, she's a liar.

PRINCIPAL (*to* MRS H). Thank you. It's about Charlie.

MRS H (*to audience*). She makes me feel like I did something wrong! Guilt trip! (*To* PRINCIPAL, *sourly.*) What's he done?

PRINCIPAL (*to* MRS H). Do you know Mrs Campbell?

MRS H (*to* PRINCIPAL). Yes. (*To audience.*) Boring cow!

PRINCIPAL (*to* MRS H). She teaches maths.

MRS H (*to audience*). She bored me to death!

PRINCIPAL (*to audience*). You can see this is going to turn out badly already!

You get the idea. Encourage them to play with this idea of sharing their thoughts and looks with the audience, whilst at the same time keeping the scene going. Some of the dialogue will overlap and it will be rough, but the idea of sharing with the audience will be implanted.

Starting the Show 1

We are going to use the opening chorus to *Henry V* in a few different ways.

I chose this chorus because it begins a play (so your group need not be familiar with the whole play), and it illustrates succinctly the relationship between actor and audience, and how the audience was encouraged to *imagine*. This links us to the theme of the workshop.

- Have the group make a circle. Get one person to read a line, then the person on their left reads the next line, and work around the group until the whole speech is finished. Help with pronunciation and meaning.

- Ask them to notice, if someone does not pick up their line on cue, how everything 'dies' and the energy evaporates. Tell them it is their job not to let that happen. Having done that, get them to read the text through again. It should be smoother.

- If everyone knows the line they are saying, you might like to try the *Radiating and Receiving* (*Throwing the Ball*) exercise in Chapter Two in order to get them to radiate the lines out into the space and the group. Assure them they now know the line! Tell them to remember who speaks before and after them, then ask them to make a new circle. Line 1 throws to 2, 2 to 3, 3 to 4, until the end of the speech is reached. Try this through a couple of times. Check that everybody registers when the energy goes down.

Starting the Show 2

- Now split the text into a few sections (I have done it for you below), and your group into teams with 5 or 6 people in each.

- Each team should perform their piece with a group identity, as, for example, teachers, gossips, actors, the ghosts of dead soldiers, news reporters, or anything else you might think of that might be appropriate.

- Tell them it is important to still make contact with us, their audience. They are speaking to *us*. Each team can split the speech up between them however they like. For instance, in Team 1, on line 1, the whole group might say 'FIRE!' Let them be creative with this, but remind them they are telling us the story. Whatever type of character they are playing – gossips, teachers, etc. – they still need to speak to the audience as the characters.

- Get them to perform these pieces to the rest of the group.

- *Flyback*. Ask them what they found out. What they will find immediately they do this, of course, is that whatever *type* they are playing makes the delivery and feel of the speech sound very different.

Michael Chekhov calls this type of approach using archetypes, and this will be explored in more detail in Chapter Fourteen. It is powerful and non-intellectual. This exercise should be a lot of fun. I would recommend, as this is an early workshop, that you focus on their ability to share with the audience and tell the story, rather than language and imagery.

CHORUS

> 1.
> O for a muse of fire, that would ascend
> The brightest heaven of invention,
> A kingdom for a stage, princes to act
> And monarchs to behold the swelling scene!
> Then should the warlike Harry, like himself,
> Assume the port of Mars, and at his heels,
> Leashed in like hounds, should famine, sword
>   and fire
> Crouch for employment.

> 2.
> But pardon, gentles all,
> The flat unraisèd spirits that have dared
> On this unworthy scaffold to bring forth
> So great an object. Can this cockpit hold

The vasty fields of France? or may we cram
Within this wooden O the very casques
That did affright the air at Agincourt?
O, pardon! since a crooked figure may
Attest in little place a million,
And let us, ciphers to this great account,
On your imaginary forces work.

3.
Suppose within the girdle of these walls
Are now confined two mighty monarchies,
Whose high upreared and abutting fronts
The perilous narrow ocean parts asunder.
Piece out our imperfections with your thoughts.
Into a thousand parts divide one man
And make imaginary puissance.

4.
Think when we talk of horses, that you see them
Printing their proud hoofs i'th' receiving earth.
For 'tis your thoughts that now must deck our kings,
Carry them here and there, jumping o'er times,
Turning th'accomplishment of many years
Into an hour-glass: for the which supply,
Admit me Chorus to this history,
Who prologue-like your humble patience pray,
Gently to hear, kindly to judge our play.

Closing

- Ask the group to stand still and close their eyes, and to focus on their breathing, in through the nose and out through the mouth.

- Talk quietly about how we have almost gone back in time to make a bridge between Shakespeare's time and our own. Ask them to think about one thing they found out, either about themselves or Shakespeare's theatre, which was new to them.

- Tell them they need to bring themselves back into the present and to listen to the sounds around them, the breath of others, anything they can hear outside. Really give them time to imagine these things. Don't rush, unless you feel someone is getting giggly or can't cope with the quiet.

- Focus back on the breath.

- Ask them to open their eyes.

Chapter Four

> Speak the speech, I pray you, as I pronounced it to
> you…
>
> *Hamlet*: Act Three, Scene Two

You are your instrument. This might be a cliché, but like all clichés it has some truth in it. Likening training for theatre to training for sport or learning an instrument is always a useful analogy for young people.

I feel that in order to touch the visceral and magical power of Shakespeare, you and your young actors are missing something if you do not engage with the language. It is on that that the whole alchemy rides. In my experience, I do not know of any group that cannot at least engage with poetic phrases, occasional lines or short exchanges.

To do that, you have to help the group unlock some of their vocal power. We are not getting into the area of changing accents or any kind of standardising of the voice: our job is to *free* the voice. Of course, the voice needs to be clear to give value to the language, so there is some mechanical work in the following exercises.

I have included two workshops on voice in this and the following chapter to help you along the way. My goal here is for the group to experience the *importance* of voice rather than to generate immediate expertise. To achieve expertise, these exercises need regular practice. Some of the building blocks for these exercises, which ideally need to be carefully constructed in a dedicated voice course, will be combined in one exercise. Success will be more limited but it will come faster. Both workshops will certainly get students to recognise, enjoy and open their voices up. What is important is that voice, body, imagination and feelings are all connected for a good performance.

There will be no floor work in this book (an important building block for the voice), and I suggest if you wish to go into the voice work in more depth, you get hold of my book *Teaching Voice*.

This is very much an active workshop. Using the body to provoke and enrich the voice can massively accelerate progress, provided the group commits. I have, time after time, seen young people gasp at the way they say a line when they are actively engaging with the body at the same time.

Breath, diction and resonance will be the focus here. In the next workshop (Chapter Five), I will focus more on emotional response to poetic language and how to decide on breathing and emphasis. My approach is always to make this work energetic and enjoyable, to get as far away from 'Speech and Drama' as possible. Given that our goal in this book is ultimately to work on a Shakespeare project, we need to focus our efforts on reminding young people that Shakespeare can be much more accessible and powerful than they might think. I always try to employ some application of our exercises to text at the end of all the workshop plans, so that the young people get a sense of where the exercises might ultimately be leading them.

The Workshop

The warm-up described in Chapter Two is always useful, but I suggest you keep that for your other general sessions or rehearsals. We might repeat a couple of those exercises within this session.

Wu Shu

This was something I was taught by a facilitator, Sharon Cromwell, and it has stuck with me. If your group needs waking up it is one of the best exercises ever. Make it a game.

- Get your group in a circle, still and ready. Say, 'Go with me'.

- Bring your arms into the middle of the circle, and say, 'Go gently.'

- Bring your fingers to your temples and *very very gently* tap your temples with your fingers for about 15 seconds or so.

- Then bring your hands over your scalp, tapping the scalp with your fingers, now much harder. Go over the back of the head and into the back of the neck. Bring the fingers back over the head, still tapping, and back to the temples, where you must go back to tapping *very gently.* (*Important Note*: Banging your temples hard can cause injury.)

- Repeat this movement from the temples to the back of the head. (Do this four times.)

- Now put your right arm into the space; everyone follows. Swing the other arm behind you and over your head, as if you were throwing overarm, letting out an open '*ah*' sound at the same time. Bring the left arm round, then tap the right arm with your left hand vigorously. Tap down the arm from the shoulder, right to the fingers and back to the shoulder. (Do this four times.) Be vigorous. Tell the group to relax their shoulders. Some will inevitably rise.

- Repeat the procedure, waking the left arm. (Do this four times.)

- Now bring your hands up to the top of your chest, and say something like 'Nice and gentle', and tap down the chest to the pelvis, this time with both hands. (Do this four times.)

- Now bend your knees as if you are going to run a race and put your hands at the top of your thighs. Raise your hands and make a big '*ah*' as you start tapping at the top of the thighs. Tap down the thighs vigorously down to your feet, and back up to the tops of your legs (four times). At the end, jump to face the other way and put your hands on your behind.

- Cry 'Go!' and tap down the behind and the backs of the legs to the heels and back (four times). Encourage energy.

- At the end I like to get everyone to jump back and stand absolutely still. I ask them to listen to their breathing and how their bodies are awake. You will find that standing still is almost impossible for some people, who will want to straighten their tops or adjust their hair.

- I ask them to notice the silence, to look around at each other and notice how we all look quite powerful.

Easy Stretch

- Ask the group in the circle to find a partner across the circle. I find even with a mature group this can be tricky and requires everyone to come into a tighter circle and point at their partner before moving out again. Ask them to smile broadly at their partner. Ask them to notice what happens when they do this. They immediately feel freer, sending out their energy. Tell them they have to keep smiling throughout, sending their energy out to their partner. If you do this, you achieve three things at once: you get the group to radiate their energy, acknowledge the group, *and* exercise the shoulders and arms.

- Ask them to knit their fingers together and hold their hands in front of their chests. Then, as they breathe in, to turn their hands and stretch up. As they breathe out, they need to bring the hands back to the starting position. Ask them to keep the stretches easy. (Do this four times.)

- Ask them to push their knitted hands out in front of them and push their chest to the back. Try and get them to release tension, to let go. Then tell them to bring their hands back towards the chest. (Do this four times.)

- Ask them to shake their bodies out vigorously.

Puppet

- Now ask them to hang down from the waist. Get them to breathe and let the weight of the body take the upper body further to the floor. The legs should be straight and shoulder-width apart at least.

- Ask them whilst in their hanging-down position to let go, releasing the knees, so they release the back further. They should go floppy and loose like a puppet, bending over from their waists. Ask them to shake their head and shoulders *only*, and let out a moaning sound. Do it for them so they are not embarrassed.

- Ask them to consider whether that is a freer sound. Then, *very slowly*, ask them to bring themselves to standing, curling up the spine vertebra by vertebra. The head and neck should be the last to go into place.

- You might like to repeat this twice.

Teaching Tip: Encourage slowness.

Head Rolls and Yawn

- Ask them to drop the head to the chest and then very slowly roll the head to the right, to the back, to the left and back to the front in a circle. (Four times each way.)

- As they roll their heads to the back, their mouths open, now tell them to let their jaw relax; as they do, ask them to let out a moan or a yawn. Do it with them so no one is embarrassed.

Shoulder Chugs

- To vary the tempo a bit, so they do not go to sleep, give the instruction, 'Shoulders *up*', 'Shoulders *centre*', 'Shoulders *down*' (four times). Do this quite quickly, like a game. And smile. Enjoy it.

- Now ask them to roll their shoulders in a circular motion, first one way and then the other (four times).

Rubber Face

- Put your fists in front of your face. Then, as if you are stretching the face, pull the fists apart and imagine you are stretching the face horizontally like a rubber mask.

- Bring your hands together, then pull them vertically and stretch the face vertically.

- Now try on the diagonal, both ways. Make a sound as you do it.

Now that we have done a short warm-up of the body and woken the voice a little, we begin working on the breath. You might like to explore a few of the warm-up exercises in Chapter Two, in particular *Breath Dance 1*.

Meet Your Breath

- Ask the group to stand in a circle and explain that today you are going to look at some issues of voice. Remind them that voice was very important in Shakespeare's world because language, poetry and sound were the main vehicles for the imagination. In addition, although the acoustics were good in the Globe, there were no microphones! You might also tell them that voice is still important now, and that how you speak tells us not only where you are from, but how confident you are, how you might be feeling and whether you want to communicate with others. It is vital for acting but important in many other spheres as well.

- Explain that the breath is the fuel for everything we do and without it we can do nothing. Ask them to consider that sometimes when they are going to sleep they notice that the breath falls more deeply into the body and helps relaxation.

- Ask them to put their fingers to their lips and breathe in through the nose. Get them to breathe out through the mouth, blowing on their fingers, and as they do, to move their fingers away from their mouths.

- Ask them if they felt their breath on their fingers.

- Now ask them to repeat the exercise, breathing in again through the nose, but this time blowing against their fingers, as if they are blowing out the candles on a birthday cake. (Do this three times.)

- Ask them to bend their knees slightly so they are almost sitting on the air and put one hand on the tummy. (*Important Note*: This is on the belt line and not on the ribs.) Ask them to put the other hand to the lips and breathe in through the nose. As they breathe in, ask them to imagine they are *breathing down* and that the tummy is filling up with air, making it expand. Then, imagining the sound is coming from that place in the belly, pull the tummy in and let the breath come up out of the mouth and onto the fingers. It is as if the breath is coming from the tummy, coming up through the body and going out through the mouth. This exercise involves the basic diaphragmatic breath, vital for voice work of any kind. If you are not familiar with this it is described in detail in *Teaching Voice* (*Breathing Exercises* (1): *Basic Breath* and *Breathing Exercises* (2): *More Fuel for The Body*, pages 43–44).

- Remind them to breathe down into the tummy and tell them to try not to tense their chests or raise the shoulders. Keep telling them to let the shoulders go. Some will be able to do this; some will need practice.

- Ask them to draw the fingers away from the mouth as they breathe out and ask them to imagine their breath is filling the room. Perhaps they might imagine their fingers are pulling the thread of breath from their mouths.

- Now ask them to *breathe down* into the tummy, and this time exhale on an '*ah*' sound. Tell them they must keep the sound going until they have to take a breath. Tell them it is not a contest to see who can go on for longest but to notice what happens to the voice when they run out of breath.

- Ask them what happened to the voice as they ran out of breath: that it became weaker, less controlled.

- Ask them now to breathe in and try these two lines quite loudly, without taking a breath after the first line:

  Two households, both alike in dignity,
  In fair Verona, where we lay our scene...

  Prologue to Romeo and Juliet

- Ask them what they noticed: 'The line got weaker, fizzled out' might be the response. This shows them *why* they need to know where to breathe. Ask them to try this again and take a breath after 'dignity'. The result will be easier.

- You might then try asking them to breathe after 'households', 'dignity', and 'Verona'. For some that will work better.

Teaching Tip: Shakespeare is like doing opera. If you are intending to *perform* substantial amounts of the text with your group, then some of the speeches require these kinds of technical decisions (when to breathe) to give your young actors freedom and power to be effective. Ultimately you need to explore with them how to split the speech up. This might appear counter-creative (it certainly seemed so to me when I was training as an actor), but for young actors it is *essential*, especially if they are using a lot of the text. We will return to this topic in the next workshop. For now, it is enough that they acknowledge the importance of the breath.

At this point you might try *Radiating and Receiving* (*Throwing the Ball*) from Chapter Two. This exercise is one of my staples and is useful for breath, connecting the body to the voice, and connecting the actors to each other.

Resonance

Before you start this series of exercises, you might explain that the more resonant the voice then the less effort is needed for your voice to carry, the more interesting it sounds, the more powerful it will be and the more you will be able to share your feelings and those of the character. Do these exercises with them.

- Move the hand to the top of the head. Breathe in. Focus on where the hand is and send the sound up there. Hum into the hand as you breathe out. Try and make the hand vibrate with a '*mmmmmmmaaaahhh*'. Direct the vibration there.

- Put the hand to the bridge of the nose. Breathe in. Hum into the hand. Try and make the hand vibrate with a '*mmmmmmmaaaahhh*'. Direct the vibration there.

- Put your fingers lightly to your lips. As you breathe out and start to hum, bring your hand from your lips to about a foot in front of you. Focus on the hand as if you were singing into a microphone.

- Now put the hand on the chest. Breathe in. Hum into the hand. Try and make the chest vibrate with a '*mmmmmmmaaaahhh*'. Direct the vibration there.

- Now ask them to see if they can move the resonance from one area to another; to move their hands and the sounds around and to play with '*mmmmmmmaaaahhh*'. They breathe when they need to. Ask them what they notice. Where do they resonate best?

- Finally, ask them to put one hand on the tummy and the other on the lips. Start the '*mmmmmmmaaaahhh*', bring the fingers on the lips to a foot in front of them, then extend and open the arm and let the sound fill the room. Tell them to breathe into the tummy when they need to. Next ask them to put their focus into the room, opening both their arms, intoning the line, 'Two households, both alike in dignity'. Ask them to fill the room with their words. Get them to say the line a few times, then bring to a close.

- *Flyback*. Get them to talk about how their voices sounded. They are fuller, more resonant and open.

Diction Warm-up

Without clear diction it is impossible to hear what someone is saying, and if you can't hear what they are saying you are not going to want to listen to them in the theatre. Suggest to them how important it is to be clear when they are working or doing presentations in school or college; that this work has many more uses. Keep it physical, strong and fun.

- Shampoo. Ask them to massage their scalps vigorously as if they were washing their hair. (For young people who have just done their hair, this can be challenging!) Get them to massage into their necks too and even the shoulders a little.

- Massage the jaw. It might help for them to reimagine the melting of the hinge of the jaw we did earlier in the *Head Rolls and Yawn* exercises.

- Rinsing. With hands on the face, get them to draw down their hands vigorously as if they were getting water off it. Get them to make a '*fuh*' sound as they do it. (Four times.)

- Blow through the lips (for twenty seconds or so). Really loosen the lips.

- Tongue flicking. Flick out your tongue like a lizard. (Four times.)

- Chew fast/chew slow. The change of tempo is good. Again, it reminds you how different a new pace feels.

- Tongue circles. Circle the tongue each way with the tongue on the outside of the teeth. (Four times.) Then repeat, this time on the *inside* of the teeth. (Four times.)

- Tongue directions. Tongue to your nose/to your chin. (Four times.)

- Tongue across side to side. (Four times.)

- Rinse the face again to finish.

T–L–D

- You need to lead. These are all tip-of-the-tongue exercises. Say '*tuh*' as you point across the circle; they say it and point.

- Say '*luh*' with a flap of the hands; they say it and flap.

- Say '*duh*' with a punch; they say it and punch.

- Then start in with the sequence below. Do the sounds with them, or with call and answer (i.e. you say them, they repeat).

- '*Tttt-tttt-tttt-tah.*' (Four times.)

- '*Llll-llll-llll-lah.*' (Four times.)

- '*Dddd-dddd-dddd-dah.*' (Four times.)

- Then: '*Tttt-llll-dddd.*' (Six times.)

- Then: '*Tttt-llll-dddd, llll-dddd-tttt, dddd-tttt-llll.*' Imagine they're written in front of you, if that makes it easier. (Four times.)

- Then do: '*Bbbb-bbbb-bbbb-bah*' and '*Kkkk-kkkk-kkkk-kah*'. Notice how with '*buh*' the sound is focused at the front of the mouth. '*Kuh*' is at the back of the mouth. Then try: '*pppp*' and '*gggg*' similarly.

- Ask them to do '*Buh-duh-guh*'/'*Puh-tuh-kuh*', slowly at first and then speed up.

Teaching Tip: For these basic but crucial exercises, I cannot over-emphasise how important it is to get them to use their bodies as much as you can. It enlivens and changes the sound, often getting them to speak in ways which they had never considered. Let them dance around, making it fun, as long as the sound stays together. You might use the *Consonant Characters* exercise in Chapter Two at this point, as a way to emphasise this physical connection to sound.

Diction with Words

When inexperienced directors speak loftily about bad diction, they often expect even inexperienced young actors to be able to fix it themselves. Here is an exercise to help them improve their diction. We will take the line, 'Where civil blood makes civil hands unclean'.

- Ask the group to repeat the line all together a few times, trying to be as clear as they can. It will most likely be very unclear even by the third or fourth try. This is partly because we need to train ourselves to hear bad diction. *We* think we are being clear when we are not.

- Tell them that each person is now going to work alone. They are going to speak the line very, very slowly, over-enunciating every consonant very definitely and clearly. Tell them it will not sound 'normal'.

- At first they will go too fast. Make them go very slowly. Notice especially consonants at the ends of words. Be as persistent as you can to make sure every single sound is pronounced.

- When everyone has every single sound in the line, ask them to speed up a little. They will find they can enunciate more clearly.

- Now ask them to go up to normal speed. They might lose a little clarity but it will be better than before.

Two Households

Two households, both alike in dignity,
In fair Verona, where we lay our scene,
From ancient grudge break to new mutiny,
Where civil blood makes civil hands unclean.
From forth the fatal loins of these two foes
A pair of star-crossed lovers take their life,
Whose misadventured piteous overthrows
Doth with their death bury their parents' strife.
The fearful passage of their death-marked love,
And the continuance of their parents' rage,
Which but their children's end naught could remove,
Is now the two hours' traffic of our stage;
The which if you with patient ears attend,
What here shall miss, our toil shall strive to mend.

As I said earlier, I always like to end with a piece of application. I have chosen the Prologue from *Romeo and Juliet*. The story is familiar, which is helpful, and some may have studied it at school.

- Get the group in a circle. Read the piece through with them. Explain any words they don't understand.

- Get each member in the group to read a line, one after the other, taking up the cue as smoothly as possible until you reach the end of the Prologue.

- After reading, tell them to note moments where the energy sagged because people did not pick up the cue quickly enough. Ask them to notice that this is not a good idea; that it is a real example of what happens when we let go of energy; that all intensity evaporates, like water slipping through our fingers.

- Ask them what this speech *does*. It tells the story. It tells us everything that is going to happen and that it is going to end in blood and tragedy.

- For this exercise, initially focus on the goal of getting them to tell the story clearly to the audience.

- Put them in teams of 5 or 6 people and tell them they are going to perform the speech to the rest of the group, splitting the text between them so that everyone gets to speak. How they do this is up to them but not to be too clever; their main job is to tell the story.

- Give them only 5 to 8 minutes to prepare. Tell them this is only the first attempt and we are going to add something afterwards.

- Let them show their pieces. Don't develop the piece yet, simply ask the others whether they thought the story was clear. Could they hear? If not, why not? Are the actors too buried in their scripts? Perhaps it would help if they all went slower? Make one or two suggestions per group and send them off to do another 5 to 8 minutes.

- Let them show again.

- Now give each team a particular identity, as we did with 'O for a muse of fire!' in *Starting the Show 2* (Chapter Three). They could be actors, ghosts, reporters or police officers, for instance. Above all, make the team identity appropriate to the material. Don't let them send it up. Get them to work on this for a final showing. They will be impressed by the different feel of each presentation, brought about by simply committing to these broad choices of *how* they speak the text.

Teaching Tip 1: Don't let anyone sit down too long to pore over the script. Explain that, if they do, the energy leaves their bodies and it is much harder to get up again. Also a small word about feedback: always ask the watching group for some *positive* elements about the performers before you or they make any constructive critical comment. Always try to get the student audience to explain *why* something didn't work for them; that way everyone can learn.

Teaching Tip 2: It can be handy to have a piece of text that everybody knows. Something I have found is that you can use the same piece in many different ways to emphasise different aspects of developing the work. This piece below, for example, could be used for breathing, emphasis, atmosphere – and a whole range of other skills.

The Golden Hoop

This is a beautiful Michael Chekhov exercise which does not employ voice, but enables the group to make a final act together and get a sense of what they are learning.

- Everyone stands in a circle. You suggest to them, 'We are going to imagine that in front of us on the floor there is a large golden hoop almost as big as this circle we are in. In it is all the promise, learning and excitement of the workshop. You are going to look into this hoop and see yourself doing movements in the workshop, or moments when you saw other people doing something funny or amazing. Consider what you learned and saw. Let this last for a minute or two.'

- Now explain to them (demonstrating as you do), 'When someone wants to bend down slowly and pick up the hoop, the whole group goes down with them. We all pick up the hoop together. When everyone is standing with the hoop at their waists everyone looks around at everyone else in the circle. Feel that moment. Don't miss anyone out. Then, all together, we will slowly throw the hoop up into the air like a balloon and watch it float away.'

- Having demonstrated, you then do the exercise as a group. Try not to be the person who instigates the movement down to the hoop, but at the beginning you might have to be. When you have sent up the hoop, stay staring at it floating away for a moment and then bring the arms down slowly. Say 'Thank you.'

Chapter Five
Voice Workshop Two:
Voice and Shakespeare

> And crown what I profess with kind event if I speak
> true!
>
> *The Tempest*: Act Three, Scene One

This workshop is really two workshops in one, in that it focuses partly on working imaginatively and through the body, before we move on to more technical issues of breathing, emphasis and annotating the text. As I stated earlier, we must introduce the technical skills in order to free our young actors and give them confidence, whilst at the same time developing the imagination to take them out of themselves in order that they can be truly creative. There is always a trade-off between these two priorities when we do productions.

Later in the workshop we are going to work with Ariel's speech from *The Tempest* which begins, 'All hail, great master, grave sir, hail!' (Act One, Scene Two). You might like to explain that Ariel is a magic spirit who has created a tempest at the bidding of his master, Prospero, a magician and the person to whom he is talking. I chose Ariel as it is a fantastic character and therefore, to my mind, freeing, especially for the voice. Another good text for this session might be Puck's speech, 'My mistress with a monster is in love' (*A Midsummer Night's Dream*: Act Three, Scene Two) which we will also look at in Chapter Ten.

The Workshop Part One: Imagination, Voice and Body

Warm-up

I would suggest you use the warming-up plan from Chapter Two and repeat some of the exercises found in Chapter Four (Voice Workshop One), particularly those around the diction work. Spend about 15 to 20 minutes on this. What you are trying to do is invigorate the body and connect the breath and voice to it. If the group is listless or drowsy then something like *Wu Shu* is a good start, or you might like to start more quietly and focused with something like *Beach Ball* or *Breath Dance 1*.

Breath Dance 2

An extension to *Breath Dance 1*, this exercise provides an important sense of connection between acting partners. It will prepare us for more work on radiating and receiving.

- Tell each person to find a partner and ask them to stand looking at each other about three feet apart. Ask them to synchronise their breathing, in through the nose, out through the mouth.

- After maybe four breaths, as they breathe in, each moves an arm, then sustains the stillness and then breathes out and makes another movement with the arm. As before, the movement and the breath have to be connected. They cannot move unless they are breathing in or out. Tell them they are not 'mirroring' the other performer but complementing them. They are *relating* to the other. So we have two people breathing in and out together and moving in a synchronised way.

- Tell them now to engage more of the body as they move in these waves of synchronised 'in–out' breathing.

- Tell them not to be clever at first and try to catch each other out, but relate to each other with simple movements and regular, even breaths. Keep the breathing steady and suggest that they enjoy working together, with a 'Feeling of Ease' (a Chekhov term) rather than competing.

- Ask them to note the moment when they change their movement and their breath from an 'in' to an 'out'. There is a moment of suspension or sustaining, a moment which has all sorts of possibilities within it.

- Once they get proficient in this, you might ask them to change the tempo of the breath, which means, of course, that if they breathe in quickly they have to move quickly; a gasp, for instance, makes for a fast movement.

- Let them try this more adventurous option of changing the pace.

- Ask them to bring the exercise to a close, not to just stop when you say so.

- Ask them what it felt like.

Tempo

There's a version of this exercise in *Teaching Voice*, but what follows is more detailed and explores deeper feeling through movement. It is to help the young person start to explore a sense of pace. Note that again, instead of the voice, we start in the body.

- Ask them to find a real impulse to walk; that can be an odd thing to instigate, so here is a way for them to find it.

- Get them to stand in a circle and feel an impulse to walk ahead. Maybe suggest they pick a spot to walk to in the room and tell themselves, 'I really want to go there!' Ask them to feel that impulse very strongly but not to move until you clap your hands. You'll see some of them straining to move. Clap your hands. Get them to stop after a couple of steps or there'll be a collision!

- Ask where they feel that impulse in the body. People generally say the thighs, pelvis and/or the chest.

- Now ask them to find the impulse in the body again, walk around the room briskly and keep it going. As they walk, tell them to start saying aloud what it *feels* like to walk fast. They

67

might say 'rushed', 'nervous', 'excited', 'uneasy', 'confident'. Don't be concerned if the words are conflicting. Tell them to keep walking. Now ask them to say a couple of lines of text, for example:

> All hail, great master, grave sir, hail! I come
> To answer thy best pleasure.

- Ask them to run around the studio, then get them to stop. Now ask them to walk very, very slowly. Ask them how the change in tempo affected how they felt. They might say 'excited', 'positive', 'angry' or 'afraid' when they were running; 'sad', 'serious', 'important', 'careful' when they were moving slowly.

- Now get them to run and say the lines at the same time. They will sound energised and excited. Now get them to stop and walk slowly. They will be serious, solemn, perhaps nervous.

- Ask them to stop and share what they noticed.

Teaching Tip: If it isn't working for some of the group, try getting them to walk forward with an impulse, as they point with a finger, walking to a point they want to get to and speaking as they move. Pointing is a great way to get focus in the voice. It is another easy example of the body helping the voice, and this time even exploring the emotional content of what the person is feeling and saying.

Radiating and Receiving (*Throwing the Ball*)

If you haven't used this exercise (page 30), then you should. Use the opening of the Ariel speech again.

Verbing the Body/Speaking the Text

This exercise is based on Chekhov's 'Psychological Gesture'. Provided the young person is connected to their body, there will be an earthy and immediate contact to the way they speak, which is absolutely essential when you are working with imagery.

- Ask everyone to stand in their own space.

- Suggest a verb: an action that they can do strongly with the body, like 'punch'.

- Invite them to perform the action without speaking. Make sure the movement is vigorous and engages the whole body. If the movement is small and without impulse, nothing will happen and they might feel foolish. Remind them of how invigorated they were by the walking exercise.

- Invite them to breathe in through the nose and out through the mouth and let out a sound as they punch. You will suddenly feel like you are in a martial-arts class. Let them continue with this for a couple of minutes.

- Now get them to say 'punch' on the out-breath as they punch with the body. Get them to do this a few times.

- Then ask them to say 'punch' *as if* they were punching with their bodies, but to stay absolutely still, to simply *imagine* they are punching. You will note how much more powerful the word sounds.

- Ask them what the action did to the way they said the word and what it felt like. Some might say it 'got them into' what the word meant. Do reassure them that they may need a few tries to get this. It's instinctive for most people, but if anyone is unconnected to the body or is half-hearted they will not feel it as strongly.

- Try a few more action words: 'squeeze', 'open', 'wash', 'tear', 'embrace'.

- Shake out.

- Now take the lines:

    All hail, great master, grave sir, hail! I come
    To answer thy best pleasure, be't to fly,
    To swim, to dive into the fire, to ride
    On the curled clouds.

- Get them to look at this text. (If you want to use another, just make sure it is one with many expressive verbs within it.)

- Ask them to use the words 'fly', 'swim', 'dive' and 'ride' in the same way as we used the other words in the exercise. Explain to them that they are not pretending to fly! They are making a movement that excites their imaginations to connect with flying, which in turn affects the voice. This might sound complicated to explain but it is important to head off any feeling that this might be silly, as they cannot really fly. If they understand the process and enter into it wholeheartedly, then the benefits to their dialogue in both expression and commitment will be enormous.

- Ask them to drop the external movement and *imagine* they are flying, diving, etc., as they speak the words.

- Now ask them to try all four lines, really emphasising those verbs and speaking them first *with* the movement and then *without* it.

- Look at a few and ask for comments. Some people will be better with these word/voice/movement connections than others. Explain that everyone will have strengths and weaknesses in the work.

Two Qualities: Flying and Radiating

Ask them to stand in their own space. Tell them we are going to look at two basic qualities of movement, as described by Michael Chekhov, which are going to help them be more flexible with their voices and bodies in quality and feeling. One is *flying* and the other is *radiating*. I chose these two particular qualities to approach first because I thought them appropriate for the speech. The other two core qualities, *moulding* and *floating*, we will meet in Chapter Six (Qualities and Gesture).

Please Note: In Chekhov Technique, *radiating* is also about transmitting our energy (as in Radiating and Receiving). Radiating in this context means to move with a sense of 'fire'. If there is any confusion you might call it 'fire' or 'flaming'.

70

Flying

- Invite them, with their eyes closed, to imagine they are flying. Ask each person to feel this and let it affect their body. Should anyone lose the feeling, then just make the suggestion to bring the attention back to a feeling of lightness.

- Allow the whole body to be affected and let flying movements happen. Ask the whole group, without losing concentration, to open their eyes and keep the movement going. Ask them to be aware of anywhere in the body that is not affected and to put their attention there and let out a sigh. Get them to 'fly' around the room.

- Now ask them to make a sound as they fly, then to use a line such as, 'All hail, great master, grave sir, hail!' All being well, you will find their voices have a very light, flying quality. If they don't, ask them to make the feeling of flying stronger. This should put this quality into their voices.

- Ask them to drop the external movement but keep that flying sensation inside them. Ask them to speak the line as they did when they were flying. It should sound light, swift and ethereal.

Radiating

- Invite them, with their eyes closed, to imagine their bodies are flaming, as if they were a superhero. They are invincible and the fire is coming from their eyes, face, fingertips and the whole body.

- Ask them to bend at the knees slightly; this enables the radiating to affect their legs. Remind them to breathe and feel through the whole body. Any time the sensation is lost, ask them to bring it back to this idea of fire. Invite them, without losing concentration, to open their eyes and keep the movement going, moving around the room in this fiery way.

- Now ask the group to add a sound (these sounds are usually strong and sharp), then to add the same line, 'All hail, great master, grave sir, hail!' Let them do this a few times. It will be very noisy!

- Ask them to stand still but to keep that sensation of fire strongly inside them. Tell them to speak the line again, 'All hail, great master, grave sir, hail!' Let them do this a few times. It will be very full of life and anger.

- Talk to them about how using these movement qualities can affect the mood, tempo and feeling of how they speak. Explain how this can be especially useful for characters who are not like us.

Flying and Radiating with Text

Let's see if we can put this movement quality into practice with text:

- Put the group into teams of 4 to 6. Tell them that each team is going to have six lines of the text, which they can split up however they like, but that every word must have the quality of *flying* or *radiating*.

> All hail, great master, grave sir, hail! I come
> To answer thy best pleasure, be't to fly,
> To swim, to dive into the fire, to ride
> On the curled clouds. To thy strong bidding, task
> Ariel and all his quality.

- Give them just 10 minutes to do this, splitting the text using these two qualities. Suggest they use whole lines with one quality, then change the quality for the next one. Try and get them to leave the script behind. Encourage them to use their bodies and imaginations.

- You may well have to reawaken the qualities. Really push them to go as far as they can with their imaginations and bodies. They will feel they are overdoing it. They won't be. Remember you can always pull it back in performance. First, they have to *find* it.

- Have them show each other the pieces and note how using the different qualities affects the text.

Imagining the Image

You might like to get into imagining the image. Remind people that before the internet, television or movies, people created their own images from language. Here is Ariel's full speech. I have left out the lines where Prospero speaks, which explains the occasional short line.

> All hail, great master, grave sir, hail! I come
> To answer thy best pleasure, be't to fly,
> To swim, to dive into the fire, to ride
> On the curled clouds. To thy strong bidding, task
> Ariel and all his quality.
> I boarded the King's ship: now on the beak,
> Now in the waist, the deck, in every cabin
> I flamed amazement. Sometime I'd divide
> And burn in many places – on the topmast,
> The yards and bowsprit would I flame distinctly,
> Then meet and join. Jove's lightning, the precursors
> O'th' dreadful thunderclaps, more momentary
> And sight-outrunning were not; the fire and cracks
> Of sulphurous roaring, the most mighty Neptune
> Seem to besiege and make his bold waves tremble,
> Yea, his dread trident shake.
> Not a soul
> But felt a fever of the mad and played
> Some tricks of desperation. All but mariners
> Plunged in the foaming brine and quit the vessel;
> Then all afire with me, the King's son Ferdinand,
> With hair up-staring (then like reeds, not hair),
> Was the first man that leapt, cried 'Hell is empty,
> And all the devils are here.'

- Let the group have notebooks and pens in front of them. Tell them you are going to read the speech for them, which describes the tempest. They will have their eyes closed.

Every time they get an image or feeling or smell they should open their eyes and write it down.

- Read the speech, slowly but with power.

- See what they come up with. For instance, when asked for feedback, someone might say they saw boots sliding on the slippery deck of a ship or people panicking, imagined the smell of fear, black clouds, huge forks of lightning, or someone running with a lifejacket. Tell them that all these images are important because they will really assist in the way the speech is spoken.

- Remind them that Ariel has to bring the storm to life for us, even though we might assume that he is showing what fun he had creating the storm as well.

- Ask each person to take any image in the text they really like and imagine it, then speak the phrase aloud. If you like, you can get them to speak it one by one, or all to speak at once. Ask them what they noticed. They should notice that the imagination coloured what they said.

The Workshop Part Two: Iambic Pentameter, Emphasis and Breathing

It is now time to look at the text in a more technical way because, without it, lots of the more imaginative work might not be possible. There has to be a balance. For instance, if actors are not vocally clear, which requires practice, they are not going to be able to create a good performance.

Iambic Pentameter

Here might be a good place to introduce the form of iambic pentameter. In some ways, I am quite nervous about introducing this concept because it can be like a straitjacket and, instead of freeing the young actor and allowing imagination, it can constrain her. If you look at performances from decades ago on YouTube, people sometimes overemphasise the rhythm, making their delivery stilted.

You might ask why bother to mention this aspect of the work at all? The answer is that the rhythm gives the language a form and poetic strength; it heightens what everyone is saying and takes it to a different, more universal level, whilst at the same time being very close to our natural speech rhythms. In a production, it is useful at least to acknowledge this rhythm as it can really help with the acting, so long as you don't push it too much. Also, knowing a bit about iambic pentameter helps with emphasis and memory.

Explain that Shakespeare's verse is set up as having five feet per line:

> di DUH di DUH di DUH di DUH di DUH

So:

> All <u>hail</u>, great <u>master</u>, <u>grave</u> sir, <u>hail</u>! I <u>come</u>
> To <u>answer</u> <u>thy</u> best <u>pleas</u>ure, <u>be't</u> to <u>fly</u>,
> To <u>swim</u>, to <u>dive</u> in<u>to</u> the <u>fire</u>, to <u>ride</u>...

So far, so good. Ask them to clap it out with you. The problem comes, though, with the next line:

> On the <u>curled</u> <u>clouds</u>...

Explain how, when we emphasise the word 'the' in the line, which *should* be the next word to be emphasised, it sounds wrong. So we cannot stick so rigidly to the pattern. We have to be playful with this rhythm. Tell the group that it is simply useful to sense the rhythm is there and to use it when it feels right.

Some of the songs in Shakespeare are written in different rhythms, along with certain spoken passages. Puck's speech beginning 'Now the hungry lion roars', many of the Witches' speeches in *Macbeth*, and Feste's song 'Come Away, Death' from *Twelfth Night* are good examples. Some scenes are written in prose. These are usually in scenes with poorer people or comedians.

However, this is as far as I would go. It really depends on the purpose of your session and how far you wish to go with this academic exploration. There are many voice and poetry books which set out to explain this rhythm in more detail. I am not suggesting you ignore it totally; I would far rather you got people on their feet. They have enough to concern themselves with acting, working on an old text, and training their voice.

I would suggest you spend about 12 to 15 minutes on each of the next sections.

Working with Emphasis

When we work on Shakespeare in particular, it is essential that we appreciate which words are carrying the sense or meaning. (I have called them 'sense-words'.) Sometimes, as an audience, we do not always receive the full image, but we get a powerful sense of what is going on through the emphasis of the important words and the power of the actor. Here is a fun exercise you might try.

- Explain that we are now going to work on emphasis. Tell them if you do not emphasise the 'sense-words', the audience will lose the thread, however passionate and imaginative you are when you speak.

- Give this example. Let's take the words 'I come / To answer thy best pleasure'. Try stressing the word 'I' over the rest of the sentence. It sounds like Ariel is very arrogant. If you emphasise another word, the intention will sound different.

- Looking at the first half of the Ariel speech, ask them to decide which words to emphasise in order for the text to make sense, underlining the words in pencil so they can change it later.

- Working in pairs, get them to test out the emphasis on each other by reading aloud. Does what they are saying make sense to their partner? Does it sound right?

- After a few minutes, listen to a few. If any do not make sense or the emphasis is too weak (the most frequent problem) ask the young actor to repeat the line and stamp on the floor when they speak the word that needs stronger emphasis. You will find the emphasis improves a lot. If not, get the young actor to try it again. You will be surprised how strange some of their choices can be.

- Tell them they might not stick to their chosen emphasis once they know more about the character and what the character is doing, but they need somewhere to start from.

Working with Breathing

- Now ask them to return to their pairs and, using the same text, to work on where they need to breathe. This is trickier because everyone is different. If you have good breath capacity, you may wish to go all the way down to 'clouds' without taking a breath. This is not going to be a likely possibility, so you need to look at how you split it up and mark the text. You might need to help them and do it with them. What you want to achieve is not unqualified success, but to develop the understanding in your group that *where you breathe* affects your ability to perform and create the pictures for the audience. It depends how well they understand the whole concept of breath being the fuel for the voice and whether you have explored this in the earlier workshop.

- Tell them it is not a contest for who can say the most words without running out of breath! It is about giving the actor a sense of freedom and power.

- Mark the places to breathe on the text. Let's look at the following section. Here are some choices I might make. The | marks a place to breathe:

> I boarded the King's ship: | now on the beak,
> Now in the waist, the deck, in every cabin
> I flamed amazement. | Sometime I'd divide
> And burn in many places; | on the topmast,
> The yards and bowsprit would I flame distinctly,
> Then meet and join. | Jove's lightning, | the precursors
> O'th' dreadful thunderclaps, | more momentary
> And sight-outrunning were not...

- Notice that I have not chosen to breathe at the end of any line. Ariel is excited and the piece is full of flying movement. Breathing mid-line keeps the flow of the text going and makes the text sound free.

- Listen to a few. Notice that not everyone makes the same choices and that many choices work.

Finishing Up: Song Circle

I love singing, especially in what has been primarily a voice and text class. This is one of the most magical exercises I know to finish a session well. Here are the rules.

- Form a circle. Tell the group that when you have finished talking, you are all going to hold hands and close your eyes. You will lead. You are going to sing a line like, 'Hell is empty / And all the devils are here!' – or something else from the piece you have been working on which is not too long.

- *You* sing the line the same way over and over; make the tune *easy*. If possible, try leaving a few beats between the end of the sung line and the beginning of the repeat, so there is a silent space.

- The group, with their eyes closed, will sing the same line with you, over and over. Gradually, if anyone has the desire, they can start to harmonise with the original tune. They can use pieces of the line or just single words if they want. All being well, something quite magical and quite intricate can develop. If it doesn't the first time you try this exercise, then keep at it. All you need in the group are one or two good singers to make it sound exciting.

- Everyone must sing. If there is someone who right now feels they *can't* sing, tell them to stay with the base line, which you should not leave. If that is hard for them, suggest they speak or whisper the line in rhythm. This can sound great over the singing.

- You might open your own eyes during the exercise and notice who cannot manage to keep their eyes closed. You might want to follow this up later, reinforcing that it is important to commit to the exercises to get the full benefit and enjoyment from them.

- When do you stop the song? Only you can judge. But do give it enough time to catch fire! On the other hand, you don't want them getting giggly and disrupting the end of the session.

- When you feel it is time to stop (and you need to explain this before you start) you will squeeze the hand of the person on your right. They will squeeze the hand of the person on their right and so on, so the squeeze goes round the circle. When you feel the squeeze come back to you, you know everyone knows.

- Tell them that when they get 'the squeeze', it does not mean 'Oh great, it's over': they have to listen and bring the music down slowly. When everyone has stopped singing and there are a few seconds of silence, you let go of the hands, open your eyes and clap. All applaud each other and the session is ended.

Chapter Six
Acting Workshop One:
Qualities and Gesture

In action how like an angel…

Hamlet: Act Two, Scene Two

This workshop plan is the first of two which focus on elements of the Michael Chekhov Technique. The technique works on a psycho-physical principle, which means that we can find most of what we need for acting a character from the imagination and the body. It means the character is not 'all about *you*', as we might say in modern parlance, but it *emerges* from an imaginative response to the text. What it means from the young actor's point of view is that it frees her; she does not have to base her interpretation on some personal life event, which can be painful, nor try and make the character as much like her as possible, which can be limiting. The character has its own life. All this sounds rather mystical but it isn't. All the exercises in the Michael Chekhov Technique are based upon the way we respond to things in everyday life. It is worth telling your group this.

Importantly, this approach is invaluable because it finds imaginative ways into exploring character that are also authentic and transformative. We will touch more on this aspect of the work when we look at rehearsal processes.

Remember we are all conditioned into making an intellectual response to everything. Initially, Chekhov Technique is not about thinking at all. The intellect has a place, of course, but it comes into its own *after* the initial creative work has been done. It can be hard to get people just to respond intuitively through the imagination and body. It is a case of 'Play first, think after'.

Chekhov considered acting as a primary creative art, not merely an interpretive one. In other words, the actor has a real contribution to make and is not just there to fulfil the director's instructions! This is integral to all theatre work, but particularly when we are trying to encourage the development of our young people; only then will they feel valued, own the work, and so develop depth. The Chekhov work is extremely accessible to many young people and can provide transformative experiences quite quickly.

Chekhov Technique explores movement and energy; it states that all acting *is* movement. Even when we are still, there is an *inner movement*. When we stand still, this inner movement can be frantic. Consider what happens in a crisis, when you are under threat: your mind might be racing, you can feel the energy flying around inside like fireworks, but your body can appear calm.

One of the main rules about this work is that you *commit*: commit to the movement, the image, the atmosphere and the instruction. That is all you have to do – and your acting will become free and surprising. Many a time have I witnessed actors and students startled by how they said a line when working with Chekhov Technique because it was not how they had expected to say it.

The three main areas we are exploring here are Radiating and Receiving, Qualities and Psychological Gesture. These are all areas we will return to, particularly once we start to work on project and production. Feel free to put this workshop into two sessions if you feel it is too long.

Warm-up

Let's begin by using some exercises from Chapter Two (Connecting Up). I would suggest *Beach Ball*, the *Head Rolls and Yawn* exercises and *Breath Dance 1*. When doing these exercises, suggest that they try and move with a Feeling of Ease. This is one of Chekhov's principles (see Appendix). It is a more effective way to look at the idea of relaxation.

Perhaps one way of introducing this might be to give the instruction to raise the arm tensely and bring it down tensely. Then to try and do it with a Feeling of Ease. Everyone can notice the difference. The thing about tension is that we need *some* tension in the body to give us the sensations and feelings we get from movement, which in turn goes into our speech. However, too much tension ruins the sensation and makes the performer tense.

Easy Walk

- Ask them to walk around the room. They are not to look at each other. Each is alone. They are walking easily. You will soon spot who is tense and where they are tense. If it is okay to say it, point out to people when they have tense shoulders, when they are clenching their fists or pushing their head forward.

- Ask them to experience the room as if they have never been in it before; as if they are seeing it for the first time.

- Tell them to remain 'easy'. Look out for people who become aimless and floppy, looking as if they are not engaged. Really try to get them engaged in their surroundings. Talk about the room, things you notice yourself.

- Ask them to notice something in the room and go to it. Ask them to really look at it, consider what interests them about it. As soon as the object or the detail no longer holds them, get them to walk around the room and find another.

- When they fix on an object or detail, suggest it is as if they are inviting it in, almost like they are absorbing it. Tell them that concentrating or focusing is not about really screwing up the face and trying very hard. It is not about trying to remember.

- Bring the exercise to a close. Ask them to *flyback*. How did they feel? Did they get bored? Did they notice that they stayed 'easy'? How was it to concentrate in this way?

Teaching Tip: Tell them that you are just dipping your toes into finding a Feeling of Ease, and you are also awakening a different form of concentration; one that isn't about remembering facts, but about *experiencing*. It is a very creative aspect of our life. Suggest that when they are walking to lessons, lectures or work, they might like to focus on walking there with a Feeling of Ease.

Open the Hand/Close the Hand

- Ask everyone to stand still. Then ask them to hold out one hand and open and close it. They can do it fast or slow. Get them to notice whether they feel differently when they do it at different speeds. You will find that many of them will. Tell them to change hands if one gets tired or get them to use both.

- Now ask them to open and close their hand *sadly*. This can be very powerful, as immediately in the room you will start to feel a sombre atmosphere. Ask them to add a sound with the opening and closing. Tell them not to force it, to concentrate only on moving the hand *sadly*.

- Tell them to keep going, but now to say, as they open and close the hand sadly, 'To be or not to be, that is the question.' (You can use any line for this exercise, but as we are focusing on Shakespeare, I thought we should use one of his.) Have them repeat the line several times as they open and close the hand.

- Ask them to stop. After anything potentially intense, get them to really shake out the whole body. Occasionally this body work causes a strong reaction, and it is important to acknowledge this, without being scary about it.

- *Flyback*. What happened? Some will say something like, 'The way I moved made me feel really sad, so I said the line sadly.'

- Now ask them to open and close the hand, this time *greedily*. Most will move faster and sharper. Tell them to add a sound. There will be growls and guttural noises. Try and get them to keep the sound open, with not too much tension.

- Now put the line into the mix. Tell them to keep opening the hand greedily and say, 'To be or not to be, that is the question.' It will radically affect how they say it.

- Shake out, then try the line *lovingly*.

- Shake out, then try it *angrily*.

- Shake out, then try it *peacefully*.

- *Flyback*. Standard responses will be that some qualities were easier than others. Everyone has this issue. Tell them this is natural. We all have varied access to different feelings, even from one day to another. Also, we might feel quite strongly that to feel *hate* is wrong, so we block it, yet many characters hate and this needs to be accessed by the actor. Another problem might be that we start asking ourselves questions in our heads like, 'What does moving hatefully *mean*?' These questions are completely useless and we have to stop asking them.

Teaching Tip: What you will notice, especially if this is a new way of working for you, is that moving the body with a quality helps the young actor to connect to the text in a meaningful way. Moving with a quality gives them an immediate connection.

Stacatto/Legato

This is a standard Chekhov exercise which works brilliantly for focus and discipline, sustaining and qualities of movement. It's a great warm-up too. You will need to lead them in this sequence until they get the hang of it.

- This series of movements needs us to move in each of the six directions: to each side, back, front, up and down. There needs to be space between each member of the group.

- Ask them to stand facing front, hands by the sides, knees slightly bent and focusing ahead.

- Then ask them to move to the right by taking a small step, turning the body to the right, then lunging to the right, with their arms extended. Tell them they must try and imagine the energy streaming out of them into the space between their arms.

- Now ask them to return to the original position and stand still but still be focused in the exercise. No 'zoning out' is allowed.

- Then ask them to move to the left by taking a small step, turning the body to the left and lunging to the left, with their arms extended. Tell them they must try and imagine the energy streaming from them into the space between their arms.

- Ask them to return to the original position and stand still.

- Now ask them to raise their arms and reach up, looking up into the air.

- Ask them to sustain the energy moving upwards for a second.

- Then ask them to return to the original position and stand still.

- Ask them to reach down, bending the knees a little. Ask them to sustain the energy between their arms downwards for a second. This is not a 'flopping' movement: they are *reaching* down.

- Then ask them to return to the original position and stand still.
- Now ask them to move forward. Get them to take a small step (either foot will do) and reach forward.

- They are sending their energy forward. Sustain for a moment and come back.
- Finally, ask them to take a step backward and reach back with the arms. When you look at someone in this position, it is as if they are protecting something or someone. Sustain.

- Then ask them to return to their original position and stand still. They have completed a round of the exercise.

- Now get them to do it on their own.

Teaching Tip: There are some things to watch out for, especially if you make this exercise part of your regular warm-up practice and more than just a drill.

Try and encourage them to keep their knees soft, so they bend them and engage the whole body in the stretch. This also helps to keep their feet firmly on the floor (which is important).

Watch out for any tense, raised shoulders. Watch out for any bent arms. They need to get a sense of the energy coming through their arms right to their fingertips. Elbows are frequently sources of tension.

This exercise has many possible focuses and add-ons. Maybe for now just get them to try doing the exercise slowly or quickly. See where that goes!

The Ideal Centre

The following Chekhov exercise on the Ideal Centre is described in *Teaching Voice*, so some readers may already be familiar with it. I am repeating it here for those who have not come across it because it is wonderful for well-being and wholeness. It is also essential for projection of the voice, even though it isn't a voice exercise as such. As you describe the imaginative journey, give the group time to imagine. Do not rush. Repeat phrases now and then.

- Ask your group to stand with their knees slightly bent, feet firmly on the floor, to close their eyes and feel the energy of the earth beneath their feet. Suggest their legs are reaching into the earth like the roots of a tree.

- Ask them to imagine the energy of the earth beneath their feet as golden, benign and moving, full of potential, full of power. Then suggest they feel that same energy in their bodies: a moving, warm energy coming up through the soles of the feet and moving up through the whole body. Ask them to feel that it is energy not only in the body but also coming from it, and suggest they stay with that feeling for a moment.

- Now ask them to imagine that the sun is in their chest, strong and warm; to imagine that it is the centre from which all impulses come: movements, thoughts and feelings. Ask them to try not to force this, nor to think, and just to focus on the presence of this warm heart centre: easily and totally accessible. If they lose it, tell them not to worry; just ask them to re-establish it in the imagination.

- Ask them to focus on their middle fingers and take the mind on a journey from there to the warm chest centre, through palms, wrists, forearms, elbows, upper arm, shoulders, and then across the chest to the centre. Then focus on the ends of the big toes and take the mind on a journey up through foot, ankle, calf, knee, thigh, pelvis, belly and spine up to the golden sun-centre.

- Suggest they try, with eyes closed, to slowly move one arm. Ask them to try and stay connected to the Ideal Centre; indeed, it is as if the centre is making the arm movement happen. Then ask them to start moving the other arm as well. Then suggest they move the upper body, all connected to the Ideal Centre. Ask them to open their arms. When the arms are wide, ask them to open their eyes and imagine that the warm Ideal Centre is filling the whole room. Bring the arms down and see if you can retain that imagination/sensation.

- Invite them to explore the sense that this energy is beaming out from the face, especially the eyes; tell them not to force it, just to imagine it. If a person feels that the sensation is waning then suggest she just goes back to imagining the Ideal Centre and that the connection to it will return.

- Ask each person to share their energy with every single person in the room. Look at them. If someone gets a bit giggly, it's okay, but ask them to be aware of an interplay of energy between the members of the group. Tell them this is our old friend Radiating and Receiving. It is the basis of all real communication.

- Ask how they feel. Ask them to try and maintain the Ideal Centre for the next exercise.

Radiating and Receiving in Pairs

Next, we encourage the group to get a sense of how radiating and receiving affects their *acting*, rather than it simply being a 'feel-good' thing. These days, if I go to see a play and there is no radiating and receiving between performers, or between performers and audience, I simply want to leave the theatre and go home because it is absolutely intrinsic to the communication that is theatre.

Get them to use the lines below, using one line per throw (you can also use lines from whatever play you are working on). If you want to give some context, tell them that Ophelia is returning letters and love tokens to Hamlet, after their potential romance is now over (Act Three, Scene One).

OPHELIA. I pray you now receive them.

HAMLET. No, not I. I never gave you aught.

OPHELIA. My honoured lord, you know right well you did.

- Put the group into pairs and let there be about six feet between each partner. Get them to throw and catch to each other with the invisible ball, perhaps adding a sound as they throw.

- Then get them to add the Hamlet/Ophelia lines above as they 'throw' to each other.

- Now ask them to stand about three feet apart. Tell them they are going to say the lines looking at each other, not moving now but *imagining* they are throwing to one another as before while they speak.

- Tell them to take very long pauses and see what happens between the two partners. Some of them might get giggly because this provokes quite a personal response. Tell them it's okay to be giggly, but still to focus on the exercise.

- Many will not take pauses as long as they ought to; you might, using one pair who seem okay with the exercise, take them through it in front of the group, really making them wait between 'I never gave you aught' and 'My honoured lord', and let them feel the energy flow between them.

- Do this exercise for a few minutes.

- *Flyback*. Ask them what they felt. Ask how it felt to take long pauses and to really feel the energy of the partner. Did your partner affect the way you responded? The answer to *that* is, of course, a resounding *yes*.

Two Qualities: Floating and Moulding

We are now going to look at two qualities of movement, as described by Michael Chekhov. One is 'floating' and the other is 'moulding'. We have already explored the other two basic qualities of movement – 'flying' and 'radiating' – in Chapter Five (Voice Workshop Two) when we looked at Ariel's speech from *The Tempest*. Working on these core qualities will give their bodies access to lots of feelings and sensations. Moulding, for instance, can evoke a tragic intensity. Floating can evoke feelings of love and intoxication that will be useful for *Twelfth Night*, a play we will look at in later sections of this book. However, do not attach these feelings to the exercises before you do them; let the young actors find them.

Floating

- Ask them to close their eyes.

- Invite them to imagine they are weeds in a small stream, constantly being moved by the water. Ask each person to feel this in their whole body. Should the connection vanish, just ask them to gently bring the attention back to the water, allow the whole body to be affected, and let floating movements happen.

- Ask the whole group, without losing concentration, to open their eyes and keep the movement going.

- Now ask them to make a sound as they float, then later, to use the line: 'What means your lordship?' All being well you will find their voices have a very strong floating quality. If they don't, ask them to 'turn up' the floating. This should put the floating quality into their voices.

- Now ask them to stand still but to keep that floating feeling inside them. Ask them to give the line, 'What means your lordship?' It sounds light, floating and loving.

Moulding

- Ask them to close their eyes.

- Invite them to imagine they are trying to move their arms and upper bodies through thick clay or mud.

- Ask them to sink their knees so they feel that the effort is also affecting their legs. Remind them to breathe and feel this through the whole body. Any time the attention is lost, bring the attention back to moving through clay.

- Invite them, without losing concentration, to open their eyes and keep the movement going. Now ask the group to add a sound (these sounds are usually deep and full of effort) then to add a line: 'What means your lordship?' Ask them to stand still but keep that feeling of moulding inside them. Tell them to give the line again: 'What means your lordship?' It sounds dark and full of tragedy.

Teaching Tip: Reinforce the fact that they must engage with the imagination first, before they start moving. They must try to imagine they are floating/moulding and then the voice, movements, sensations and feelings will really be affected; they won't have to fake it. Explain how using these qualities of movement can be useful for character development. Might Ophelia principally be a floating character or a moulding character? (She might be something else!)

Psychological Gesture Revisited

Explain to the group that we are now going on to look at what the character is doing in the scene. They have already had some experience of how useful the body can be. We are now moving on to explore in greater depth something called 'Psychological Gesture', which we first encountered in Chapter One (Tools and Pathways).

Psychological Gesture is a physical manifestation of the character's intention: what is really 'going on' for them: what they are doing to themselves, the other characters or the audience. We might say that Ophelia is *offering* in the example from *Hamlet* used above. But she might be *pushing away* and this would make Ophelia quite different. Once decided on and practised, the gesture can then be imagined and internalised. It gives a strong flavour and intention to the character and her text.

I think it would be useful to introduce Psychological Gesture to your group since it will prove a great help to young actors trying to get to grips with both *character* and *journey*. I might suggest if you wish to pursue this work in more depth you consult *To the Actor* (Chekhov: 2002) and, even more importantly, explore possible workshops you might attend.

Psychological Gesture 1: 'Happy Birthday'

- Here is a lighthearted way to start. Get everyone to stand in a circle. Get them to sing you 'Happy Birthday', and ask them to move their arms as if they are tickling you at the same time. They make the gesture of tickling you from where they are standing, wiggling their fingers and probably giggling.

- Now ask them to simply *imagine* they are performing the tickling action and sing again. You will notice that their singing is playful and erratic.

- Get them to sing you 'Happy Birthday' again and, at the same time, ask them to make the gesture of jabbing at you from where they are standing.

- Now ask them to *imagine* they are jabbing at you and to sing again. You will notice that their singing is now aggressive and arrogant.

- Now ask them to jab and then say to you, 'I never gave you aught' as they jab. Then ask them to drop the physical action, and imagine it, and say the line again.

- Now ask them to consider an embrace. They do not have to embrace anyone, just the air in front of them. After they have done it a few times, and perhaps added a sound, ask them to say the same line as they embrace. The line will be tender and quiet. Then ask them to drop the physical action and simply imagine it, and say the line again.

- Bring their attention to how full of intention and feeling their voices were.

My experience is that this works like magic for many people. To begin with, it is just surprising and acts as a release. With practice though, exploring gesture in this way empowers, gives understanding and makes the student feel that she can bring feeling to the text. I repeat, though, exploring gesture does require practice.

Psychological Gesture 2: Pulling and Pushing

Here's an exercise with some rules for Psychological Gesture along with some other things to look out for.

- Ask each person to stand alone. Make sure they have a good stance, and that their feet are firmly on the floor. Try and get them to maintain their feet on the floor so the frame is strong and they get a strong sensation in the body when they make the action. This is a rule for Psychological Gesture. (There aren't many, but that's one of them.)

- Ask them to practise a *pull*. They can do it however they like. Tell them that, as much as is possible, they should engage the whole body. What I mean is they shouldn't just leave one arm limp by the side; everything is working. Also encourage soft knees, so the lower body gets engaged in the movement. They need to make the pull *big*.

- Initially they might pull very frenetically and continuously, afraid that if they stop, any feeling they have built up will simply fizzle out: rather like a child who tries to blow up a balloon, runs out of breath, and is convinced the balloon will deflate.

- Now ask them to try *sustaining* the movement. For example, when they reach out to pull, tell them to stay there for a moment to really register what that *feels* like in the body. And when they pull back, to notice what it feels like when they have pulled back as much as they can. These moments of sustaining can be very powerful.

- The whole gesture needs to be engaged throughout. In other words, the actor must not let the energy die between cycles. It is *all* part of the one gesture.

- Once they are settled on a pull they are happy with, ask them to say, 'Are you honest?' as they pull.

- Now ask them to *imagine* they are pulling, but standing still. Notice how that affects their breathing. Now ask them to say again, 'Are you honest?' Tell them to keep the voice fairly big, or there's a possibility they will lose the intensity.

- Ask them to shake out.

- *Flyback.* Some people will say it is hard to maintain that powerful pulling sensation when still. Tell them it will come with practice.

- Try exactly the same process with a *push*. When you have gone through the same process, get them to shake out.

- *Flyback.* The most important thing is that they notice that giving a *push* or a *pull* will change how they feel and how they speak, and that a *push* is very different to a *pull*.

- When you return to this exercise another time, you could try a whole range of different actions: *tearing, smoothing, gathering, embracing, stabbing, revealing, beckoning...*

This is just the start of exploring the wonder of Psychological Gesture.

Psychological Gesture 3: Application (A Snippet from Hamlet)

Here is a short sequence from Act Three, Scene One of *Hamlet*. This is to give the group some idea of how to use Psychological Gesture when they are working on a scene.

Please Note: I know I am going to say this a few times, but you and your young actors need to *know the text* in order to apply these kind of techniques. It is of very limited use if anyone is holding a script. If you don't have a group which is good at learning or the time does not allow, use the same pieces over the weeks for different experiments in this work: they do not need to be long. If you are principally working on *Macbeth* or *Romeo and Juliet*, say, you might wish to change the short scene I have used below. That's fine. Just choose a brief dramatic moment that your group can sense is loaded with emotional power and they can learn quickly. Don't be tempted to choose something any longer than what follows.

- Split the group into pairs. Let them take this short text and learn it quickly:

  OPHELIA. Take these again, for to the noble mind
     Rich gifts wax poor when givers prove unkind.
     There, my lord.

  HAMLET. Ha! Ha! Are you honest?

  OPHELIA. My lord?

  HAMLET. Are you fair?

  OPHELIA. What means your lordship?

- Ask them now individually to try and decide what the characters are *doing* in this sequence. On the surface this is quite straightforward. In the scene, Ophelia is returning gifts and Hamlet may be refusing them.

- Let each young actor work on a gesture for the character. Let's start with this: Ophelia makes a gesture of *giving*; Hamlet makes a gesture of *pushing away*.

- Ask each young actor to play with these gestures alone for a few minutes. Check out how they are doing.

- Then ask them to meet and stand about six feet away from each other.

- Then they perform the gesture towards each other. Encourage them to make an open sound as they make the gesture.

- Then tell them to continue with the gesture and start the text. Ask them to take long pauses in the text, sometimes sustaining the gesture. See what happens.

- *Flyback.* Ask them what they noticed, especially within the pauses. Ask them what other actions the characters could be doing. Suggest that the characters might be doing something psychologically to each other, above and beyond just giving back or rejecting presents. For instance, Hamlet might be *tearing* or *pushing down*, and Ophelia *throwing*.

- Give them another two specific actions. Let's try Ophelia *throwing* and Hamlet *tearing*. Repeat the process.

- Now let's try Ophelia *lifting* and Hamlet *embracing*.

- If they are ready for it, you might suggest they pick actions for themselves.

- Here we have a whole number of variations on the scene: each intense, each viable.

- If you have actors of reasonable ability, you might get them to show one of their versions and then take them to the next stage...

- Get them to do the gesture, then do the text with the gesture; then ask them to *imagine* the gesture as they say the text. Ask them to take their time, to allow big pauses. Now ask them to repeat the scene, imagine the gesture, yet feel free to move around the room.

Changing the Quality of the Gesture

Have a group chat now and explain how they have spent the session, firstly exploring how to radiate and receive energy (and text) in a rooted and powerful way; how to find the feeling for the character through the body; and how, through Psychological Gesture, they have found out about what a character might be doing. Tell them that with Psychological Gesture they can find out what they believe a character is doing in part of a scene, in a whole scene or even for a whole play. They can also explore not only *what* they might do as the character, but also find different ways *how* to accomplish it.

- If you have time, ask them to go back to Ophelia *giving* and Hamlet *pushing away*.

- Now ask them to change the quality of that movement. Ask Ophelia to *mould* the gesture. Get her to repeat it a few times, then speak. She may, for example, be returning the gifts *suddenly*, *reluctantly*, or perhaps *angrily*.

- If you ask Hamlet to *float* the gesture, he might speak his lines *sadly* and *gently*, as if he were ill.

Ending the Session

The Golden Hoop exercise from Chapter Four (Voice Workshop One) might be a useful way to end the session, as it grounds and focuses the group, bringing them together.

Chapter Seven
Acting Workshop Two:
Exploring Atmosphere

Denmark's a prison…

Hamlet: Act Two, Scene Two

Atmosphere exerts an extremely strong influence on your acting.

Michael Chekhov, *To the Actor*

Two Types of Atmosphere: Personal and General

We have already touched on General Atmosphere: first in Chapter One, which includes an introductory explanation of it, and again in Chapter Three (Shakespeare's Theatre) where we focused mainly on how the atmosphere of different locations affects the characters' behaviour, mood and speech. The latter is a small though important aspect of what atmosphere can do, and a great way to introduce the power of atmosphere. For me, General Atmosphere is one of the most powerful aspects of the Chekhov work and incredibly useful in Shakespeare. We shall look at it again when we explore devising and production, but for the present I want to give you a workshop to enthuse both you and your group.

One of Chekhov's axioms is 'making the intangible, tangible'. In other words, giving the audience something which they can *experience*, though not always *understand*. Like lots of seemingly abstract ideas, this element of the Chekhov work is absolutely *how things are.* Atmosphere is an invisible force which, if you trust it, can change not only your feeling about a short scene, but the direction of an entire play.

We all know what it is to walk into an atmosphere. It can be created by the people we encounter, their mood, the situation, the building they are in, what it is used for, what the temperature is, etc. There can be a multitude of factors, but at some level there is always a General Atmosphere that influences everyone in some way.

Michael Chekhov believed that performers, using their imagination, could *create* atmosphere, and that atmosphere was 'the oxygen of performance'. In addition to the obvious atmospheres which are defined by location (which we explored a little in the chapter on Shakespeare's Theatre), we can imagine anything as an atmosphere: for example, 'feathers', 'grief', 'darkness', 'earth', 'oil', 'ice'. These things are not literal, they are imaginative spurs. By that I mean you can still breathe in them and move through them. For instance, you might have asked a young actor to move into an atmosphere of vegetable oil. They might say this is impossible because no one could breathe in it. However, all you are asking them to do is experience what the imaginative prompt gives them because it can be of extraordinary value.

In addition to a sensitivity to General Atmosphere, we all have our own 'Personal Atmosphere'. Young people understand this idea very well; that sometimes a person has a strong sense of something that they carry around with them. It might be what we use to protect ourselves from harm, a mood, an assumption of what we are, or a response by other people. It might be a smell of cheap perfume, sourness, drudgery or a feeling of entitlement. Where the Personal and General Atmosphere interact is an interesting place, both in life and in drama: in plays it happens all the time. Every time a person enters a space with their Personal Atmosphere, they are tussling and adjusting to the General Atmosphere within the space.

For this workshop we are going to use the Hamlet/Ophelia exchange we used in the previous chapter and a few lines from the opening court scene (Act One, Scene Two). Choose something else if you are working with a particular play.

Begin by using the warm-up exercises in Chapter Two if you have time.

Letting It All Go

To start with, here is a version of an exercise from *Teaching Voice*. It gives the young actor the opportunity to set aside their day and, importantly for this session, introduces them to the concept of Personal Atmosphere.

- Get the group into a circle, ask them to breathe and stand with their eyes closed, feel their feet on the floor and get a sense of where the body is uneasy or even tense. Have them bring their attention to any tense spot and say to themselves, 'Just let go.' Ask them to get a sense of being in the room, of who is around them, where the walls are and what it feels like to be in this circle with the group. Ask them to listen for sounds and feel the atmosphere in the room.

- Now ask them to imagine that around each of them is a bell jar, and this bell jar is full of the day and the things they have brought into the room: memories, concerns and hopes. Get them to imagine what the concerns are like. Are they buzzing around? Are there memories that just float in? Is a thought grabbing on to them like some little creature reminding them of something they have to do? What does it feel and look like in their imagination? Does it have a colour, smell or taste?

- They are going to step forward with their eyes closed and step out of that Personal Atmosphere of their thoughts and concerns. Tell them to step forward and leave the atmosphere behind.

- Ask them to open their eyes, look around at the rest of the group and share their energy with them. It is okay to laugh or smile but not to talk. Ask them to notice if they feel differently.

- Ask them to turn back to their Personal Atmosphere. All together, with a big sweeping gesture and a shout, tell them to sweep all their thoughts and concerns away.

Molecules

- Ask them to stand still, close their eyes again and breathe in through the nose and out through the mouth. Ask them to think, as they breathe in, that all the molecules in the body are separating, and as they breathe out, they are coming back. Suggest to them that they are letting their body become a porous membrane, ready to take in the atmospheres we are going to explore.

Moving

Music is a brilliant starting point for training sensitivity to atmosphere.

- Ask everyone to find their own space and close their eyes. Tell them to keep their eyes closed for the whole exercise. You are going to play a number of different tracks and you want the group to move with the music.

- Tell them to let the music fill them up and physically move *them* rather than doing set dance movements.

- Pick very different styles of music and, for the most part, do not use music that has any words or story. Keep away from anything too familiar until you have played three or four extracts. Let each track last about 1 to 2 minutes, depending on how it is going.

- I am often astounded watching this, noticing how everyone has a bond to the music, even if their responses are different. Something intangible binds them.

- Bring the final track down, get everyone to be still, shake out the body and open their eyes.

- *Flyback.* Usual responses are that it's easy to do, but hard not to dance. Focus on the power of it.

Light and Dark

Here is a simple but powerful exercise to explore the relationship between Personal and General Atmosphere.

- Ask each person to stand on their own. Get them to work with their eyes open. Tell them they are going to define the space of their own Personal Atmosphere.

- Ask them to imagine there is a bell jar over their body which goes right down to the floor. Tell them to trace the edges with their hands.

- Tell them you want them to imagine that this is their Personal Atmosphere which they (or later, their characters) can carry around.

- Tell them to imagine it is full of golden light.

- Ask them to walk around the space with this Personal Atmosphere surrounding the body. As they walk, ask them how it makes them feel to have their own aura of golden light. Ask them to meet others and shake hands. How do they feel when their space is slightly invaded by others?

- Ask them to stop. Keep the concentration.

- Now tell them to put their arms out in front of them, with their hands up, as if they have them against a wall. Tell them that this is the extent of their Personal Atmosphere full of golden light.

- Tell them that beyond their wrists there is complete and utter darkness. Now ask them to stretch out their hands and fingers, dipping the hands into the dark General Atmosphere. What does the darkness feel like? Ask them to bring their hands back into the warm golden light of their Personal Atmosphere.

- Now ask them to walk around the room with their bright Personal Atmosphere, but knowing there is darkness beyond it.

- Ask them to stand still. Now suggest that they start to imagine that the darkness is pushing its way into the

Personal Atmosphere, really putting some pressure on it. Tell them to really imagine it. Let them walk around if they want to.

- Ask them to stand still. Now ask them to say a line from the first scene of *Hamlet*: 'Stay, speak, speak! I charge thee, speak!'

- Now tell them that the darkness is really coming in and it's only a foot from their nose. Get them to repeat the line.

- Now tell them their Personal Atmosphere is only six inches from their face and to try the line again.

- Finally ask them to imagine their Personal Atmosphere is growing and pushing back strongly against the darkness. Ask them to repeat the line a few times as they do this. You will find the lines will sound edgy and dangerous.

Teaching Tip: Getting people to work imaginatively with their eyes open is something to aim for, because it always requires a serious adjustment if you begin with eyes closed and then are asked to open them. Even the most imaginative person might find whatever they are imagining difficult when suddenly faced with the reality of the rehearsal room. So, if they start with the eyes closed, warn the young actors that, when you ask them to open their eyes, they must try to keep the imaginative atmosphere alive. If they lose the image, tell them not to worry, just connect up their imagination again and it will come back.

In the Room/Outside the Room

This exercise won't take a moment and is a good thing to do if you have another space you can easily go to nearby.

- Get everyone to stand in a circle and close their eyes. Tell them to breathe in through the nose and out through the mouth.

- Ask them to get a sense of the room they are in. What does it feel like on their faces, on their hands? What does it smell like? What does it feel like to be in here?

- Ask them to start using a word to describe this and speak it aloud. You might need to do this as well to encourage them. Words like 'safe', 'exploring', 'haven' and 'friendliness' might be spoken.

- Now ask them to open their eyes and move them to another space. Do exactly the same thing in the new space. I often take my group out to the hallway. There are many different responses. They will definitely feel differently in the new location. Don't discuss it yet.

- Then I ask them to open their eyes and come with me back to the workshop room. When we get to the doorway I ask them to enter one by one, stepping over the threshold slowly and noticing, when they come into the room, how it feels different.

- *Flyback*.

Teaching Tip: Tell them that every single time they walk into a room they are walking into an atmosphere and crossing a threshold. This is also true whenever they come onto a stage. They are crossing the threshold from the 'real world' into the 'world of the imagination'.

General Atmosphere

Now we'll move on to a General Atmosphere exercise:

- Get each person to work on their own. Remind them about atmosphere and, if you have used it, the *Creating Atmospheres* exercise in the workshop from Chapter Three (Shakespeare's Theatre). Tell them that everywhere has an atmosphere and that, as performers, we can generate this atmosphere. This can change the way we feel, the way we say things and the way we respond to others.

- Tell them also that there can be atmospheres which are not simply about *where* we are (like a railway station, a hospital or a place of worship) but that you can use something more abstract like feathers, oil or laughter: you can also use colours for atmosphere, like grey or green.

- Tell them you are going to give them a few atmospheres to explore. Tell them to fully commit and use their imaginations to take them there. Tell them to let the atmosphere really fill the body: whatever atmosphere you name they can always breathe in it. Not everyone will respond in exactly the same way but that's fine.

- Now ask them to really imagine that the whole room is full of *bubbles*. Tell them they can still breathe in the atmosphere and still survive in it, but nonetheless it is full of bubbles.

- How does it affect their breathing? What does it feel like on the skin? Does it feel nice? Annoying? Suffocating? Cosy? What's it like?

- Ask them to breathe it in and let the bubbles affect their whole being. Really push them to use their bodies. This might result in something artificial to begin with but will become less so as they commit to the exercise. One prompt I use to make this happen is, 'Turn the atmosphere up.' It keeps things in the imaginative realm.

- Ask them to add a sound. The atmosphere will give everyone a tone.

- Now ask them to say one of their lines from the Hamlet/Ophelia exchange from the previous chapter in that atmosphere.

- Now suggest they stand still and retain that atmosphere, perhaps saying that line to another member of the group.

- Shake out.

- Now ask them to imagine that the atmosphere is full of *electricity*.

- Go through the same procedure. Electricity is a good one because it encourages a lot of dynamic movement. As before, if they are not responding physically, it might be good to suggest they 'turn it up'.

- Give prompts like: How does it affect the breathing? What does it feel like on the skin? Does it feel nice? Annoying? Dangerous? What's it like?

- Ask them to add a line and say it in the atmosphere as they move around. Then ask them to stop moving and say it in the atmosphere.

- Shake out. Now ask them how that felt. Most people find this surprisingly easy; though not everyone, of course. The first and most obvious thing is that the atmosphere changes the feeling and colour of the line.

Teaching Tip: Teachers can be concerned with pushing people to move physically when they are doing this work, for fear they will not act truly and organically from inside. After all, the bodily response is supposed to come from the imagination. In the early days, though, sometimes the imagination needs a kick-start. Learn to judge this as you watch the group.

Atmosphere Application 1

We will use the following lines from *Hamlet*: Act Three, Scene One, these are the same lines we used in the previous workshop, so they should still know them.

OPHELIA. I pray you now receive them.

HAMLET. No, not I. I never gave you aught.

OPHELIA. My honoured lord, you know right well you did.

- Ask them to get into pairs. Ask them what the atmosphere might be in that little exchange: *stickiness, bitterness, confusion, goodbye* are things I might offer as possibilities.

- Get them to try one; let's say *stickiness*. Begin by getting them to work alone and let the atmosphere fill them and affect their bodies.

- Now ask them to turn to their partners and speak their lines. Tell them not to worry at first about being Ophelia and Hamlet, simply that they are in this world of *stickiness*. What does it taste or feel like? Does it make them breathe or move in a certain way? Does it have a colour? Insist they keep the physicality going and give big pauses between the lines to let the stickiness exist in the space. Atmosphere grows and is felt even more in silence.

- Now ask them to keep the atmosphere strong in their imagination, to feel it inside, but to reduce the obvious physical response.

- Shake out. Ask them how they felt. They might say something like 'weird' or 'interesting'. Try and get them to be more specific. Tell them that we might describe this meeting as 'a sticky situation'. They might each say something about wanting to leave the space in the pauses.

- Go through the same process and this time explore an atmosphere of *goodbye*.

- Shake out. Point out how the scene is transformed with the different atmospheres, both of which are possibilities for the scene.

Teaching Tip: The atmosphere is *not* the character. It is the atmosphere in which the characters *function*.

Atmosphere Application 2

Let's consider Act One, Scene Two of *Hamlet*. As we know, Hamlet's father has been killed and his uncle Claudius has usurped the throne and married his mother, Gertrude. No one is saying anything about it. Ask everyone to learn one of these two lines:

KING. How is it that the clouds still hang on you?

GERTRUDE. Good Hamlet, cast thy nighted colour off.

- Lay a long line of electrical tape at the back of your studio and get half the group to stand behind it. The others can sit and watch. It is extremely useful to get students to watch this work as they start to get a real sense of its power.

- Tell those behind the line that where they are is our studio but that when they step across the line they are then in the *atmosphere.*

- Ask the group standing behind the line to visualise that over the line is the atmosphere of *corruption.* Get them to stand at the line and put their arms over the line. Ask them what it feels like to put their hands into corruption. Is it wet or dry? Can they feel a movement in the atmosphere? What does it feel like on the skin? Get them to move their hands in it for about half a minute, then tell them to pull their hands back over the line.

- Tell them to keep their concentration, to reimagine the wall of corruption, then to stand at the line and stick their head and shoulders into it. Tell them to breathe it in deeply. What does it smell like? Is it wet or dry? What does it feel like on the skin? Is there movement in the atmosphere? What does it feel like on the face, the ears, the eyes?

- Ask them to pull their heads back over the line and into the space. Ask them to notice the feeling in the studio. How is it different from the atmosphere of corruption you created over the line?

- Now ask them to put one of their feet over the line and into the atmosphere. How does it feel on the soles of the foot? Is it wet or dry? Is it firm or slippery? Is it easy to move?

- Now ask them to bring in the other foot and the whole body. Tell them to let the body really respond to the atmosphere.

- Ask them to make a sound, then ask them in their atmosphere of corruption to speak the line they learned. Repeat both lines so they are reminded. Get them to turn the atmosphere up.

- If you are satisfied the atmosphere is there, ask them to feel it inside and reduce the obvious physical response. Ask them to walk around, to radiate and receive with the partners that they meet and say their line to them. If you are not satisfied the atmosphere is being retained, get them to go back to allowing the body to be affected.

- After a couple of minutes of living and moving in this atmosphere, ask them to step back slowly over the line and 'return' to the studio. Ask them to shake out thoroughly. Then, as we did with Personal Atmosphere at the beginning of this chapter, with a big sweeping gesture and a shout, tell them to throw the atmosphere away altogether. Get them to do this a couple of times.

- Now ask them to sit down and ask the second group to come up.

- Ask the group standing behind the line to visualise that over the line is the atmosphere of *ice*. Tell them they may be cold but they can live in it.

- Go through the same ritual as before, allowing different parts of the body to enter the atmosphere. Take your time. Give many prompts. It helps those less connected to the imagination and spurs everyone on.

- Once they are in the atmosphere and making the sound, ask them to voice their line and start to relate to one another. This will give a curious distancing and mistrust between the group, a feeling that something is not quite right. Ask them to try and be nice even though they are in this atmosphere. Perhaps ask them to laugh. If this is as far as you can go, then get everyone to walk to the line, step out, shake out and once more 'throw away' the atmosphere.

Now if you have a group who might be able to develop this further, then proceed as follows:

- Tell a member of the group that he will be Hamlet coming into the court. Ask him to have a Personal Atmosphere of *heat*, for example, or *truth*. Tell the rest of the group you are going to have Hamlet enter their atmosphere of *ice*.

- Hamlet steps into the space. Tell the others to notice him. Hamlet may use the line, 'But I have that within which passeth show.' The actors in the court, by making their atmosphere stronger, by turning it up, will antagonise our Hamlet without saying anything, whilst Hamlet tries to push his Personal Atmosphere onto the space, thus threatening the group. In turn, the court will try to overwhelm his atmosphere. Tell the group to let Hamlet win sometimes. What happens then? Perhaps the court will pity Hamlet, ignore him or be afraid in case his fire melts them. By using atmosphere, the multilayered intensity of the scene may be revealed.

- See what happens. Then get everyone to step over the line and shake out. Find out how people felt.

- *Flyback* with the group. They will be full of thoughts and feelings about it. There are some who might find this difficult but, hopefully, will be won over when they actually watch the work that others produce. What's important is that they get a sense that atmosphere is a powerful and essential tool.

Teaching Tip: You can use any scene where one of the characters is at odds with the General Atmosphere; Shakespeare is full of scenes like this. Indeed, if you consider it, even a scene where a messenger brings news is a scene where this dynamic occurs, albeit briefly. Here are a few examples: the bloody sergeant in *Macbeth* (Act One, Scene Two); Lucio's arrival at the nunnery in *Measure for Measure* (Act One, Scene Four); Malvolio in *Twelfth Night* (Act Two, Scene Three); Ophelia in *Hamlet* (Act Four, Scene Two).

Closing the Session: Three Shake-outs/Three Breaths

I suggest that you end the session with something very energetic to dispel any residual intensity, such as the following:

- Everyone is in a different part of the room.

- Tell everyone to run around the room.

- Shout, 'Stop and shake out!' Let them shake out vigorously.

- Then shout, 'Run!' Then, 'Stop and shake out!' Let them shake out.

- Then shout, 'Run'. Then, 'Stop and shake out!' Let them shake out.

- Gather all into a circle and get them to hold hands and close their eyes.

- Ask them to breathe in through the nose and out through the mouth. Do this twice more. Say, 'Thank you.'

This is the end of Part Two of this book, the Skills Workshops. I hope you will be returning to this section often because it forms the building blocks for future work, and it is only by repetition that the power of the exercises will deepen.

In the next section we will be working with devising, directing short scenes and working on soliloquies: a step closer to production.

Part Three

*Moving Towards
Performance:
Devising,
Short Scenes
and Soliloquies*

Chapter Eight
Devising a Group Project on Shakespeare

Love thee better than thou canst devise.
Romeo and Juliet: Act Three, Scene One

Devising allows students to discover themes and create short theatre pieces around the play which can either be used to make a public performance or remain in the studio/classroom. It provokes exploration, teamwork, imagination and a deeper understanding of the play you are working on.

Devising a piece allows a freer response to the Shakespearean text, using lines and short scenes from the play, interspersed with original writing, movement and music. For our example we will be using *Macbeth*, though the principles could be applied to any play. If you or your group are not yet ready to embark on a production, then this is either a great place to start *towards* a production, or it can be an end in itself.

For you, though, devising is challenging because you have to be the director, the author and the teacher. Play to the strengths of both yourself and the group and it can be very worthwhile. For instance, it can be difficult to encourage movement pieces if you are uncomfortable with them yourself.

Working on a devising project can be incredibly valuable, especially with a less theatre-orientated group, because they can come at the material in many different ways. The piece can be varied, and can be as short or as long as the group wishes or time allows. You can use as much or as little of the Shakespearean text as you like, but of course, as I have said before, to abandon the text *totally* is really not exploring Shakespeare at all, as the language is key. What devising allows you to do is to use some of the original text, whilst still giving the group the space and freedom to use their artistic talents in other directions: in other words, to play to their creative strengths.

I am going to provide you with three basic 'maps' which have different starting points to create material for your devised piece. Follow the maps and you can apply the process to any Shakespeare play you want to explore.

Please Note: Each map will take several sessions to explore and develop the piece.

This chapter provides pathways but it is not exactly a workshop plan. It will give you a lot of frames and ideas which you can follow or work with, along with the three maps. They are far from the only routes you can take.

Though you have the story of the play, you do not necessarily have to follow it. Your piece might end up as a collage of music, dance, images, original writing and short scenes from the play. You, as the coordinator/director, will be folding the students' material into it. Think of the result more as a piece of music rather than a play.

My Rules for Devising

Whilst this is not a book on devising per se, and there are many books out there on this subject, I would like to set out what my rules for devising work are, both for the group and for you.

- Once you have got the project going, investigate what skills your students have that you may not know about, especially if they involve music.

- Try and lead the project as a group as much as possible and give the group a lot of say in creating the content. This is not about you directing a play. It's about making something engaging which expands *their* ideas and explores the Shakespeare play. It gives them the chance to engage with the text without being overfaced.

- Make sure *everyone* is involved. You need to work hard at this. It is useful to have group work in your piece to accommodate the shy or reluctant. Try and make sure everyone has some responsibility in the piece.

- You need to make clear to the group that a lot of material will be created and yet some of it may not be used. This is not a value judgement on the material but it might just mean that it does not work for the flow of the piece.

- Everything the group comes up with should be tried if possible. Sometimes this is not possible because of time constraints.

- No rubbishing of other people's work or ideas is to be allowed. If something comes up which you feel is sexist or racist, however, do not let it pass unchallenged. This often happens in devising because students feel they can say what they like because the group has a lot of scope for self-expression.

- When a student gives feedback, *always* insist the comments are constructive: derogatory criticism is not helpful.

- Make sure everyone understands these rules.

Warm-up

As there is a strong possibility that your piece will involve some group movement, I am going to look at a few warm-up exercises which will enhance this approach, whilst at the same time make the young actors aware of certain principles in the work. There have already been a number of exercises to develop ensemble and the sense of the group, so mix and match from the following: *Breath Dance 1* and *2*, *Radiating and Receiving* (*Throwing the Ball*) and *Stacatto/Legato*. Incorporate a little voice work from Chapter Four, such as *Diction Warm-up*.

Group Animal

This is an oldie but a goodie. It is a version of a Chekhov exercise but there are a myriad variations done by other schools and teachers.

- Ask each person to find their own space in the room. Tell them that, in order to devise and work as an ensemble, they will need to work together. In this game everyone has to do the same action at the same time.

- Tell them they can all either:

  - Walk around with their hands on their knees.

  - Walk around with their hands on their heads.

  - Run to any wall in the room.

  - Stand completely still.

  - *Float* or *mould* around the room if you are familiar with this from Chapter Six.

- The rule is that everyone has to do these actions *at the same time* without talking. So as soon as someone has their hands on their knees, then everyone must. As soon as someone stands still, then everyone must. At the beginning, it will be very ragged. However, if they persist, they will improve.

- In my experience, the first time people do this, they get giggly, whatever age they are! Let that happen, then stop it and tell everyone they now have to do it completely seriously. Try again.

- Finally, get them to radiate and receive with each other first, just sharing their energy with the whole group, before they start. Then say *go* for one last attempt. All being well, you will get a further improvement.

- Ask them if they noticed the moments when everyone was together and working well.

Walk Across the Room 1

This exercise is important in that it really gets the group to understand focus and direction. Ostensibly, it's a very simple one but it has a lot of learning outcomes. You need a large room.

- Split the group into two. Group Two sits down to watch.

- Ask Group One to go into one corner of the room. Pick one person to be the leader and have the others stand behind her.

- Those behind should be in a group not a line, standing quite close together.

- Group One is going to travel across the room. Ask them to look into the other diagonal in order to make their journey across the space as long as possible. You need to find a sign or a light or something else that Group One can focus on. Tell them all to focus on it throughout the exercise.

- Tell them they are going to cross the room quite slowly as a group, following their leader, all concentrating on the focal point you have suggested.

- Tell them to stay behind the leader and try and get a sense of *how* the leader is crossing the space and take that on in their own movement. Is she moving lightly or heavily? Get her to cross slowly the first time.

- Say *go.*

- The result will be a really focused and interesting crossing of the space. Ask for feedback from the watching group.

- Now get Group Two to try it.

Teaching Tip: Ask the 'watching' group to notice what happens when a member of the performing group loses focus and how that draws the eye. The person who looks down or scratches their nose immediately draws the eyes of the audience and ruins the impact of the work.

Walk Across the Room 2

- This time, give the leader of Group One more ambitious instructions. Ask them to stay fixed on the agreed point of focus and move towards it with the group behind them as before. This time, though, the leader can move to the side or sometimes stand still; she can move with any quality she likes; she can kneel, crawl on the ground, or move quickly or slowly.

- The others need to stay with her. They do not have to move exactly like her, but they should feel at one with her as they all move towards the agreed point. This makes for something interesting and connected, different to the first walk in that it has an element of rhythm, change, tempo and surprise. Remind them that all pieces of theatre need these elements.

- Now get the other group to try it.

- *Flyback* and ask for feedback.

Walk Across the Room 3

- Now we are going to add some drama. This time, ask the leader of the performing group to walk slowly across the room with the others following.

- Designate one person: he is going to stop halfway across and then decide to go back the way he came, whilst the others go on. You might ask one or two of the group to notice this waverer but still choose to go on with the leader.

- Really make those that notice take their time and radiate/receive, both with the waverer and with each other as that person decides to leave the group. Taking time makes the actors really feel the dynamic of what is going on.

- Do the same exercise with Group Two.

- *Flyback* and discuss it. People are really surprised at the intensity of this exercise.

- Explain that we have performed a very simple dynamic here but it's very dramatic. You might say that the story of *Macbeth* has an element of this dynamic. He murders the King and, to start with, most of the lords go along with it. Gradually, one by one, they desert him until he is left alone. Eventually even his wife leaves, by dying and leaving him completely alone. Explain that this is only one element of the play but with devising we can take what we like.

Teaching Tip: This idea of how we can tell the inner story through *movement*, in this case how Macbeth's crime isolates him, is something worth considering as a powerful tool for *all* theatre exploration. The physicalisation of what is going on between the characters is a development of Psychological Gesture, only this time you are using it for an entire play's dynamic rather than for a character's psychological drive.

Where to Start: Finding Images

It's important that in order to begin this project, everyone ought to have read the play or at least know the story.

- Ask everyone to close their eyes. Tell them you are going to read aloud the first scene of the play between the three Witches. It is only thirteen lines long.

- Read slowly and clearly, including stage directions. They should listen, with eyes closed, with notebook or paper in front of them.

- After you have finished reading, get them to open their eyes and write down any images they saw and any feelings the text gave them. What was the atmosphere?

- Words like 'secrets', 'evil', 'foreboding', 'danger', 'an imminent battle', 'pouring rain', 'storm' and 'darkness' might come up.

- All their words or phrases are relevant to the next question. Write them down yourself.

- Ask the group to consider what the play is *about*. Answers you might get include 'ambition', 'corruption', 'murder', 'power', 'the future' and 'betrayal'.

- Tell the group their suggestions have made a rich canvas for the devised piece.

Exploring Themes: Stepping into an Atmosphere

I was first introduced to this powerful approach to atmosphere and archetype by Lenard Petit, a distinguished Chekhov teacher who has really helped me develop and deepen my knowledge and skills. His book, *The Michael Chekhov Handbook* (Routledge, 2010), explores this work in a deeply practical way. Whilst I have changed the exercises a little here, the basic approach is the same.

This way of approaching themes and archetypes encourages the young actors to stop *thinking* and instead to respond more deeply and instinctively.

Teaching Tip: *Macbeth* is a play frequently taught and done a lot with young people, but it is very dark. So really shake out after you have explored feelings and sensations through the body: it's important. If one of the atmospheres you wanted to explore was *evil*, you might suggest an atmosphere of *mud* or *slime* or *bitterness* instead. This would still have a strong effect on the actor, without having to deal with the potent abstraction of evil.

- Ask each person to work on their own. Ask them to imagine in front of them an atmosphere of *ambition*.

- Ask them: Does it have a colour? Is it thick? Can you see through it? Does it smell of anything? Tell them not to think about it, just let it come to them. Does the atmosphere have a movement, like a wind? Is it heavy or light?

- Ask them to step into the atmosphere and experience it on their skin. Is it hot or cold? Dry or wet? For instance, I might imagine an atmosphere of *ambition* to be a strong, icy wind pushing me forward, with images of beautiful and wonderful things in front of me which I want, but which disappear.

- Ask them to breathe the atmosphere in, really deeply, and let out a sound. Then ask them to allow the atmosphere to mould them into a statue of ambition.

- Now ask them to speak the line from this statue/pose: 'Away, and mock the time with fairest show' (*Macbeth*: Act One, Scene Seven).

- Ask them to repeat the line, keeping the atmosphere around them and listening to how it sounds and how they feel. Get them to say it a few times. For many people it will sound charged and urgent.

- Now tell them to step out of the atmosphere, throw it away and really shake out.

- Try this with a few of the other atmospheres mentioned above ('corruption', 'murder', 'power', and so on). Go through the same process. Use the same line so that everyone gets a sense of how the atmosphere affects the way you feel and speak.

Telling the Story

One of the things we need to do is own the story of our chosen play and tell it together. We will use this exercise in much greater detail later on when we work on production, but it is a good starting point for devising. You might need to try this exercise twice.

- Get everyone to stand in a circle. Ask someone to start to tell the story of the play to everyone else. And that is exactly what I mean: they must speak to the group directly, not into some vague space, nor as if trying to tell the story like a test or a memory exercise. (This is very hard to maintain, especially the first time.)

- Encourage anyone else to jump in and continue at any point. Don't let anyone go on for too long. It should be a group telling of the story of the play. If someone wants to contradict or add, let them do it, but keep the energy going. Stay in the circle yourself. You might need to add part of the story.

- When they get to the end, try and note for yourself how they feel about the story and what they believe the play is saying. All this may be incredibly useful to you. In spite of you having asked them, some of them will not have read the play: they may well only have watched a movie version so you have to accept some of their impressions will not be coming directly from the text.

Three Maps

In devising, even more than when you are actually doing a play in production, you and your group are in charge of the shape of the piece. If the group is inexperienced, many of these choices are going to be down to you, but give the group as much of a say as you can. Much of how this process evolves is going to be down to how much time you have. I am going to suggest three maps along with how you might develop them into short pieces. These maps will give a 'spine' (another Chekhov term) to your piece and offer support and shape. They may not necessarily follow the narrative. They are:

- Using the story as the spine.
- Using one of the characters as the spine.
- Using a theme, for example *guilt,* as the spine.

Teaching Tip: The map you choose will have a big impact on what you choose subsequently to include in your devised piece. Making three maps like this is a bit mechanistic, but you can 'mix and match' exercises and pieces from any of these maps to create other routes, as ideas come from yourself and the group. I am not telling you what to do here, just giving you some pointers. If you want to follow the maps religiously, you can, but you don't need to.

Map One: Starting from the Story

Here is a nice easy way to start building your piece. I am using *Macbeth* as an example, though the principle could be applied to any play.

It will take a while, I would say at least six sessions, if you want to bring it to performance level. It depends on how long you have been working with your group and their skill level as to how fast they can go. Where it is very successful is in getting the story into the *bodies* of the group.

- Tell them we are going to split the play into three manageable sections: a possible beginning, middle and end. Michael Chekhov has a chapter in *To the Actor* (Routledge, 2002) called 'Composition of the Performance' which gives great insight into this. See if the group can find these sections in the play for themselves. If they do not know the story then it is going to be hard for them, so you will need to deal with this. Here are three possibilities for the beginning, middle and end sections, though they are by no means the only ones:

  - From the opening until Macbeth becomes the King.

  - From Macbeth becoming the King until the murder of the Macduff family.

  - From that moment to the end.

- Split your group into three teams and give each team one of these three sections.

- Ask each team to tell the story of their section in six tableaux/stills. Every person must be in each 'still', however many characters there are onstage. They can play animals, spirits, characters in the play but not in the scene, or even pieces of architecture. Tell them they obviously cannot convey every nuance or incident; just ask them to pick what's important. They can use the script to check things out. The actors can change parts from one still to another.

- Tell them to make their gestures *big* and to radiate their energy out into the space. These tableaux are not just about what the characters *do* but *how they feel* and *what they want*.

127

- Ask each group to show their tableaux. Ask them to go very slowly from one tableau to the next. To start with, you will say, 'Next tableau' to prompt them until they get to the end of their sequence.

- Make sure they are very clear on which moments they are highlighting in the story, and help them make those moments sharper. Everyone should know who or what they are supposed to be and what they are doing. Which character are they? How might that character feel at that moment? If they are playing part of a throne, say, what does that throne *represent*? Look out for anyone who is not engaging with their full body. Ask them what the atmosphere is in each tableau.

- Suggest they make the transitions smooth between each tableau. This is no mean feat, because everyone needs to know where they are moving to and *how*. There is a lot of refinement you can do around this if you are developing the piece into something for performance and it takes time. Do suggest, though, that someone leads every transition and they need to decide who that is. Tell them the transitions are as important as the tableaux.

- After you have seen all the tableaux, ask the group to spend 10 minutes refining them with your own suggestions and the feedback they have got from the rest of the group. Show them again.

- You now have some kind of rough framework for your piece. And make no mistake: it will be rough. However, you and your group will have told the whole story of the play in pictures. Isn't that amazing?

Developing It Further

- Go back to the work on qualities of movement (moulding, floating, radiating, flying: pages 70 and 92) and see if you can use them in the transitions.

- Let's take the initial tableaux. Let's say they are:

- ○ The Witches are prophesying to Macbeth and Banquo.

- ○ Duncan arrives at the castle, greeted by Lady Macbeth.

- Let's say that the initial tableau is the three Witches prophesying whilst Macbeth and Banquo look on, amazed and nervous. Ask the performing group what the *atmosphere* is. Ask them to imagine that their whole tableau is surrounded by this atmosphere. Only pick one atmosphere per tableau and do not make things too complicated: then the magic can happen.

- Then move to Tableau 2: the next atmosphere might be one of 'relief', 'safety' or even of 'light'. Duncan has just come from the battle and is looking forward to recovery and celebration. Suggest to the performing group that they move from one atmosphere to the other as they move from one tableau to the next. Get them to try this. You will notice a change in the feeling you get from the tableaux. The performers will have an added depth.

- Get the groups to find atmospheres for the whole sequence and to practise moving from one to the other.

A Next Step: Adding Text and Song

You need a simple short sound bite from the Shakespeare text that you feel sums up the overall atmosphere of this play or indeed of whatever play you are using. It may be an underlying theme. The whole group might be involved in this search for a chant.

'Fair is foul and foul is fair,' is one of the greatest lines about a world going dangerously wrong. It is so simple yet so precise and it is about what happens in *Macbeth*. For much of the play there seems to be no morality. One might argue that Macbeth's world is not so great to begin with; treachery, war and brutal punishment, but somehow the character of Duncan appears to rise above it all. At this point we might consider with the group whether the world isn't in that kind of a mess right now!

You might try getting the groups to chant 'Fair is foul, and foul is fair: / Hover through the fog and filthy air' (*Macbeth*: Act One, Scene One) as they move from one tableau to another.

Initially get everyone to speak it, so the full power of what the play is about soaks into them. In the end, you might like to get someone to make a tune for this couplet and sing it alone.

Lyke-Wake Dirge

Alternatively, you might like to use an actual old song, such as the following haunting 'Lyke-Wake Dirge', to link the tableaux together. The song is written in northern English dialect. It goes:

> This ae nighte, this ae nighte,
> Every nighte and alle,
> Fire and fleet and candle-lighte,
> And Christe receive thy saule.

For the tune, see: youtu.be/Y3JyVHOq7PQ

Try getting the groups to show their tableaux in sequence, either singing or chanting.

Adding More Text

One of our objectives in this devising exercise is to get the group to engage with the original text and situations in the play. Tell the group we are going to use Shakespearean text, either from the scenes they show in the tableaux or lines from the play they feel might be appropriate: you might ask the group to choose their own text or else suggest text to them. Let's look at six possible tableaux that the group may have created for the 'beginning' section.

Six Tableaux with Texts

1. The Witches are prophesying to Macbeth and Banquo.

2. Duncan arrives at the castle with his troops. Lady Macbeth greets them.

3. Macbeth murders Duncan, with spirits and the Witches around him, the drugged guards sprawled on the floor.

4. The Macbeths washing their hands of blood, the others asleep around them.

5. After the murder. A scene of confusion and chaos.

6. The Macbeths are crowned. The court is kneeling. Banquo looks away.

May I stress again that I am not *prescribing* these tableaux. I am only using them as examples. See what tableaux your groups come up with. The text pieces can be even shorter than I am suggesting. The texts could even be spoken by others in the group speaking out to the audience who are *not* involved in the tableaux.

TEXT FOR TABLEAU 1

MACBETH. Speak if you can: what are you?

FIRST WITCH. All hail, Macbeth! Hail to thee, Thane of Glamis!

SECOND WITCH. All hail, Macbeth! Hail to thee, Thane of Cawdor!

THIRD WITCH. All hail, Macbeth, that shalt be King hereafter!

BANQUO. Good sir, why do you start, and seem to fear Things that do sound so fair?

(Act One, Scene Three)

TEXT FOR TABLEAU 2

DUNCAN. This castle hath a pleasant seat.

BANQUO. I have observed the air is delicate.

DUNCAN. See see, our honoured hostess.
Give me your hand. Conduct me to mine host.

(Act One, Scene Six)

Teaching Tip: Note that in this snippet I have not followed the scene structure, simply provided a few of the lines which suggest safety and happiness. I wanted to include Lady Macbeth, but I think her text is very complicated (to show she is being duplicitous). Maybe she is simply making a deep curtsy in the tableau.

TEXT FOR TABLEAU 3

In this tableau of Macbeth murdering Duncan, there is no text immediately relevant because the scene does not exist. Shakespeare, of course, did that for a reason, but that doesn't mean to say that your group might not see it as being relevant since it's the most important thing that actually happens! So the text will have to come from a related scene which lends its atmosphere to their invention. An example might be:

> MACBETH. Methought I heard a voice cry, 'Sleep
> no more!
> Macbeth does murder sleep' – the innocent sleep,
> Sleep that knits up the ravelled sleave of care,
> The death of each day's life, sore labour's bath,
> Balm of hurt minds, great Nature's second course,
> Chief nourisher in life's feast –
>
> (Act Two, Scene Two)

Teaching Tip: Remember each tableau group is composed of six or seven members; the others are watching. If you want to develop this into a performance, this text could be spoken as a chorus by other members of the group, building to a crescendo as the tableau forms.

TEXT FOR TABLEAU 4

The Macbeths washing the blood from their hands; others asleep; the Witches, perhaps, watching.

> LADY MACBETH. A little water clears us of this deed.
> How easy is it then. Hark! More knocking!
> Be not lost so poorly in your thoughts!
>
> MACBETH. To know my deed, 'twere best not know
> myself.
> Wake Duncan with thy knocking. I would thou couldst.
>
> (Act Two, Scene Two)

This text is a truncation of the end of the scene, picking the easy lines that focus on the situation.

TEXT FOR TABLEAU 5

Chaos in the castle. The body has been discovered. See everyone moving in different directions in the tableau itself.

>MACDUFF. Awake! Awake!
>   Ring the alarum bell! Murder and treason!
>   Banquo and Donalbain! Malcolm, awake!
>   Shake off this downy sleep, death's counterfeit,
>   And look on death itself! Up, up, and see
>   The great doom's image!

(Act Two, Scene Three)

Teaching Tip: For this piece you might get the whole performing group to use this text. Split it up. Be adventurous.

TEXT FOR TABLEAU 6

For the final selected text of this section, we might have the Macbeths triumphant, with the courtiers smiling superficially, and Banquo apart.

>BANQUO. Thou hast it now, King, Cawdor, Glamis, all,
>   As the Weird Women promised.

>MACBETH. Here's our chief guest.

>LADY MACBETH. If he had been forgotten,
>   It had been as a gap in our great feast.

(Act Three, Scene One)

SUMMARY FOR MAP ONE: STARTING FROM THE STORY

After this, we then move to the second group, who were working on 'the middle', using the same process. Then we work with the third group who made tableaux for 'the end'.

This is the map which requires the most organising from you. It helps the group get to grips with the energies, the themes, the story and some of the original text. You can add music and develop the movement between tableaux as much as you like.

Map Two: Using a Character as the Spine

Map Two is going to give space to the young actors to do more varied devising and writing, as well as using short pieces of the original text. We are going to focus on one character, Lady Macbeth, and use Act Five, Scene One, the 'sleepwalking scene', as the Spine with the inserted devised pieces acting as Lady Macbeth's flashbacks. The scene is reproduced below in its entirety and then again subsequently after the devised pieces have been inserted. I shall now explain how I might build this up.

Stage One

- Tell everyone that we are going to look at the story of Lady Macbeth and build a short piece about her. Tell the group that we are going to use the 'sleepwalking scene' as the Spine of it, and then insert pieces of the Lady Macbeth story, which the group is going to create using short scenes from the play, their own original writing or movement.

- As an introduction, ask everyone to make a statue of Lady Macbeth as she appears at the beginning of the play. This needs to express what she wants and how she feels, more akin to a Psychological Gesture rather than simply a woman reading a letter. Let's call it a gesture/statue from now on. She could be excited, pushing forward, thrilled with ambition. Some people will have a different take. Perhaps they see her as closing, withdrawing, scheming. Look at a few of the gesture/statues and discuss them. How does this Lady Macbeth appear? Is she angry? Determined? Downtrodden? Bitter? Some will find it hard to articulate but you might get some interesting and varied responses.

- Then ask them to consider the end of her story. Don't go to her actual suicide unless you are sure you have a group who can cope with that. You don't need to. Tell them to make a gesture/statue for after the sleepwalking scene. For me, that final gesture/statue might show she is searching desperately for comfort and solace from her torment and loneliness. It could be that one of your young actors sees her as completely closed-off and numb, like a doll.

- Now ask them to go from the first gesture/statue to the second, *very slowly*.

- Tell them they have now performed the character's emotional journey in the play. Get them to try it a few times; ask them how it feels.

- Now ask them to pick a moment in the middle of her story that is meaningful. There are many possibilities. Some will pick her curse, some will pick when she emerges with blood on her hands, when she washes them, when she becomes Queen, when her husband leaves her out of the next murder, or when she has to contain his behaviour at the banquet. Ask them to make a gesture/statue of the moment. For our purposes, let's say it is when she becomes Queen. She has achieved her goal and for a moment she is triumphant and powerful. Perhaps she is presenting herself to the world, looking down at everyone.

- Now ask them to perform the three gesture/statues. Let half the group watch the other half. Ask for comments. What did the group feel about the character?

- Tell the group that, in addition to telling us something of the possible journey of the character, these statues might be something we can use directly for our piece.

Teaching Tip: Make sure they make these gesture/statues fully. Cite graphic novels perhaps, or pictures of classical statues where every sinew is engaged in the movement and feeling. Especially watch out for a lack of connection to the lower body. A good exercise to tackle this lack of connection is *Stacatto/Legato* (Chapter Six), which you might like to integrate into your warm-up.

Stage Two

- Now get the group to read the scene below. Cast three people to read the three parts, but assure the others they will have plenty to do in the final piece. Ask the people not reading to listen to the scene with their eyes closed.

Enter a Doctor of Physic and a Waiting-Gentlewoman.

DOCTOR. I have two nights watched with you, but can perceive no truth in your report. When was it she last walked?

GENTLEWOMAN. Since his majesty went into the field, I have seen her rise from her bed, throw her nightgown upon her, unlock her closet, take forth paper, fold it, write upon't, read it, afterwards seal it, and again return to bed; yet all this while in a most fast sleep.

DOCTOR. A great perturbation in nature, to receive at once the benefit of sleep, and do the effects of watching. In this slumbery agitation, besides her walking and other actual performances, what, at any time, have you heard her say?

GENTLEWOMAN. That, sir, which I will not report after her.

DOCTOR. You may, to me; and 'tis most meet you should.

GENTLEWOMAN. Neither to you nor any one; having no witness to confirm my speech.

Enter Lady Macbeth, with a taper.

Lo you, here she comes. This is her very guise, and upon my life, fast asleep. Observe her; stand close.

DOCTOR. How came she by that light?

GENTLEWOMAN. Why, it stood by her: she has light by her continually; 'tis her command.

DOCTOR. You see her eyes are open.

GENTLEWOMAN. Ay, but their sense are shut.

DOCTOR. What is it she does now? Look how she rubs her hands.

GENTLEWOMAN. It is an accustomed action with her, to seem thus washing her hands. I have known her continue in this a quarter of an hour.

LADY MACBETH. Yet here's a spot.

DOCTOR. Hark, she speaks. I will set down what comes from her, to satisfy my remembrance the more strongly.

LADY MACBETH. Out, damned spot: out, I say. – One; two. Why then 'tis time to do't. Hell is murky. Fie, my lord, fie, a soldier, and afeard? What need we fear who knows it, when none can call our power to account? Yet who would have thought the old man to have had so much blood in him?

DOCTOR. Do you mark that?

LADY MACBETH. The Thane of Fife had a wife. Where is she now? What, will these hands ne'er be clean? No more o' that, my lord, no more o' that. You mar all with this starting.

DOCTOR. Go to, go to. You have known what you should not.

GENTLEWOMAN. She has spoke what she should not, I am sure of that. Heaven knows what she has known.

LADY MACBETH. Here's the smell of the blood still. All the perfumes of Arabia will not sweeten this little hand. Oh, oh, oh!

DOCTOR. What a sigh is there. The heart is sorely charged.

GENTLEWOMAN. I would not have such a heart in my bosom, for the dignity of the whole body.

DOCTOR. Well, well, well.

GENTLEWOMAN. Pray God it be, sir.

DOCTOR. This disease is beyond my practice: yet I have known those which have walked in their sleep, who have died holily in their beds.

LADY MACBETH. Wash your hands, put on your nightgown, look not so pale. I tell you yet again, Banquo's buried; he cannot come out on's grave.

DOCTOR. Even so?

LADY MACBETH. To bed, to bed: there's knocking at the gate. Come, come, come, come, give me your hand. What's done, cannot be undone. To bed, to bed, to bed.

Exit.

DOCTOR. Will she go now to bed?

GENTLEWOMAN. Directly.

DOCTOR. Foul whisperings are abroad. Unnatural deeds
Do breed unnatural troubles. Infected minds
To their deaf pillows will discharge their secrets.
More needs she the divine than the physician.
God, God forgive us all. Look after her,
Remove from her the means of all annoyance,
And still keep eyes upon her. So, goodnight.
My mind she has mated and amazed my sight.
I think, but dare not speak.

GENTLEWOMAN. Goodnight, good doctor.

Exeunt.

- After the reading, ask the group who were listening what the atmosphere felt like in the scene. What did they see? They might say: 'a dark castle', 'damp running down the walls', 'rats', 'wind howling through a broken window', 'darkness', 'hell', 'fear', 'secrecy' or 'guilt'. Note these images and feelings down, and encourage the group to write them down as well. Tell them they might be useful to us.

- Tell the group we may not use the full text of the scene, but use it as a spine for our piece on the story of Lady Macbeth. You might suggest it is like a series of flashbacks in a movie. Ask the three actors to spend a little time working on the characters they are playing whilst the others devise. (I devote some time to the text of this scene in the following chapter, Working on Short Scenes.)

- Tell the rest of the group that they are going to work on devising. Split them into pairs or small groups. They need to pick a moment from the play when Lady Macbeth has some kind of turning point.

- Ask them to pick lines from the play that happen around this moment they have chosen. It might be when she speaks or argues with her husband, or when she defends him at the banquet. Get them to work on these moments in their subgroups.

- Tell them to show their snippets of scenes and give support. Note down all the work they present. If you have time, offer suggestions and give them a few more minutes to show again with improvements.

- Now ask them in their subgroups to make a short piece of *original* dramatic writing (of around six to ten lines) which expresses a moment in Lady Macbeth's story they want to explore. This can be something we actually see in the play or something imagined which happens offstage. For instance, someone might write her a speech for when she takes the daggers back to Duncan's chamber and sees the body. Remember she says in Act Two, Scene Two: 'Had he not resembled / My father as he slept, I had done't.' Perhaps the ghost of Duncan might speak to her! If they want to explore writing for another character, commenting on Lady Macbeth, that might also be interesting. Perhaps Lennox or the Porter has a story about her?

- Ask them to read/show them, and give support. Note all the work down. If you have time, offer suggestions and give them a few more minutes to show again with improvements.

- Finally, you might ask them in their subgroups to make a movement piece about Lady Macbeth. (This will depend on the skills and interests of your group.) For instance, remember the gesture/statues we developed in the earlier exercise? Let's imagine that three of the young actors in various parts of the space are now moving from one statue to the next, whilst others in the group whisper: 'The Thane of Fife had a wife. Where is she now?'/ 'A little water clears us of this deed.' / 'What, in our house?'

- Ask them to show their pieces and give support. Offer suggestions and take comments.

- You now have a wealth of material to work with. You can either choose an order with the group or decide on it yourself.

Teaching Tip: It is up to you how much creative-writing coaching you might do. The *Hot-Seating for Material* exercise which follows in Map Three might be useful.

Stage Three

When you have a running order and the pieces have been selected and worked on (all this will take a few sessions), the final presentation might look something like the script below (I often think of it as a musical score).

To facilitate the shape of our devised piece, which could be much more complex than it is here, I have edited the actual sleepwalking scene quite a bit. The inserted pieces, which are like flashbacks for Lady Macbeth, I have put into italics. In our devised piece, I imagine that only Lady Macbeth can see the inserted pieces of movement, Shakespearean text, or modern student writing. There are a number of young actors playing Lady Macbeth (called Lady M1, M2, etc.) in the new devised work.

Enter slowly a number of Lady Macbeths, as the group sings the Lyke-Wake Dirge (see Map One). They stand in their first statue position, then move to the second and the third. The singing stops as we hear, whispered:

'*The Thane of Fife had a wife. Where is she now?'*

'*A little water clears us of this deed.'*

'*What, in our house?'*

The Lady Macbeths freeze.
The rest of the group provide a wind sound and moaning.

The Doctor enters: it is dark. He shudders. He says to the audience:

(*Student's writing:*) '*What am I doing here? God help me, this is not safe. Why did I agree to come? You have to realise this is a very dangerous situation for me. These are difficult times. It is hard to stay out of trouble. If nothing happens tonight, I am never coming again.'*

Enter a Waiting-Gentlewoman.

(*Shakespearean text:*)

DOCTOR. I have two nights watched with you, but can perceive no truth in your report. When was it she last walked?

GENTLEWOMAN. Since his majesty went into the field, I have seen her rise from her bed, throw her nightgown upon her, unlock her closet, take forth paper, fold it, write upon't, read it, afterwards seal it, and again return to bed; yet all this while in a most fast sleep.

DOCTOR. What, at any time, have you heard her say?

GENTLEWOMAN. That, sir, which I will not report after her.

DOCTOR. You may, to me.

GENTLEWOMAN. Neither to you nor any one.

Enter Lady Macbeth, with a taper.

At the same time, Lady M1 enters with a letter. They stop and look at each other.

Lo you, here she comes. This is her very guise, and upon my life, fast asleep. Observe her; stand close.

(*Student's writing:*) *Lady M1 addressing the audience:*

'It's happened. I've been waiting for this moment for so long. At last we are bound for greatness. I don't believe in witches but my husband is superstitious and it will help to push him. We will be truly powerful, answerable to no one. Why should my husband go on risking his neck in battle for an old fool who can't even lift up a sword?' (*She reads:*) *'They met me in the day of success.'*

Lady M1 passes and moves away.

DOCTOR. How came she by that light?

GENTLEWOMAN. Why, it stood by her: she has light by her continually; 'tis her command.

DOCTOR. You see her eyes are open.

GENTLEWOMAN. Ay, but their sense are shut.

Movement piece 1: Based on Act One, Scene Five. 'Come you spirits that tend on mortal thoughts, unsex me here.'

Lady M2 enters, tears up the letter and Lady M2 begs to be filled with cruelty. Lady Macbeth watches and starts to wash her hands. The Witches surround Lady M2. Lady M2 breaks through the Witches and starts to wash her hands. The Witches flee.

All the Lady Macbeths start to wash their hands frantically. They continue as:

DOCTOR. What is it she does now? Look how she rubs her hands.

LADY MACBETH. Yet here's a spot.

DOCTOR. Hark, she speaks.

LADY MACBETH. Out, damned spot: out, I say. – One; two. Why then 'tis time to do't. Hell is murky. Fie, my lord, fie, a soldier, and afeard? What need we fear who knows it, when none can call our power to account?

Movement piece 2: Lady M3 goes up into Duncan's chamber to place the daggers by the sleeping grooms, who groan in their sleep and laugh. She looks at the body. Suddenly the ghost of Duncan stands up and points menacingly at her. The group whispers, 'Had he not resembled / My father as he slep't, I had done't.'

Yet who would have thought the old man to have had so much blood in him?

DOCTOR. Do you mark that?

LADY MACBETH. The Thane of Fife had a wife. Where is she now?

(*Flashback scene from Act Two, Scene Two:*)

Lady M4 and Macbeth washing their hands.

LADY M4. *A little water clears us of this deed.*
How easy is it then. Hark, more knocking!
Be not lost so poorly in your thoughts!'

MACBETH. *To know my deed, 'twere best not know myself.*
Wake Duncan with thy knocking: I would thou could'st.

LADY MACBETH. What, will these hands ne'er be clean? Here's the smell of blood still. All the perfumes of Arabia will not sweeten this little hand. Oh, Oh, Oh!

Lady Macbeth leaves the space

DOCTOR. What a sigh is there! The heart is sorely charged.

GENTLEWOMAN. I would not have such a heart in my bosom, for the dignity of the whole body.

DOCTOR. Well, well, well.

GENTLEWOMAN. Pray God it be, sir.

The whole group except the Doctor and the Gentlewoman starts to knock furiously. Lady Macbeth runs back in and around the space, terrified as she speaks.

LADY MACBETH. Wash your hands, put on your nightgown, look not so pale. I tell you yet again, Banquo's buried; he cannot come out on's grave.

The knocking stops.

DOCTOR. Even so?

LADY MACBETH. To bed, to bed! There's knocking at the gate. Come, come, come, come, give me your hand. What's done cannot be undone. To bed, to bed, to bed!

Lady Macbeth goes out.

DOCTOR. Goodnight:
My mind she has mated, and amazed my sight.
I think, but dare not speak.

GENTLEWOMAN. Good night, good doctor.

Exeunt. The whispers which began the scene return. Enter a Messenger, who kneels. The whispers stop.

MESSENGER. The queen, my lord, is dead.

Silence.

Map Three: Using a Theme

This map is the most open of the three examples. It will encourage freer and wider responses around a *theme* that comes from the play, rather than a character or the story of the play itself. In fact, this is less of a map and more a series of tools and signposts.

However, this time the piece you create will be much more involved with the group's creative response to the theme rather than how they respond to the play. Paradoxically, this freedom does not make it easier but harder and might be demanding. If this is your first time at devising, you should start with one of the earlier maps.

Here, more than ever, you have the freedom to work with the group's limitations and strengths. In other words, if someone wants to draw a picture, write a poem or a song, it can easily be encompassed here. You and your group are creating a mosaic of responses to the work. This map requires much more flexibility from everyone to let go of material – and that includes you also. What I mean is, everything cannot be included: you do need a creative *frame* or *spine*, as before, if it's ultimately going to work. Do try, however, to use some of the original text, even if it is only occasional lines.

The first thing to do is to choose your theme.

For the sake of argument, let's look at *betrayal*: this is a pretty strong theme in the play, though not something we might immediately consider. Early in the play, Duncan says of the defeated traitor who has just involved the country in a bloody battle (Act One, Scene Four):

> There's no art
> To find the mind's construction in the face.
> He was a gentleman on whom I built
> An absolute trust.

Stage One: Exploring the Theme of Betrayal and Making Material

Here are a few broad suggestions.

- You might start with the exploration of the theme using *atmosphere*, suggested earlier in this chapter (see above, page 124).

- You might ask your group to find lines/moments about *betrayal* in the play. If you do, get them to physicalise the words as in *Verbing the Body/Speaking the Text* (Chapter Five). Get them to radiate and speak the lines to other members in their group. Get them to really use the language with their bodies. You might use these lines later as a moment of collage.

- You might split them into groups to make tableaux of *betrayal* from scenes in the play. You will see a lot of body language with perhaps one person looking away, separate from the group. Betrayal involves isolation, another strong theme in the play. You might point this out. Look at the tableaux: decide whether they can help you create your frame. Consider that all concepts contain an opposite; with betrayal it is honour, a desire to do the right thing. In Chekhov terms this is a 'Polarity', a potent tool of exploration in theatre. It is something we will explore in more detail when we work on production.

- Now discuss betrayal in the play. What does his act of betrayal do to Macbeth's life? It draws him into a life of deeper cruelty and desensitises him to violence. It destroys him, and though his hangers-on stay with him for a while, he is ultimately isolated.

- Now start to open things out to the group's own experiences of betrayal which they might be prepared to share, or experiences they see in the world. If something comes up that might be used for the piece, note it down. Maybe some people might want to write a poem or piece of dramatic writing from the discussion. Check out the *Vox Pop* exercise later in this section.

Teaching Tip: When asking for an experience, always ensure the contributor is fine with sharing it.

Walk Across the Room 3 Revisited

After a period of sitting down, it might be useful to do something physical. Remember the exercise *Walk Across the Room 3*? (See above, page 123.)

- Get half of the group to perform and half to watch. Have two actors playing Macbeth and Lady Macbeth respectively walk across the space with the others following. Slowly, one by one, the others leave them. The Macbeths look round to see they are alone. Then Macbeth continues to walk but Lady

Macbeth cannot move and cannot go with him. Maybe ask her to call after him, 'My lord!' He keeps walking. Finally, Macbeth is totally alone.

- *Flyback*, and discuss how gradually the lords change sides: they betray *him*. It is interesting to consider how betrayal is a matter of conscience. It's not always a bad thing: Macbeth is the King after all, but then again he is evil and the forces of good are rising. You have created this whole dynamic through *movement*.

- Try this exercise again. Consider now *how* people leave. Macduff and Lennox do not leave in the same way, for example, nor at the same time in the story.

- This is an example of how to use an exercise as a dramatic piece within your devised work. The exercise below could create material to go with it.

Hot-Seating for Material

Hot-seating is a tried-and-tested way to explore character, but can also be a good way to make material, as it really encourages spontaneity in the young actor/writer.

- The young actor/writer decides to work on a character, in this case Lennox, the young lord who eventually changes sides. Tell everyone we are going to look at this character, focusing on the subject of *betrayal*.

- Tell everyone that we are going to interview Lennox about his actions in the play, which can also include imaginary episodes the young actor might invent as the questions continue.

- For writing purposes it's good if the young actor can record the Q&A on their phone. Get the actor to ask permission. I do not encourage using phones for anything in workshop, but in this case it's useful.

- Decide where we are in the play when we interview the character. Is it at the beginning of the story? Or when he is about to leave Macbeth's court? Perhaps it is after the banquet? This is important or the actor will be confused and vague.

- The young actor playing Lennox sits in a seat in front of the group. Stay with the group and ask questions yourself as well, if things go quiet. Give a moment for silence to settle.

I am going to provide a fictitious script of this here, to indicate and highlight one or two things that might come up. The group asks questions; Lennox answers.

Q. What is your name?

A. Lennox.

Q. How old are you?

A. Eighteen.

Q. Are you a servant?

A. No, a lord. I have a lot of servants, and as the lords go, I am pretty rich.

Q. Were you in the last battle?

A. Yes.

Q. Where are you now?

A. I am in my room after the banquet.

Q. What happened?

A. The King... well, the King wasn't well. It was pretty disturbing.

Q. Go on.

A. He was... seeing things... ghosts.

Q. Go on. Do you think he was tired?

A. He's never tired. I have seen him fight and kill three men one after the other in battle... he's never tired.

Q. So what do you think?

A. What do you mean?

Q. What's going on? Is he ill?

A. Dunno.

Q. Is he well enough to be the King?

A. I'm not talking about that.

Q. We won't tell anyone.

A. I'm scared to say it.

Q. Go on.

A. I... I think he murdered Duncan.

Q. What are you going to do?

A. People are talking.

Q. What about?

A. Why weren't Macduff and Banquo there at the banquet? They are soldiers, honourable guys, men who do the right thing.

Q. So. Are you going to join an uprising?

A. What if I am?

Q. Aren't you betraying the King, the office of the King, by plotting against him?

A. I have to do *something*...

Teaching Tip: In this example, note how the questioners begin with basic questions first, to get the young actor in the zone. Note how important it is to place the character in a moment in the play, because the character would answer differently if he was, say, Lennox at the start of the play. Indicate to the group in the discussion afterwards how complex the act of betrayal can be. The final few lines could be made into an interesting monologue by the young actor and elaborated on. A student's created monologue on Lennox's story might sit well with the *Walking Across the Room* piece, above. Perhaps you might also use the characters of Macduff and Ross, and create monologues for them too.

Rhythm Circle

Another way to create material of a different sort is through a *Rhythm Circle*, using various lines from the play.

- Let's take Macbeth's lines, 'Stars, hide your fires, / Let not light see my black and deep desires!'

- Ask the group to get into a circle and split them into four teams. Ask the whole group to beat out a 4/4 time by clicking their fingers or tapping their feet. Ask one team initially to whisper, 'Stars, hide your fires' to the rhythm. Ask them to keep repeating it in rhythm.

- Then give another team 'Let not light see my black and deep desires!' still within the 4/4 rhythm, and add them so now both teams are chanting their different lines at the same time.

- Now add another team: 'Who should against his murderer shut the door.'

- And finally, 'False face must hide.' The whole group is chanting now, using the different rhythms they have found in the texts.

- Get the teams to build this up to crescendo. Then stop it and let everyone get their breath back.

- Now ask each team to add a fairly simple movement to their rhythmic line. Make sure the movement has resonance with the line and is full of energy.

- Ask the whole group to learn each other's movements and lines.

- You can now conduct, having two groups merge, then separate, then at times having the whole group moving and speaking using one of the lines. Finally perhaps, get everyone to end with 'False face must hide what the false heart doth know.'

- Bring it down to a whisper. The effect of this is like a rap using the Shakespeare text.

- This is an excellent way to build up a whole sequence, which can be as simple or as complex as you like, with choreography and singing. Perhaps ask the group to make a tune and *sing* their lines.

Vox Pop

- Ask each group member to write down in no more than a sentence what they believe an act of betrayal is or feels like to them. Have them speak aloud what they wrote, one by one.

- If you feel that might not be comfortable, perhaps put the papers in a hat instead and ask each to pick one out so it can be anonymous.

- You might well be able to use some or all of these within your final devised piece. You can intersperse the young actors' sentences with texts from the play.

Stage Two: Finding a Beginning

In the earlier maps we have had the whole story of the play or one of its scenes as the spine. In this case there is less to hold on to, so I am not going to give you a concrete suggestion because it is more dependent on what the young people give you to work with.

Having gathered a massive amount of material from exercises we have done throughout this chapter, you could be excused for thinking, 'Well, this is all very well, but how do I put something together?' It is useful for you to have an 'artistic frame' in which you can place some of the material you have created. Consider when you do, that you are *composing*.

We might say that for this devised piece we are thinking as much about the young people's experience of the theme, and how they feel about it, as the way it manifests itself in the play.

We have to find a *beginning*: for instance, you might begin with the group coming slowly onstage and every so often they all

152

look behind them; you might begin with each person coming towards the audience and saying 'Trust me'; you might begin with a *Rhythm Circle* on betrayal (see above), with two actors miming a fight in the centre. Finally, you might begin with one person, as Lennox, sitting on a chair and writing a letter to his parents about the situation at court and what he witnessed at the banquet. This could then be framed by a chorus of people offering their *Vox Pop* on betrayal behind him, then adding some lines from the play itself on betrayal... and so on. Each beginning is valid; each different.

Stage Three: Where the Beginning Leads

Choose a beginning which is effective and everyone is enthusiastic about. Having decided on it, you might ask, quite legitimately, 'Where do I go from here?' I suggested earlier that you were *composing*, so look for a flow in the pieces you and your group choose to use. Add and change. Use your intuition. If you can really involve the group in these decisions there is more chance they will *own* the work.

Many pieces, be they devised or not, make a great beginning then lose their way. The piece can be greatly focused by considering a journey for it. A way to clarify a journey is to discuss with the group: ask them, 'How do we as a group feel about betrayal as it is portrayed in the play?' The play is not very positive about honesty and innocence; the honest and innocent die. Someone might say that the play suggests that no one can be trusted; that whilst we are trying to be good and honest, traitors emerge and you constantly have to 'watch your back'. Ask questions like: Do we want the piece to support that statement or challenge it? Would we like the audience to get that message, that the world is untrustworthy? Finding their 'take' on this theme can give you a journey for your piece, at the same time as making clear that what we are trying to communicate is very important for the creators and a potential audience.

Michael Chekhov believed that we, as artists, should have a responsibility to know what we are saying when we make theatre, and I believe, in the educational context, this is even more vital.

Conclusion

It's important to remember that, however you devise (and whatever the standard of the final piece), provided you have used the play as a basis, you will have allowed your group some exploration of Shakespearean language, of the relationships and characters, of the atmosphere of the play, the imagery and the themes, and have explored it in a dynamic, accessible way. You have also, particularly in the final map, built some bridges from the themes in the play to the group's everyday lives.

In addition, it can be a valuable stepping stone towards making a production. In the next chapter we are going to look at exploring short scenes, again from *Macbeth*, which you might perhaps put into this project, use for teaching acting and/or hone your own directing abilities.

Chapter Nine
Working on Short Scenes

Thus, then in brief…
> *Romeo and Juliet*: Act One, Scene Three

Initially, even for quite experienced actors, looking at a big slab of text can be a daunting thing, especially if it is written in seventeenth-century verse. A good place to start can be with short, manageable scenes.

I want us to look at three very short scenes which are nonetheless packed with character, action, atmosphere and flowing energy. Short scenes are excellent for teaching acting (and directing). No scene we look at in this chapter is longer than twenty lines. We are going to stick with *Macbeth*, as you can then use this chapter easily in conjunction with the previous devising chapter.

We are going to look first at some general issues that come up when directing a scene and some exercises to enhance and focus these skills. Many of these exercises we have done already, and rather than going over them again I will refer you back to where to find them. (An index of all exercises in this book can also be found in the Appendix.)

Even though it is Shakespeare, I am starting from a psycho-physical base. In other words, I am not having us pore over the script. Start from a physical place and then you will find out things about the characters and situation. The language is precious and vital, but even if you are looking at images, explore them through the body first. Act first; think later.

Secondly, we are going to look in detail at three scenes. We are going to work with different elements for each scene. Whichever starting point you choose will immediately influence the direction of the scene. For instance, if you approach the scene starting with a General Atmosphere, the scene will have a different feel than if you were starting with Psychological Gesture. It is important to consider as a director what you want the actors to achieve *first* to make the scene live.

Some General Points

Knowing the Lines

It is most helpful if the actor can be free with the body from the start. You are seeking to keep the actor's body and imagination open. If they are focusing down, holding a script, with the hands trapped, it is impossible to do anything.

If they are reading from a phone (something utterly forbidden in my workshops) it is even worse, as they frequently lose their place and then anything they are trying to create is gone.

Here are some points to remember about words and learning:

- Young actors can be daunted by learning lines. Tell them as soon as they know the lines, they can do anything and can be truly creative and free from fear.

- Working on short scenes ensures there isn't too much text to learn. If the piece is in verse, suggest they use the rhythm to help them memorise.

- With Shakespeare there is the added problem of *meaning* which frequently holds things up, so it is helpful if you can read the piece through for meaning and work on emphasis with them if you need to. Looking for definite changes in thought, subject or feeling can also help.

- Do not feel the young actor has to know the meaning of every single word at this stage; they don't!

- Remind them that once through this initial stage of learning and understanding, it is the feeling, the character, the imagery, the atmosphere and the story that are going to be our concern. The actor and the language are carrying all that to the audience.

- If they have yet to learn the text, then there is a common process you can go through which I call 'ghosting', which leaves the actor free.

Ghosting

If, for whatever reason, the group do not know the lines, then how can you spend that first session? Well, you can approach it more intellectually and go through the breathing points and emphasis. You can also use the *Radiating and Receiving* (*Throwing the Ball*) exercise with one or two lines that they can learn on the spot. Perhaps get them to read slowly and try radiating and receiving, without throwing, text in hand, really elongating the silences in the scene: that way they can still get a sense of what the other actor is giving them and what is going on in the silences.

I am going to describe below what I call 'ghosting'. I first learned this from the actor Bruce Myers, and have found it incredibly useful to free actors physically when they don't know the lines.

- The performing actors give their scripts to two readers. The actors radiate and receive towards each other and are free to move around.

- Reader 1 reads a line clearly and flatly.

- Actor 1 repeats the line, responding to his acting partner with conviction; in other words, he acts it.

- Reader 2 reads the response by Actor 2 clearly and flatly.

- Actor 2 repeats the line with force and conviction towards her acting partner.

- Reader 1 reads their next line.
- Actor 1 speaks the line, and so on until the end of the scene.

Teaching Tips:

- The readers must not be timid; they need to read clearly and loudly, but with little or no emphasis or feeling. They are not trying to be invisible; they are trying to free their partner-actor from the script.
- They can follow their actors around the space.
- The reader must not read more than a line at a time, otherwise the actor might be struggling to remember and cannot be free. The only time that changes is when the reader needs to get to the end of a phrase or sentence.

Keep this exercise in your toolbox because it is extremely useful. It enables a physical dynamic between the actors, frees the body: which also frees the voice. It allows a myriad of interpretations because the actors are liberated from the script. It also highlights to the young actor how much more they can achieve when they know the text!

Issues of Physical Contact: The Way I Deal with It

In the drama studio there needs to be an atmosphere of trust as we explore the play, ourselves and our character. As someone who has worked with young people for a long time, I am aware one has to be mindful of things going on in their lives that we don't know about. However, I am beginning to fear that young people are afraid to touch each other, which for theatre can be extremely problematic. In *Physicalising the Psychology* (an approach we use later in this chapter) it is sometimes required that the actors have to touch, push or hold each other. So how do we resolve this, particularly with young adults? After several people, in a recent class I taught, kept asking permission to hold someone or touch someone's hand, I made a series of rules, as follows:

- I say that this is a safe space and that no one is allowed to do anything inappropriate to anyone else.

- At the same time, we have to recognise that we are acting and to explore character and relationship, some physical contact must be allowed: the condition is we ask permission and it is granted. This cannot happen every single time physical contact occurs because it breaks the energy of the movement.

- At the start of the session I ask whether anyone feels unwell or would mind *theoretically* being held or pulled around the room, or whatever might be required. If everyone says they are okay, then I remind them they can change their mind later in the session: just to let me know. If this action was likely to be something strenuous I would perhaps ask again. Basically, however, when we have agreed *once*, permission has been given for the session. There is no need to keep asking!

The Three Short Scenes

I want us to imagine we have warmed up, perhaps using exercises from the *Connecting Up* section of Chapter Two and finishing with *Radiating and Receiving* (*Throwing the Ball*). Ask them to use their text and throw the imaginary ball. Then, once they have thrown, ask them to sustain and stay extended, until their scene partner answers them.

You might try, as part of a voice warm-up, *Verbing the Body / Speaking the Text* (Chapter Five) on some of the verbs within the text of the scene you are going to be working with, just to remind the actors of the importance of connecting the body and voice to the language.

Acting and directing are both about making decisions. These are not decisions to last for all time. They are decisions *for now*. If you are using these scenes as a studio exercise with your whole group, and you have time in the session, you might ask each pair to find *two* ways to play the scene. Psycho-physical exercises give you a lot of choices which, whilst they are a gift, can be confusing. As one of my own teachers, David Zinder, told me when I was training, eventually you will just *know* which of your choices is right.

Short Scene One: 'We will proceed no further in this business'

It is night. Macbeth argues with Lady Macbeth about the murder of the King, who is staying with his entourage at Macbeth's castle. He has left the feast to be alone and consider his conscience. Lady Macbeth leaves the feast to look for him.

Make sure your actors know exactly what has happened so far in the story. I am going to assume your actors know the lines.

The scene is Act One, Scene Seven.

Enter Lady Macbeth.

MACBETH. How now! what news?

LADY MACBETH. He has almost supped. Why have you left the chamber?

MACBETH. Hath he asked for me?

LADY MACBETH.   Know you not, he has?

MACBETH. We will proceed no further in this business:
He hath honoured me of late, and I have bought
Golden opinions from all sorts of people,
Which would be worn now in their newest gloss,
Not cast aside so soon.

LADY MACBETH.   Was the hope drunk
Wherein you dressed yourself? Hath it slept since?
And wakes it now, to look so green and pale,
At what it did so freely? From this time
Such I account thy love.

In our exploration of this scene, we will be using *Radiating/Receiving*, *Applying a Quality* and *Physicalising the Psychology*.

160

Radiating and Receiving

- The main element of this scene is the conflict between Lady Macbeth and her husband. It's useful to note that she interrupts Macbeth's troubled soliloquy when she comes in. For me this fact alone would make me explore this short scene with radiating/receiving first, because something immediately 'happens' between them when she comes in.

- Let them do some radiating and receiving, throwing the ball and using the text, so they get to both run the lines and make connections to each other. Now ask the actors to speak the text facing each other, radiating and receiving, leaving very long gaps between each line. If they go very slowly, they will notice what happens between the lines. They will also notice moments when Macbeth is losing, and feels strongly that he wants to look away, before rallying. How and if he feels this will depend on how the actor playing Lady Macbeth responds and speaks. This one exercise can create an absolute riot of nuance and subtlety: for instance, you might discover that Lady Macbeth is not as confident as she is sometimes portrayed.

- After you have done this a few times you might discuss making a choice about what is actually going on between them.

- Have an idea yourself, but try and get a decision from the actors.

Teaching Tip: Notice how we are working here. We explore on our feet, then *flyback* and consider *afterwards*. This is an absolute bedrock of the Chekhov work.

Applying a Quality

- Ask your actors, what is the *quality* of the exchange? How are they reacting to each other? Try and make it come from *them*. Ask them to try 'secretly', 'desperately', 'angrily'. Tell them to really commit to whatever quality they choose, whilst still radiating and receiving with their partner. You will see how simple and powerful this is.

- Don't worry that this might make the scene play on one note because it is always *their* sense of what the particular quality might suggest that powers them. In addition, there are always other influences, the images of the text or the way an acting partner responds, which are constantly flexing and changing the quality. On the rare occasion when acting with a quality sounds flat, it is usually because the actors are not committing to the quality sufficiently.

Teaching Tip: Something that is amazing about the Chekhov Technique is how you have simply to commit to the image or the idea. Once you do that, the acting can soar. If you choose a quality that doesn't feel right, you can change it in a moment.

Physicalising the Psychology

This is an extension of Psychological Gesture, but is more visceral and interactive. It's easier than Psychological Gesture because in this case the young actor has an actual physical obstacle or confrontation with the other actor. It is immediately freeing and works incredibly fast.

- Ask the actors: What is Macbeth *doing*? We might say he is trying to push his bad thoughts behind him and move forward. This might be a Psychological Gesture in itself. But basically he is *trying to escape* from his honour, from the murder, from what his wife is saying, and from his guilt. What is Lady Macbeth *doing*? Perhaps she is trying to grab him, pull him or hold him?

- To begin with, ask two other members of your group to hold Macbeth. They need to keep him firm. Macbeth needs to escape. Tell the actor to try and get away from his captors; then the scene begins and Lady Macbeth comes in.

- Initially, if they really commit, Macbeth will sound terrified and Lady Macbeth powerful. Perhaps she comes right up to him like a prison warden as she taunts him.

- However, perhaps that is not the right balance. Discuss it with your actors afterwards.

- Try it the other way, with Lady Macbeth being held. That is obviously wrong for the whole sequence, but it might not be if the pair of 'captors' gradually let her go during Macbeth's speech about 'golden opinions'.

- Just *doing* this really makes us consider how far Lady Macbeth is responsible for the murder. Who is the dominant partner?

- Try it this time without the captors: Macbeth moving agitatedly around the space and Lady Macbeth chasing him. Again, this is not necessarily how you would present the scene, but it might be what is actually going on *psychologically*. There is a phenomenal amount of energy going between the two of them.

- One thing is clear: he seems unwilling to tell her how he feels. Now try again, with him ranging around and her chasing him as before; this time, he moves agitatedly until he turns and faces her and says, 'We will proceed no further in this business.' Then he stands his ground. She might start to push him physically when she begins, 'Was the hope drunk...' You will find that *physicalising* this scene releases the voice and the emotions. When I get people to work this way with the whole body, the group watching often gasp as they feel the release happen with the actors.

- Most of these psycho-physical scenarios will not necessarily be seen by an audience, though some of the physicality may well remain, smaller but intense. However, I have often retained this kind of strong physicality completely in the performance when it has been the only way a young actor could give the scene effective commitment and energy.

- Once you have explored the broad sweep of this approach, I would advise going back to the beginning of the scene. What happens between the two of them when Lady Macbeth enters? Does she know he is faltering before she speaks? What happens in that silence before her first line?

- Knowing specifically what happens to the actors' energy in the pauses is a very mature performance skill, but most young actors can do it through radiating and receiving. In

Chekhov terms, it is 'making the intangible, tangible' for the audience.

- I would want to have some feedback on how the couple feel after the little scene is over. How stung is he by her rebuke? How hopeful is she that her emasculation of him will spur him on? So, ask them how the characters feel when they have finished the scene. This will guide us as to our decision-making.

- Finally, ask the pair to work on two options to show the group. Tell them to make definite decisions. For example, they could present two versions of the scene, one where Macbeth is broadly dominant and one with Lady Macbeth in more control.

Short Scene Two: 'Words... That would be howl'd out in the desert air'

The Scottish lords have fled to England and want support for an army to reclaim Scotland. We join the scene where Ross reveals to Macduff the horrible fact that his family have been killed by Macbeth: Malcolm looks on.

What we are mainly looking for is the sense of *truth* in this moment of breaking terrible news. What we are *not* looking for, especially with young actors, is getting them to try and find the feeling directly through their own life experience. For acting, we want the expression of emotion to be authentic, but we are going to find it by using a physical gesture and, later, by speaking the subtext.

I cannot stress enough how dangerous the idea of 'emotional recall' is when searching for emotional truth. Using their own lives directly can bring up difficult unresolved emotions. Secondly, this direct life experience they use to summon emotion often cannot be sustained, so by the second performance it 'wears out'. Furthermore, just using their own memories and traumas over and over again somehow belittles their real-life experience. It is far better to get them to find sensations and feelings through the imagination and the body.

Whilst these feelings can be intense, they can be much more easily shaken away: this is one of the main reasons I chose the scene below.

The scene is Act Four, Scene Three.

> ROSS. Would I could answer
> This comfort with the like. But I have words
> That would be howled out in the desert air,
> Where hearing should not latch them.

> MACDUFF.   What concern
>   they?
> The general cause? Or is it a fee-grief
> Due to some single breast?

> ROSS.   No mind that's honest
> But in it shares some woe, though the main part
> Pertains to you alone.

> MACDUFF.   If it be mine,
> Keep it not from me, quickly let me have it.

> ROSS. Let not your ears despise my tongue for ever,
> Which shall possess them with the heaviest sound
> That ever yet they heard.

> MACDUFF.   Humh! I guess at it.

> ROSS. Your castle is surprised; your wife and babes
> Savagely slaughtered. To relate the manner
> Were on the quarry of these murdered deer
> To add the death of you.

In this exploration of the scene we will be using *Psychological Gesture, Falling* and *Speaking the Subtext.*

It is worth saying that Macduff, having heard this news, cannot initially speak at all, and it is Malcolm who speaks next.

After an initial *Radiating/Receiving* exercise with the text, I might start here with Psychological Gesture. What is Ross *doing* here? He is presenting news. It is as if he has this horrible gift in his pocket which he has to give to his friend.

Finding Emotional Truth with Psychological Gesture

- Tell them we are trying to find the psychology; the *what* and the *how* of this scene. Get the two actors playing Ross and Macduff to face each other and radiate and receive, speaking the lines to each other. If you want to add 'throwing the ball' as each speaks their lines then do. Get them to do this a couple of times.

- Now tell the actors they are going to speak the text and, as they do so, the actor playing Ross should hold 'the news' behind his back. He has to present this to Macduff, who is watching him. He presents the information as if he is holding it in his hands.

- Watch how your actor performs this act. It will probably be slow and tentative. Maybe he will re-conceal his hands behind his back, or may certainly want to. Perhaps he presents it but does not want to open his hands to reveal the information.

- When Ross has presented and opened his hands, Macduff might consider taking the 'gift' from him. See what happens between them.

- *Flyback*. Ask the actors how they felt. The actor playing Macduff may well say that he knew the news was going to be terrible (and even what it was) before it was spoken. This is a good acting discovery.

- Don't be afraid to try this exercise a couple of times. Tell the actors it may not work in exactly the same way each time. Suppose Ross offers it more quickly the second time: the actors will speak differently and feel differently, and the moment will change.

- Ask the two actors to now work on two interpretations of the scene using Psychological Gestures.

- Afterwards, suggest they try *internalising* the physicalisation as they play the scene.

Falling

Another way to explore this scene might be to imagine you are 'Falling', a Chekhov term, one of the 'three sisters', as he called them, of Falling, Balancing and Flowing. They are physical manifestations of psychological states: *falling* in love, *falling* into despair, *falling* from grace. We all know the strange sensation of falling, that mixture of being totally in the 'now', experiencing freedom, terror and loss of control in equal measure.

Falling (literally) can be challenging for everyone. Our very being makes us want to stay balanced and stay erect. Allowing ourselves to tip, and get that sick feeling in the solar plexus, is undoubtedly a strong element of the moment of getting or giving terrible news.

But try it and see.

- Ask them to imagine they are falling and to tip slowly forward, saving themselves only at the last moment. Try it a few times.

- Ask them to hold on to that feeling and then ask the two actors to try the scene.

Teaching Tip: Some people will not be able to do this. If they can't, don't force it. What this does allow us to experience is that emotion has direction.

Speaking the Subtext

This is not a Chekhov exercise, but it does explore subtext and tone. I'm sure some of you know it already. This exercise can be very useful for those actors who are less free in their bodies and who tend to respond more verbally.

- Tell them you are going to give them lines which denote how the characters may really feel in this moment, in other words the subtext: how they feel, not what they say.

- Let's say that Ross's subtext line is, '*I have to tell him now.*' Let's say Macduff's subtext line is, '*Something terrible has happened.*'

- When they speak each of their subtext lines, the actors have to say it like they mean it or the exercise won't work. The subtext has the same status as the main text of the scene.

- Tell the actor to 'top up' with the subtext line (in italics in the example below) and say it as many times as they want. So it might go something like this:

ROSS. *I have to tell him now.* Would I could answer
This comfort with the like. *I have to tell him now.*
                       But I have words
That would be howled out in the desert air,
Where hearing should not latch them. *I have to tell him now.*

MACDUFF. *Something terrible has happened.*
                           What concern
   they?
Something terrible has happened.
The general cause? Or is it a fee-grief
Due to some single breast?

ROSS. *I have to tell him now.*   No mind that's honest
But in it shares some woe. *I have to tell him now.*
Though the main part pertains to you alone.

And so on to the end of the scene. Let them use other subtext lines of their own choosing if it helps. You can see how this might be applied to any scene you might be dealing with.

Short Scene Three: 'When was it she last walked?'

It is night in the castle. Lady Macbeth's Waiting-Gentlewoman has asked a Doctor to come and watch with her, as her mistress has been sleep-walking. This is one of the scenes we have examined in the previous chapter on devising (page 137).

Let's imagine we are at Shakespeare's Globe Theatre in the open air, and on come two characters we have never met. Interestingly, there is no description of where we are, merely 'A room in the castle'. So the actors need to bring this dark, intangible atmosphere onto the stage with them, and fill the stage with it, even before they open their mouths. Whilst the scene is generated by the dialogue and the situation, there has to be something 'in the air' from the beginning.

This extract is from Act Five, Scene One.

Enter a Doctor of Physic and a Waiting-Gentlewoman.

DOCTOR. I have two nights watched with you, but can perceive no truth in your report. When was it she last walked?

GENTLEWOMAN. Since his majesty went into the field, I have seen her rise from her bed, throw her nightgown upon her, unlock her closet, take forth paper, fold it, write upon't, read it, afterwards seal it, and again return to bed; yet all this while in a most fast sleep.

DOCTOR. A great perturbation in nature, to receive at once the benefit of sleep, and do the effects of watching. In this slumbery agitation, besides her walking and other actual performances, what, at any time, have you heard her say?

GENTLEWOMAN. That, sir, which I will not report after her.

DOCTOR. You may, to me; and 'tis most meet you should.

GENTLEWOMAN. Neither to you nor any one; having no witness to confirm my speech.

Enter Lady Macbeth, with a taper.

Lo you, here she comes.

Our focus here will be on *Working with Atmosphere* and *Plot*.

To me, unlike the other scenes we have looked at in this chapter, the paramount thing to explore here would be the *atmosphere*.

Why is that? Well, sometimes it is not helpful to follow a literal naturalistic route with Shakespeare because it was not something with which he was overly concerned. For instance, why has the woman not told the Doctor all this information about Lady Macbeth over the last two cold nights they have waited for her to appear? If she has, why is the Doctor asking her to repeat it? It simply defies analysis and will only confuse the actors. The Doctor and the Gentlewoman's dialogue gives us a good bit of information to prepare us for the arrival of the wretched Lady Macbeth and, most importantly, is there to create a dark, uneasy atmosphere. This does not mean the two watchers have no characters at all. They do, but their prime contribution is atmosphere.

You might go back to Chapter Seven (Exploring Atmosphere) for support before you try this.

Working with Atmosphere

- Ask them to read the scene, radiating and receiving, and then share what the atmosphere felt like. They might say 'ominous', 'I saw damp castle walls running with water', 'candles flickering', 'fear' or 'danger'.

- Get them to try the scene using one specific agreed atmosphere in the studio space. Try 'darkness'. Really encourage them to take their time establishing it, working alone at first. Get them to really feel the atmosphere in the room strongly as it invades their bodies and not to worry about the characters.

- Now ask them to still feel the atmosphere but reduce how much they show in their bodies.

- Now ask them to come together and run the scene.

- Remind them that the main thing they have to focus on is the atmosphere and what it is doing to them.

- *Flyback.* Come up with another idea. Perhaps try 'cold' or 'fear'. Go through the same process and you will find the scene changes.

Plot

Having established an atmosphere, it is time to look at the plot and the information we need to convey to the audience. Whilst I would not start with this kind of sit-down textual exercise unless I had to, I am aware that some of you might want to.

It can be important to analyse for plot-points with Shakespeare because it is often assumed that the audience knows what happens. Young actors (and often seasoned professionals) forget to convey these new pieces of information which develop story and character, evoking both surprise and shock. It is rare that I suggest forensic examination of the text with young actors; it is too like school or college and can stunt creativity. At the same time, you must not forget about it, even if you do not start with it.

- Get them to sit down and discuss what we find out within the text. Tell them that nothing is too small. The characters have been watching for two nights. This is the third night. This subconsciously prepares the audience that *tonight* something is going to happen. (Think how often 'three' or 'thrice' is mentioned in this play, taking us back to the Witches' scenes.) They are probably waiting for the Queen; she is disturbed, has been sleepwalking, and this has happened several times. Macbeth is away fighting. They are both nervous and irritable. The Gentlewoman refuses to repeat what she has heard the Queen say. It would be dangerous since there are no other witnesses. This emphasises both the danger and the fact they do not trust each other.

- Now ask them to repeat the scene, making sure the plot-points you have discussed are there and try and retain the atmosphere at the same time.

The Danger of Over-Embroidery

This scene has pitfalls which we could extend throughout our whole approach to Shakespeare. Make sure the actors do not over-embroider the scene with detail. Perhaps, the actor might suggest, the Doctor has brought food, a stool and a blanket to make his wait more comfortable? This seems like a clever and funny idea, realistically believable, and may well have been tried in many professional productions. It makes the actor playing a small part feel as if he has made a contribution to the work. However, his dialogue does not support this idea, the Doctor is clearly worried about what he is going to see, and it does little to prepare us for Lady Macbeth's entrance. I am not here trying to quell spontaneity and ideas like this should always be tried. However, they have to be in keeping with the scene. The characters are clearly *waiting anxiously*. If you play against that, you might well be sacrificing something.

Interestingly, within that action/quality of *waiting anxiously* there are a range of options. The Doctor could be *angry* or *kind* to the Gentlewoman; she could also be angry at being somewhat disbelieved, perhaps afraid of discovery, or she could be in despair at the plight of her mistress. There are many possibilities.

The Three Short Scenes: Conclusion

This examination of three short scenes has, I hope, opened up a wide range of directing ideas and tools for you. I have used all these processes with young actors and they can be subtle, dramatic and powerful. We will visit some of them again when we look at our production of *Twelfth Night*.

Find out the most important thing you need to achieve in each scene. This will vary depending on the scene, the level of ability and how much time you have. Try and achieve that primary element first. Notice that I started with atmosphere in the third scene because I believe that is the most important thing to explore. Once achieved, consider the next thing of importance and use one of the exercises given, to develop it with your actors. Don't overface the actors nor give them too much to work with at once.

Remember if you are using a Chekhov acting tool that the young actors need some practice in it first before you apply it to the scene. They need some level of experience or it may not work and risks putting them off forever.

If you feel you have to start with reading through solely to clarify meaning, then do so. Just remember, it is not the only way to start. In my recent production of *Twelfth Night* with undergraduates, a linguistically complex play, we had no full read-through at all, we began with story and character first. We worked on the language as we progressed through the play.

Chapter Ten
Working with Soliloquies (and Long Speeches)

Now I am alone…

Hamlet: Act Two, Scene Two

Of course, when you are acting, you are never alone. The audience is *always* with you.

Working with soliloquies can be a rewarding experience, both for you and your young actors, whether you are working on pieces in their own right or within a production. Look on them as fabulous opportunities for the actors to directly contact and involve the audience in the dilemmas of the characters, rather than big word blocks of usually famous quotes. Consider all that was said and explored in Chapter Three (Shakespeare's Theatre).

In the first part of this chapter, I will as before, begin with some more general 'how-to-start' exercises with your group, which might be interesting if you are preparing the group for a production or having a workshop simply to explore soliloquies. To use these early exercises, get everyone to learn a short soliloquy (between eight and ten lines) perhaps from a play you are studying.

In the second part of this chapter, we will look in more depth at two soliloquies of different types and, in addition, at a long speech delivered to another character which, whilst not strictly a soliloquy, requires much the same approach. They are:

- A questioning soliloquy: Viola from *Twelfth Night*: 'I left no ring with her. What means this lady?' (Act Two, Scene Two).

- A narrative soliloquy: The Chorus from *Henry V*: 'Now entertain conjecture of a time' (Act Four).

- An aria speech: Puck from *A Midsummer Night's Dream*: 'My mistress with a monster is in love' (Act Three, Scene Two).

What Are Soliloquies?

Soliloquies are speeches given to the audience. The character is usually alone onstage, but even if he isn't, he is talking to the *audience* rather than the other characters. The character, often in crisis, is often trying to decide what course of action to take and shares the dilemma with the audience. This makes these speeches very *active*. Even if the character is not in crisis, the audience exists within the character's world: he involves them, asks them questions, and makes them confederate in his decisions.

Some soliloquies are more of a device, like the Chorus in *Henry V*, Rumour in *Henry IV, Part 2* or Time in *The Winter's Tale* which speak to the audience in storytelling mode. They allow the audience to cover long stretches of time or location, and importantly provide and provoke atmosphere.

Things for You to Consider

Talking to the Audience

Who are the audience? What might their attitude be to the character confiding in them? We might ask how much the audience itself is a *character* in the story. For instance, in a recent workshop, working with a soliloquy from *Richard III*, a young actor suggested that Richard desperately needed the audience on his side. We might argue that the audience has an active role in the play as Richard's friend or carer. As things go wrong he starts to lose that support. It is interesting to consider what role the audience is playing because it will influence the way Richard speaks to them. In Macbeth's case, it feels to me that Macbeth is constantly *justifying* his actions, as if he knows the audience to be disapproving from the start. We are almost his conscience. Whilst we may not want to make this the most important aspect of the character, it is something to bear in mind and gives the actor something positive to focus on, other than the dangerous naturalistic concept that he is only talking to himself.

This idea, that the character is merely talking to himself rather than sharing his problem, belongs to another realm of more 'realistic' theatre entirely. Some professional actors do a kind of 'zoning-out' when they look at the audience, a fake acknowledgement, a generalised stare and glazing over of the eyes, which satisfies them that they are staying in character and playing 'for real'. The thing with soliloquy is that you have to bring your character, your atmosphere and your dilemma into the whole auditorium. You are both your character in his world *and* addressing the audience in the theatre. You are doing both simultaneously, talking to yourself and talking to them. It is generous and open. This does not mean to say that the moments of introspection aren't there. Sometimes the character realises something for himself and the energy is more held, but it always goes back out to the audience. Simply put, there has to be a movement of energy between character and audience; back to our old friend, radiating and receiving.

Creating a Journey

It seems to me essential that whatever sort of soliloquy it is, the character takes us on a journey; in the narrative soliloquy this is obvious: the character is telling us a story. In the questioning soliloquy the character feels differently at the beginning to how he feels at the end. The speaking of the soliloquy has, if only temporarily, resolved something. A classic version of this is the Act Two, Scene Two soliloquy in *Hamlet*, which ends with the couplet: 'The play's the thing / Wherein I'll catch the conscience of the King.' At the beginning of the speech Hamlet is distraught, wringing his soul and raging with himself; by the end he has resolved a plan of action.

I am going to offer a way to finding this route through the speech with *gesture*. It means the young actor can explore soliloquies in a physical way.

The Technical Aspects

At some point, the actor has to understand that if they have no breath to speak, or their breath is running low, then they will not be able to radiate through the voice. I would like the young actor to get the *feel* of the soliloquy right first, the argument and the journey, before diving into breathing marks, phrasing, emphasis, clarity and diction. *Please Note*: We are not neglecting these issues, just not doing them first. I find young people generally prefer working this way.

There are exceptions. Check out the soliloquy and consider the young actor. If we look at the Chorus to Act Four of *Henry V* which begins, 'Now entertain conjecture of a time', you will note that there are some tricky breathing passages and unusual words to tackle. In this case, maybe start with a little technical help if she seems to need it, but you must be the judge here.

A Few General Exercises with the Group

So let's get started. I am going to presume that each member of the group has *learned* a short soliloquy of eight to ten lines, and done some kind of warm-up. Never be tempted to miss a warm-up, even if you have to keep it short. As we have looked a lot at imagery in earlier chapters (not that it isn't crucial) I am going to focus here on rhythm, tempo, and when the character's energy moves from introspection to direct questioning of the audience.

Radiating the Whole Text (Line-learning)

This exercise does two things at once. It lets them run the lines and practise radiating and receiving, eventually to a group.

- Split your students into teams of 4 to 6 and ask each of them to share their speech with the rest of their team. The others can be grouped *around* the speaking actor, *not* in a line like a conventional audience. Let them be at least three metres away from the speaker. Afterwards, *flyback*: ask the listeners whether both the words and the feeling are reaching them.

- After everyone has had a turn, let a few people have a turn in groups of 10 to 12. It will feel different.

- *Flyback*. Ask what the performers felt. Was it easier or not in the bigger group? Some might say it was easier because they felt supported by the group; others might say it was harder because they had more people to include. Ask perhaps if they felt the connection with their 'audience'.

Tempo Revisited

Use the exercise *Tempo* from Chapter Five (Voice Workshop Two) which gets the tempo of the speech into the body. Talk about the importance of changing tempo in speeches, particularly soliloquies. Suggest they note how moving and speaking at different speeds immediately influenced *how* they spoke and *what* they felt.

Directions (Backwards and Forwards)

Rhythm and direction are elements we need to find by practical exercises rather than discussion, especially in the first instance. Here is an exercise you can employ, using the body and allying it to text. It has evolved from the concept of the 'Six Directions' from Chekhov Technique. It's a way to get people to really understand and feel movement and tempo in a speech. We need to find out when the character is primarily speaking to the audience, when the character's energy is more reflective or internal, whether they are reaching out to the audience or pulling back for a moment to think or contend with their own feelings.

Ultimately, of course, you may not use these directions openly in a production; though I might ask the young actors to keep them if I felt it was the only way to get the necessary intensity and variety. Remember you are not dealing with professional actors, and your young actors may need the physical actions to support them.

- Suggest they walk forward quite fast. Ask them to name how they are feeling. They might say things like 'proud', 'strong', 'focused', 'confident'. Some will be different but don't worry about that.

- Now ask them to speak their text as they walk. You will find it full of the qualities they have named. Suggest they keep the lines going. Tell them they can repeat the same line or two if they don't know the speech properly.

- Now ask them to stop and then ask them to walk backwards. Ask them to name what that feels like. Most will say words like 'nervous', 'disempowered', 'afraid', 'out of control'. However, some people like the feeling as they walk backwards and feel freed. Ask them to speak some of their text. The words should be full of the qualities they have mentioned. For the most part, they will sound more thoughtful, less powerful.

- Now ask them to explore walking forward to speak their first line and then walk backwards and speak the next line. For this to work well, they need to get the impulse to walk, so they need time to let that feeling come to them before they speak. Tell them that the impulse and the body are leading how they speak. (See *Tempo*, Chapter Five, page 67.)

- Let's take as an example a moment from *Romeo and Juliet* (Act Four, Scene Three), where Juliet has been left alone to go to bed, but is preparing to take the potion which will send her into a death-like sleep:

  > Farewell. God knows when we shall meet again.
  > I have a faint cold fear thrills through my veins.

- The young actor might walk forward quickly on 'Farewell'; then walk back slowly to say, 'God knows when we shall meet again.' Then she might walk slowly forward as she says, 'I have a faint cold fear thrills through my veins.'

- This exercise can create an extraordinary amount of variety in feeling and in the way the text is spoken. Get the group to experiment with this backwards and forwards motion, seeing how it affects how they speak the lines.

- If you feel your group is able, you might try seeing what it's like for them to speak their lines while reaching up and crouching down, moving sideways in different tempi or making turns.

Teaching Tip: Walking backwards is difficult for some, especially if two people crash into each other. A way to deal with this is to demonstrate with someone else. Walk backwards into them, feel the backs together and just follow the energy until you disentangle; don't apologise or break the atmosphere by giggling. This is going to depend on the level of experience of your group.

Some Time on the Text

It is now time to look at the text in a bit more detail. Ask the group to split into pairs and just mark up on the text where they feel/think the speech changes direction emotionally or in its argument. Please note that we are doing this after some real physical exploration of the speech. They might be quite outlandish with their choices, depending on their level, so be prepared. Let them try their choices, still in their pairs, and maybe have some individual actors try them out before the group. If they have brought a piece that tells a story, then it's easier because the speech is governed by 'and then this happened, then that happened'. With an emotional, questioning monologue it is more challenging.

Barracking the Actor

- Ask your group to sit and be an audience for someone's soliloquy.

- Tell the group they can interrupt the actor at any point with an answer, a question, a moan or a cry of support, prompted by what the actor is saying to them. For example, a line from one of Hamlet's soliloquies, 'O what a rogue and peasant slave am I!', might provoke the response from the audience of 'Why what's the matter with you?' or, later in the same speech, 'I'll have these players / Play something like the murder of my father / Before mine uncle', and the response might be, 'Brilliant! Go for it!' This exercise can get quite rowdy but indicates immediately whether the character/actor is truly radiating to the audience.

- After the speech, ask the audience whether they felt the actor was speaking to them, and how the actor felt when people shouted at him.

Teaching Tip: If you sense the actor is not radiating to the audience, get him to reach out physically to the audience (and I mean really *reach*, not just holding his arms out) as he speaks the text. You will immediately notice a difference. Make sure that if there are questions in the text, that the actor asks them, *really* asks them.

One-to-One Work: Two Soliloquies and a Long Speech

This section is for one-to-one work, perhaps with a little help occasionally from other actors who may be around.

Be aware that what I suggest below need not be exercises for one session. Indeed, you may want to repeat them. Let's suppose for now that the actor has learned the speech and understands it reasonably well. Let's also assume the actor knows the story and specifically what has just happened in the play.

A Questioning Soliloquy: Twelfth Night (*Act Two, Scene Two*)

This brings us to our first soliloquy from *Twelfth Night*, what I have called a *questioning* soliloquy, where the audience is asked to consider what the character should do. Further examples of questioning soliloquies might be: Brutus, 'It must be by his death… ' (*Julius Caesar. Act Two, Scene One*); Hamlet, 'O, what a rogue and peasant slave am I!' (*Hamlet: Act Two, Scene Two*); Helena, 'How happy some o'er other some can be!' (*A Midsummer*

Night's Dream: Act One, Scene One); and Isabella, 'To whom shall I complain?' (*Measure for Measure*: Act Two, Scene Four).

Viola, disguised as a man, 'Cesario', works as the servant to Count Orsino, with whom she is secretly in love. He, however, is in love with the Lady Olivia and sends Viola/Cesario to speak on his behalf. After her first interview, Olivia falls for Cesario, the man Viola is pretending to be. Then Olivia sends her own servant, Malvolio, chasing after Cesario to return a ring purportedly left as a love token from Orsino, but really as a ruse to get Cesario to return. Malvolio, having thrown the ring on the ground, leaves: and it is now that Viola delivers her 'questioning' soliloquy:

> I left no ring with her. What means this lady?
> Fortune forbid my outside have not charmed her.
> She made good view of me, indeed so much
> That methought her eyes had lost her tongue,
> For she did speak in starts, distractedly.
> She loves me sure. The cunning of her passion
> Invites me in this churlish messenger.
> None of my lord's ring? Why, he sent her none.
> I am the man. If it be so, as 'tis,
> Poor lady, she were better love a dream.
> Disguise, I see thou art a wickedness,
> Wherein the pregnant enemy does much.
> How easy is it for the proper false
> In women's waxen hearts to set their forms.
> Alas, our frailty is the cause, not we,
> For such as we are made of, such we be.
> How will this fadge? My master loves her dearly,
> And I, poor monster, fond as much on him,
> And she, mistaken, seems to dote on me.
> What will become of this? As I am man,
> My state is desperate for my master's love;
> As I am woman, now alas the day,
> What thriftless sighs shall poor Olivia breathe?
> O time, thou must untangle this, not I.
> It is too hard a knot for me t'untie.

Creating a Journey Warm-up

Here is a version of an exercise from Michael Chekhov's *On the Technique of Acting* (1991). It's simple, but wakes up the body for psycho-physical connection.

- Ask the actor to stand simply in a natural position. Maybe they might start with their arms folded. Tell them to feel inside what it feels like to stand like that: if they have their arms folded, it might make them feel sulky or difficult.

- Ask them to listen to the body, then say the first line of their text.

- Now ask them to change position. Let's say they put one hand on the back of a chair and point with the other. Maybe they are leaning on the chair. Ask them to repeat the line. It will sound different: perhaps a bit 'fake-casual', as if they are pretending not to care.

- Ask them to change position again. This time perhaps they kneel and raise their arms. They look up. This would perhaps make their text sound spiritual and epic.

- Try asking them to move to other positions. Tell them to notice how changing the position affects how they feel.

Creating a Journey for the Speech

- Ask the actor to create a gesture/statue of the character at the moment before she starts the speech. Explain this is not a realistic statue; it is more about what the character is doing and feeling. It's like a 'still' Psychological Gesture. For instance, in this case, the character might be trying to look through fog, pushing her arms forward and to the side. She is trying to solve a mystery.

- Get the actor to try the line out as she moves into this 'searching gesture' and ask what it feels like.

- If it doesn't feel good for the actor, try something else. Don't be afraid to try a number of possibilities. Perhaps the statue might have a suggestion of *grabbing*. This will make for a more vibrant delivery of the line and make Viola more forceful but also more desperate, which may suit the actor and you.

- Once you have found a gesture/statue that you like, move on now to find one for the *end* of the speech. A possible choice might be a statue with an *imploring* gesture.

- An alternative ending might be for the actor to be pushing away to either side. Try it and see how different it feels: more angry and frustrated.

- Now find a moment in the *middle* of the speech when everything changes. Let's take the moment when she says, 'I am the man.' She might have a pushing-away here, or a closing of the whole body. Ask the actor what it feels like in the position she has chosen. If her answer doesn't correspond to the gesture/statue then it means that she has an *idea* that she has yet to put into her body.

- Finally, ask the actor to go through the sequence of movement, from one pose to the next (*beginning/ middle/end*). Through this exercise you have made a physical journey through the whole speech. Ask her to be aware of embodying the poses and noting where she feels the sensations in the body.

- Now ask her to try speaking the speech as she moves from one pose to another.

Teaching Tip: Ask the actor, once in her 'pose', to find out what feelings and sensations it gives her. Ask her where her energy is going. For instance, in the first 'searching' pose, the upper body might be pushing forward and the lower body reaching into the ground, the legs still, trying to give balance. This often happens when we are trying to move forward but are feeling fearful of moving on. These are subtleties you will find for yourself if you work more with Chekhov Technique.

This exercise has given you a broad *beginning, middle* and *end* of the speech. Furthermore, you can change it in a flash with different poses and gestures until you find something you feel is right!

Ultimately, though, you and the actor have to make the decisions. Working this way gives you a lot of possibilities: you simply have to decide which one suits the actor, the speech and (if you are doing one) the production.

Directions Revisited

The questioning soliloquy involves thinking about backward and forward energy. This is not necessarily about moving around the stage but about *internal* movement. When we are talking to someone, our energy moves constantly back and forth (radiating and receiving). We speak to someone in a conversation and our energy is mostly forward.

But consider when, in 'real life', you receive a shock or something hard to digest. Where does the energy go? It usually goes *backwards*. Or consider when you realise something, or remember something: you are reaching back and you bring the memory *forward*. We need to find that kind of movement in the piece. It immediately makes your piece engaging, interesting and truly alive. We have tried to find this through an earlier exercise with the whole group walking backwards and forwards. Now it's time to apply it more specifically.

So let's explore:

> I left no ring with her. What means this lady?
> Fortune forbid my outside have not charmed her.
> She made good view of me...

First of all, let's consider again what has just happened. Malvolio, probably rather sanctimoniously, has left the ring as instructed. He is delighted to do Olivia's bidding and ward off this new arrival in their midst. He leaves. So the ring is on the floor.

- Ask the actor to see the ring. Ask her if she wants to pick it up or not. See what she does, but if she does not know, perhaps suggest she walks slowly back from the ring and then slowly goes forward and picks it up.

- Now ask her to get an impulse to move forward and speak: 'I left no ring with her.' Then get an impulse to move back and say: 'What means this lady?' Then get an impulse to move forward, then say: 'Fortune forbid my outside have not charmed her.' Then get an impulse to move back and say: 'She made good view of me.' Do this a couple of times in this format.

- Now ask her to *imagine* she is walking backwards and forwards, but stay relatively still and speak the text. You should notice a reality that was not there before.

Teaching Tip: Ask the actor to try this several ways, going backwards and forwards at different times and through the speech. Remember they have to really connect to the body to make this work fully. Walking backwards and forwards like this gives a real flexibility and sense of conversation and movement to the character's speech. If such movement is too much for presentation, then use it merely as a tool for her to find this energy and the actor can then be stiller. When you ask her to *imagine* she is making the movement, you will find some of the physical movement will stay and help the actor connect to the character, the text and her problems.

I have sometimes used these physical manifestations of energy and psychology, and kept them in productions with young actors, in order that they can find a life in the scene. You need to consider the level of your group here and what your priorities are.

Try this with the actor walking sideways: this is most effective for those characters who are evading something, like Macbeth, for example. Try looking at the opening of 'If it were done, when 'tis done...' (*Macbeth*: Act One, Scene Seven).

Characters Working Stuff Out

For this exercise you will need two more performers: one to play Orsino, and one Olivia. This is simply another way to externalise the psychology and explain the text clearly. You might even be able to present this piece in this way in a production, if you wanted to be particularly light-hearted. Beware, though, because doing it this way in performance might make Viola seem to the audience much more in control than she actually is. It's up to you.

Let's take this passage:

> How will this fadge? My master loves her dearly,
> And I, poor monster, fond as much on him,
> And she, mistaken, seems to dote on me.
> What will become of this? As I am man,
> My state is desperate for my master's love;
> As I am woman, now alas the day,
> What thriftless sighs shall poor Olivia breathe?
> O time, thou must untangle this, not I.
> It is too hard a knot for me t'untie.

- Ask Viola to *explain* this problem to the audience as she speaks the text, using the actors playing Olivia and Orsino, referring to them as she speaks as if they were specimens at a lecture. This is immediately funny.

- Try making it more physical. Perhaps try to get Olivia to grab Viola, and Orsino to grab Olivia, as Viola is speaking to the audience. Notice how much power this gives to Viola's dialogue: because we are physicalising her predicament.

- Try the same thing again, but now make Orsino and Olivia sighing, floaty and romantic, with little or no physical contact. Notice what a difference that makes and how it changes the dynamic of Viola's speech: how we get the other characters to interact affects how Viola feels and how she delivers her text.

- You might look at Helena's speech from Act One, Scene One of *A Midsummer Night's Dream* where using the characters of Demetrius and Hermia in the speech might enliven the text, Helena's predicament, and the actor's delivery.

Teaching Tip: This approach is particularly useful when there are comparisons between people or qualities. Using it will immediately solve some of the issues of the meaning of the text and which word to emphasise. Of course, I am not debunking the technical, old-fashioned way of going through the text and underlining the emphasised word, but this more physical approach will take you a long way to getting your young actor to make sense of the text, and at the same time empower them with intention. It may also remind them of that most important of performance skills: to enjoy yourself.

What Is She Doing?

Make sure you have done the *Psychological Gesture* exercises from Chapter Six if you are to utilise this effectively. You are physicalising the psychological action of the character.

- Ask the young actor what Viola is *doing* in the speech, and ask her to create a dynamic Psychological Gesture for it. In this case she might be *searching*, reaching her arms forward and pushing her body forward.

- Ask her to try and find a gesture that goes with the *whole speech*. Keep it simple.

Teaching Tip: If the actor cannot find this in her body, you can ask her to verbalise it first, as that might be easier; then ask her to find the gesture.

The Opening Moment: The World and the Audience

The opening moment in a soliloquy is always a big one, whether you are using it for a stand-alone piece or in a production. Whenever we are 'left alone' in real life something happens: whether we choose to be alone and so leave the banquet, the house or the bed, or whether someone leaves *us* and, as with Viola, we are left alone on an Illyrian street, the atmosphere changes.

Viola, in disguise, confused, in love with Orsino, having survived a shipwreck and having lost, as she believes, her only remaining relation, is faced with this bizarre outburst from Malvolio as he throws her ring to the ground and leaves her alone. Furthermore, she is in a city she does not know well, a city of lethargy, sickly mourning, romanticism, drunkenness and unrequited love.

Finally, let's consider what the character is bringing with them in their soliloquy, in other words, what surrounds them, their world, their atmosphere, and how they are moving through it. We need to remember that when the character talks to the audience, they are still playing the character. They are in the character's world *and* in ours. This might sound obvious but it is something at the heart of Shakespeare, Chekhov Technique, and acting in general. It often happens that actors giving soliloquies forget where the character is in the story and what atmosphere is surrounding them.

As I write this, I can see Illyria like a maze of colourful but confusing streets. (There is a nice design concept.) When Malvolio confronts her, Viola is perhaps lost or, at the very least, trying to remember how to get back to the Duke's palace. An atmosphere of hot, bright, tangled streets may suggest the character's psychological state.

Finally, who are we, the audience? Perhaps we are the people she needs to help her keep her sanity. We are not so much her friends as her counsellors. Sebastian uses the audience in a similar way later on. If we give the audience a definite role, we can help the actor to find a journey for the character more easily. They needn't be 'the people of Illyria', or 'the drowned people of the ship', which would be far too specific and completely unbalance the play, but you and the actor might instead ask yourselves what they have to offer the character. Are they counsellors, for example? Critics or friends? Deciding this with your actor can really help their interpretation.

A Narrative Soliloquy: *Henry V* (The Chorus to Act Four)

This wonderful speech is another piece of Shakespeare that I was introduced to very early on. I have only used the first half of it. What I found wonderful about it was the way the words created the atmosphere and provoked the images in my mind. In this text we are going to explore General Atmosphere first, Psychological Gesture, and then make a physical examination of some of the images.

Use exercises from the Voice Workshop in Chapter Four, in particular *Head Rolls and Yawn*, the *Diction Warm-up* and *Resonance*, as a warm-up: do more if you have time.

Unlike the earlier piece from *Henry V*, which we used in Chapter Three (Shakespeare's Theatre) this is a moodier and more atmospheric piece that prepares us for the powerful Act Four, and *atmosphere* will be key to an effective performance.

It's the night before the Battle of Agincourt.

Enter Chorus.

> CHORUS. Now entertain conjecture of a time
>> When creeping murmur and the poring dark
>> Fills the wide vessel of the universe.
>> From camp to camp through the foul womb of night
>> The hum of either army stilly sounds,
>> That the fixed sentinels almost receive
>> The secret whispers of each other's watch.
>> Fire answers fire, and through their paly flames
>> Each battle sees the other's umbered face.
>> Steed threatens steed, in high and boastful neighs
>> Piercing the night's dull ear; and from the tents
>> The armourers accomplishing the knights,
>> With busy hammers closing rivets up,
>> Give dreadful note of preparation.
>> The country cocks do crow, the clocks do toll,
>> And the third hour of drowsy morning name.
>> Proud of their numbers and secure in soul,
>> The confident and over-lusty French

Do the low-rated English play at dice,
And chide the cripple tardy-gaited night
Who like a foul and ugly witch doth limp
So tediously away. The poor condemnèd English,
Like sacrifices, by their watchful fires
Sit patiently and inly ruminate
The morning's danger; and their gesture sad,
Investing lank-lean cheeks and war-worn coats,
Presenteth them unto the gazing moon
So many horrid ghosts.

What's the Atmosphere?

It is not always useful to start by asking, 'What's the atmosphere?' because sometimes people can see that as a challenging question, especially if they are not used to consciously imagining it. Instead, when tackling this piece with someone who has understood it, at least superficially, I would rather ask the question, 'If you had to give this speech a title, what would it be?' I might get: 'The Night before Battle', 'Soldiers Wait to Die' or 'Fear and Darkness'. Immediately we are going in the right direction.

Crossing the Threshold

'Crossing the Threshold' is a Chekhov term that means exactly what it says. As people we move from one atmosphere to another, when we come into a room, walk into a situation, get on a bus or go to a library. When you go on a stage, there is an atmosphere there, different from the one offstage. Anyone who has ever been on a stage has felt that feeling.

- Put a line of tape on the floor.

- Ask the actor to stand on one side of the line. They must feel that they are 'offstage'.

- Tell them that when they pass over the line they will be 'onstage' in the atmosphere of the speech: ask them what that might be. They might say: 'fear', 'dark', 'cold', 'waiting'.

- Let's go with *fear*. Ask the student to really look at what that atmosphere looks and feels like, then to step over the line and experience it.

- Tell them: 'Remember that the fear is outside you. It is influencing you, it doesn't mean you *are* afraid.'

- Then ask them to start speaking the text in the atmosphere. It should have an ominous, nervous feel. If it is too difficult, try something more literal, like 'darkness' or 'coldness'.

What is the Chorus Doing?

Notice that I have not explored who or what the Chorus *is*. We could, of course, say that it represents the Common Man or Woman, a News Reporter, a Teacher, a Soldier, a Lecturer, an Actor or a Storyteller. Initially, who she is is not too important. That is something you can layer on later. What the Chorus is *doing*, though, will be useful and an interesting complement to an atmosphere.

- Let's go back to finding a gesture. What is the Chorus doing? We might, for example, say they are *beckoning*, pulling the audience in to look at this sight.

- Ask them to try the gesture slowly, with a heavy *moulding* quality (see Chapter Six). Remember to encourage use of the whole body.

- Ask them to make an open sound as they move. An open sound is one that isn't tense or strained.

- Then ask them to speak using the same quality of sound. Get them to try the first few lines as they make the gesture.

- If that doesn't feel right, try *floating* (see Chapter Six). You will notice a lighter, softer, more dreamlike feel comes into the voice.

- Remind them that *how* they do a gesture will affect how they feel.

- Now get the actor to stand still and simply imagine they are beckoning, still keeping that feeling in their voice.

- Decide what might be the right gesture for the Chorus *for now*.

Physicalising Imagery

In this speech we will look at particular images and 'physicalise' them. I said in Chapter One that, 'The imagery powers the workings of the actor's imagination, and charts the character's emotional journey.' (You might want to go back and take a look at this section on 'Images'.) Here we are going to look at how to explore this practically.

- Let's try the line 'creeping murmur and the poring dark'. Ask the actor to make a gesture/statue for *each* word. As they move into each statue, they speak the relevant word, letting their movement govern how they say it. Tell them not to leave out 'and' or 'the' but make a pose for them too which perhaps emphasises what the words *do*. For instance, 'and' is a joining word, so the actor might bring their hands together slowly; 'the' is an identifying word, so perhaps the actor presents their hands outwards as they say it.

- Now get them to speak the words at the same time as they use the gesture/statues they have created, retaining a sense of each individual word. If any statue does not help them to fill the sound with meaning, help them to find another.

- Then ask them to *imagine* the movements, stand still, and then say the words as if they were still moving. It will sound exaggerated and odd. Don't worry.

- Now ask them to smooth it out slightly, to connect the words up into one phrase. You will see where this is going. The words will take on a stronger resonance and power. You may even get a sense of their direction and energy, e.g. 'creeping' might have an energy that moves slowly forward whilst 'poring' might have a strong energy downward.

- Still standing still, get them to speak the phrase faster, keeping a sense of the whole phrase whilst retaining some of the colours and rhythms they have found when they were physicalising the words.

- If this proves successful, you might try: 'busy hammers closing rivets up' or 'piercing the night's dull ear'.

Breathing and Emphasis: A Quick Look

First of all, you will need to check out the breathing and emphasis section of Chapter Four (Voice Workshop One).

Let's take an example from this speech. The first three lines *might* be spoken on one breath. It gives the opening a gentle, ominous flow. It is, however, very hard to speak these three lines on one breath without losing power at the end. This is more than a technical matter as the actor almost literally vanishes before your eyes as they run out of breath.

When you are working with young actors, the most important thing is that they become aware of the breath and don't run out of it. If you are doing a voice workshop, you can get the actor to work on extending their breathing capacity; if not, get him to work within his comfort zone. The actor needs to practise any decisions they make about where to breathe.

Here are the breathing places I would suggest (shown here with bold vertical strokes):

> Now entertain conjecture of a time |
> When creeping murmur | and the poring dark
> Fills the wide vessel of the universe. |

Note that I try not to breathe at the end of every line in order to try and maintain this feeling of the glutinous, ominous darkness.

Looking at emphasis, ask your actor which are the important words to emphasise on that third line. Usually I might say 'vessel' and 'universe', but in this case, I think 'fills' and 'wide' might be more important than 'vessel'. 'Universe' is still important, though.

An Aria Speech: *A Midsummer Night's Dream* (Act Three, Scene Two)

Puck's crowing, ebullient speech, where he tells Oberon how he has put the ass's head on Bottom and how the enchanted Titania has woken, only to fall in love with him, is a great example of what I call the 'aria speeches' in Shakespeare. They do not further the story much but they do tell us something about the character. More importantly, they transform events to create an expansive world in the audience's poetic imagination. They are often among his most beautiful and vibrant speeches. Other examples might include Enobarbus's 'The barge she sat in... ' (*Antony and Cleopatra*: Act Two, Scene Two) and Mercutio's 'Queen Mab' speech from *Romeo and Juliet* (Act One, Scene Four).

When I did a production of *A Midsummer Night's Dream* with Galway Youth Theatre, I pondered the purpose of this speech whilst I was doing my edit. From a practical point of view, it occurred to me that if there was an interval in the performance prior to this scene, this speech would be a great warm-up to get the audience back into the story. The scene before this one ends with Titania taking Bottom to frolic in her bower. It makes a nice ending to a Part One and that is ultimately how we did it.

Let's look at the speech, ignoring the asterisks, for a moment which relates to *This Way and That Way* described below.

PUCK. My mistress with a monster is in love.*
   Near to her close and consecrated bower,*
   While she was in her dull and sleeping hour,*
   A crew of patches, rude mechanicals,
   That work for bread upon Athenian stalls,
   Were met together to rehearse a play
   Intended for great Theseus' nuptial day.*
   The shallowest thickskin of that barren sort,
   Who Pyramus presented in their sport,
   Forsook his scene, and entered in a brake,
   When I did him at this advantage take:*
   An ass's nole I fixèd on his head.*
   Anon, his Thisbe must be answerèd,
   And forth my mimic comes.* When they him spy,*
   As wild geese that the creeping fowler eye,
   Or russet-pated choughs, many in sort
   Rising and cawing at the gun's report,
   Sever themselves, and madly sweep the sky,*
   So at his sight away his fellows fly;*
   And at our stamp, here o'er and o'er one falls;*
   He 'Murder' cries, and help from Athens calls.
   Their sense, thus weak,* lost with their fears
      thus strong,*
   Made senseless things begin to do them wrong;
   For briers and thorns at their apparel snatch –
   Some sleeves, some hats; from yielders all things
      catch.*
   I led them on in this distracted fear,
   And left sweet Pyramus translated there;
   When in that moment,* so it came to pass,*
   Titania waked, and straightway loved an ass.*

Telling the Story and How

- The first thing to find in this speech, presuming we know who Puck is and what has happened, is the story.

- Ask your young actor to say what Puck is *doing*. He may be 'showing off' or maybe 'bonding with Oberon'. (These two actions would provoke a very different delivery.) For our example, let's go with 'showing off'.

- Ask your actor to tell you the story 'showing off'. He can improvise the text and simply tell you.

- Check he is radiating to you, and to others if they are there, as well as to Oberon.

- Was the story clear?

Teaching Tip: If there is a character in the scene listening to the speech it is useful that you put someone there to stand in for them. In this case, it is Oberon; he does not do very much, but he is not doing nothing. Perhaps he is radiating enjoyment to his servant or impatience that Puck gets to the point.

Therefore, with speeches where the character is speaking to someone other than the audience, the actor has to fully imagine the other character and their responses. The actor is doing a duologue on their own.

This Way and That Way

This is another tried-and-tested exercise, and one you will probably know. It really helps to clarify the story.

- Ask the actor to speak their text as they walk and, every time there is a new element of the story, they are to turn and start walking in another direction.

- Tell them to mark those new elements not only by changes of direction but in speed of delivery and tone. It encourages variety of pace and feeling.

- I have marked the text with an asterisk where there might be a change of direction.

Shaping the Speech and Breathing

- Separate the speech into a beginning, middle and end. I suggest you help the young actor with this process, if you have time. Some speeches can be a bit overfacing for young actors. The 'Queen Mab' speech in *Romeo and Juliet* (Act One, Scene Four) has this effect too. Both speeches are long and the character in both cases is very excited, so the actors try to ride on that energy. The result is that the words can become incoherent and the young actor appears weak. Try and give them a structure.

- As before, you need to help them decide where to breathe. These speeches really *do* need to be considered as arias. If the breath is controlled, the speech is empowered and the acting can be empowered also.

We have now concluded this part of the book, and move on to the work of directing a play and the issues that can emerge. I will be talking about directing Shakespeare, but the issues raised could relate to any play: Shakespeare is a great place to start learning this art.

Part Four

Making the Play with Young Actors

Chapter Eleven
Preparing the Production

> The play's the thing…
> *Hamlet*: Act Two, Scene Two

Now we are going to look at aspects of making a whole production, beginning with the logistical and creative decisions we have to make at the start. Later, we shall explore certain scenes and issues in *Twelfth Night*, beginning with a preparatory week based on my own process which includes issues of story, character, language and atmosphere. Many of the issues we will address apply *generally*, so don't feel fazed if you are doing *Julius Caesar*, for instance.

Some of you might find some of my process, especially around auditions, rather lenient – but remember we are not dealing with a conservatoire course, but a youth theatre, college course or school.

The production of *Twelfth Night* I refer to was publicly performed at the O'Donoghue Theatre at the National University of Ireland Galway in 2018, as part of an undergraduate programme. My approach was not dissimilar to the many youth theatre productions I have done.

So let's begin.

Which Play Do I Choose?

You and your group want to produce a Shakespeare play. By this I mean not a production that is predominantly devised as a mosaic with pieces of text and other creative stimuli such as dance or pieces of art, as we have discussed in Chapter Eight (Devising a Group Project on Shakespeare). You are looking at directing the whole play. The question is, which one do you choose?

Things to Consider

- You need to pick something the group will connect to. This is obvious, I know, but some of the Shakespeare plays are more challenging than others in this regard. If you have a choice, pick something which has topical themes or themes that will really resonate with your group. Your group has to be enthusiastic about it or the audience will not connect with it. One way I won a youth theatre group over to *Macbeth* was by telling them that together I wanted us to make it as terrifying as a horror movie.

- What are the goals of involving them in this play? This might affect your choice of play; perhaps the group is studying it. There is no doubt that working on the play in performance can give a much deeper understanding of text, imagery, themes and theatrical power than any purely intellectual exploration.

- Pick a play that will be within your capabilities as a group. Don't be tempted to just do one of the plays *you* like, necessarily, unless you are very confident you can bring the group with you. What would suit *them*? Is your group comedic or serious? How many good performers do you have? A play like *Hamlet* or *Macbeth* has a few central roles and a lot of supporting roles: this might suit your group best. Some people want to be involved but not overawed with too much text. *Twelfth Night*, however, is a real ensemble piece with many people getting equal stage time: everyone needs to be fairly strong.

- Really look at your available rehearsal time. If you have a generous amount of time and a good group, you can tackle something ambitious.

- Alternatively, you *might* explore a strongly edited version, where you only perform a portion of the story which could make something like an hour's performance. For example, consider looking at *A Midsummer Night's Dream*, but only telling the story of the fairies and mechanicals, for instance. This is something I have done myself and it makes for an effective and lovely piece, using all Shakespearean text. *The Tempest*, *A Midsummer Night's Dream*, *As You Like It*, *Pericles* and *The Winter's Tale* lend themselves to this kind of severe editing because the characters come on in groups and their scenes can be taken out with the minimum of difficult editing choices.

- Whether you use these 'team-plays' to make a short Shakespeare production or not, choosing one of these plays with groups of characters eases the scheduling of rehearsals.

- Look at the original length. We are going to look at editing and transposing later as a separate issue but be aware you are going to need to edit extensively, whatever the level. *The Comedy of Errors*, *The Tempest* and *Macbeth* are all fairly short.

Production and Design

I am not going to go into too much detail about how I find and work with the production team because, in a way, it is not within the scope of this book and varies, depending on whether you are a youth theatre, school or college. I have often been lucky to have had a good production team and occasionally highly skilled teachers to work with them. When I haven't, I have kept the technical aspect of the production *as simple as possible*. Remember that young people might want to design a set or costumes but unless they have the requisite skill, it will be problematic.

In terms of design, the most important things are:

- To find a design that the team is capable of fulfilling.

- That you and the team always work imaginatively.

- That the design team, director and actors all create a harmonious vision of the play: what I mean is that the design should never work against what the actors create.

It is vital to have a good stage manager who organises time-keeping and is the first port of call for actors who are late arriving – and can also record the blocking of the scenes and keep the 'book', so that you do not have to worry about all that. Ideally I like that person to have an interest in directing and treat them like an assistant director.

Auditions

Audition One

Except in special conditions with a vulnerable group, I would always have auditions. The audition gives you a chance to really get a sense of what your potential young actor is like outside of the group. However, thanks to the culture of stress-inducing television talent shows, the young person may well be completely stressed coming in to an audition and not give of their best. The only way to handle this is to be kind and patient, even when they have not come properly prepared to do their piece. However, be very aware that the decisions you make around casting are decisions you and the rest of the group are going to have to live with. This might not be an issue of ability but also reliability or other difficult behaviour. In addition to talent you are looking for actors who will be good in a team.

- Always give each young actor at least 15 to 20 minutes per audition and ask them to come prepared with a piece from Shakespeare of about twenty lines. I always encourage them to think 'out of the box' and not necessarily to do something from the play we are doing. They do not usually heed this advice because they want to do a piece from the part they want and show me how well they can do it!

- Be organised from the start. Make strict audition times and get people to sign up for them. Get a member of your stage-management team to assist you so that you can focus on what matters; getting the best from your young actor. Organise the times so that you can take reasonable breaks, because auditioning young people is tiring. I want them to feel, if they have tried their best and been prepared, that they will remember the audition as something valuable in itself. I am not so inclined, however, when they have not prepared their piece.

- Ask them to arrive 10 minutes early so they can get settled and look at an already-prepared rehearsal schedule with *all* your potential rehearsal times and to record on it any conflicts they might have with it. Tell them that if they have a few conflicts, it does not mean you won't cast them, and that if you want them, you will try to work round them. Warn them, though, that if they have too many other commitments, it might make casting them problematic. I ask them to sign the rehearsal schedule document as an acknowledgement of their commitment. Of course, this has no real weight, but it does make them understand that you are taking it seriously and you expect them to take it seriously too. Always make time at the end of the audition to talk to the person a little, both about how they performed and the schedule.

- Have a space on the document for them to write down their particular skills, especially about singing or musical proficiency, vital for a play like *Twelfth Night* which has a lot of songs in it. You want to utilise the skills they have. Finding these skills often makes for a work that can be beautifully integrated, and makes performers who may not be great actors feel that their other talents are contributing to a strong piece.

- If you are working from a limited pool, as we always are, be it a class group, youth theatre or college production, you need to be very canny about the casting. Try not to have too many set ideas about the play or the characters. This is particularly true around gender. For instance, when casting *Twelfth Night*, I originally saw Feste in my imagination as a cynical male busker in his fifties. For some time I thought, 'How could that character be anything else?' The more I looked at the play and considered my young group, the more I let go of this view. In the end I cast a feisty young woman who was the embodiment of mischief, with a beautiful singing voice. It was not the only time the cast and crew changed my view of the play fundamentally.

- If the role is vocally demanding, you need to make sure you have someone who is up to that challenge, no matter how much they may suit the role emotionally or physically. If you cannot hear an actor you have a problem.

- Also you need to cast people, especially in main roles, who are going to show up at rehearsals and who are going to work. Unreliable people, however good they are, are a serious liability.

- After chatting with them a little and trying to put them at their ease (the tension is often very evident) I ask them to stand up and do their piece, working as far away from me as possible. I ask them what the piece is from and what's happened before the speech begins. Depending on the level, I do not criticise them if they don't know (I might talk to them about this afterwards in the final chat). I ask them to take their time and prepare and not to rush. If they still rush, I often make them start again.

- If they forget their lines, I sometimes let them start again. I have the stage manager on hand to give prompts. If the situation is very bad and I feel the person is simply nervous and not just lazy, I ask the stage manager to use the *Ghosting* exercise (from Chapter Nine) so I can get some sense of what the person might be like. If the person shows some ability, then I might still cast them in a small role.

- Let's suppose the young actor knows the speech well and has made some decisions about what they are going to do with the piece. What am I looking for? I want to see if they are convincing and performing well; if the character is struggling with something in the piece I want to sense it in the way they are acting. I want to hear them clearly and, ideally, I would like to feel that the piece had a beginning, middle and an end.

- You need to test out how well they take direction. I suggest you consider one aspect of the speech you feel is wanting and see if you can explore and improve it with them. If the voice is dull, I might explore some of the image/language work we have done in earlier sessions on a couple of lines. On the other hand, if the beginning of the piece is weak I might ask them to work with a gesture/statue, and so on. Only try to improve *one* aspect of the audition speech. You want the young actor to succeed. Trying to improve too many aspects will probably tell you nothing and the actor will get confused.

- If, afterwards, you ask them to read from the play, do give them a few minutes to look it over. Get your stage manager to read any other parts with them so you are free to watch. It will let you hear them read a part you feel might suit them and give you the chance to find out if they have bothered to read the whole play. Remember, though, some people find sight reading incredibly tricky.

- I would suggest that if you are in any doubt you might recall them for the group audition.

Audition Two: Group Work

I would always give yourself the opportunity to watch them work again and, this time, in a group of 6 to 10 people. This gives you the chance to watch them as team players. Have your stage manager or a colleague watch the session as well so she can discuss the session with you afterwards. I would always try and have at least two possible candidates for each character. Someone might also surprise you, and you might want to cast someone completely different in a role. Try and stay as open as you can.

For me, this group audition is as much about preparing *them* for the way the production is going to be created, working physically, as it is about casting. Below are some pathways you might take, with a few examples of my own.

The Group Audition

- In my experience, these group auditions are a lot of fun but very competitive. Try and get everybody focused with some group exercises and an emphasis on the Feeling of Ease. The *Breath Dance* exercises are very good to use for this kind of thing.

- Consider what you need to know about the strengths of these young actors and what skills they are going to need to perform the play. I would always use *Radiating and Receiving* (*Throwing the Ball*) in a group audition, a little diction work, ensemble games and singing. There might be something fundamental I need to find out. In an ensemble exercise, for example, I added the idea that the auditioning group had to line up quickly in order of height. The actors who eventually played Viola and Sebastian, who are meant to be identical twins, stood side-by-side in the middle of the room together: that's a very literal thing, though.

- More importantly, I might want to introduce something more elemental and core to the story. For instance, were I looking for a cast for *Romeo and Juliet*, I might split the group into two teams, one Capulet and one Montague. I would ask them to limit anything they might say to using sound only or perhaps the name of their group. Ask them to circle the room, test each other out. I would put a chair in the middle of the room and suggest that both teams want to sit in it; to explore how they could take the territory of the chair without fighting, perhaps offering the seat to the other team and then not letting them sit there. No actual fighting, of course, is permitted. People get very creative with this; one group might carry the chair away. I would get them to notice how the two groups test each other, mock each other, even by the way they say their opponents' name. Afterwards I would ask them how they felt. Did they feel closer to their team yet somehow also close to the other team as well, even though they despise them? A feeling of adrenaline? Addiction? There will be moments of real tension which suggest the sense of edgy, playful danger that exists between the families in the play.

- Another example might be to put a Juliet in one group and a Romeo in another. Then, have their groups surround them. Their groups have to stop them reaching each other. Juliet and Romeo lunge forward. Don't let it get rough, of course, but let the lovers feel how strong the opposition is to their love.

- What I am doing here is finding a physical way to get them to engage *emotionally* with the issues of the play. These kind of physical exercises show me how well they can work off the script, whether they can touch these emotional truths. It also shows them some of the ways we might work.

- When I was auditioning for *Twelfth Night*, one of the exercises we explored was making a tableau for comedy and one for tragedy. I did this because I wanted them to understand the difference (our production was going to exhibit strong elements of both), and at the same time watch how well they worked instinctively as a group.

- Everyone stands behind a line and steps forward together into an atmosphere of comedy. They do this without thinking and very quickly, form a tableau. Ask them what they noticed. Everyone's energy is out front; high and going forward.

- Now ask them to stand behind the line and, as they pass over it, they come into an atmosphere of tragedy. Without talking, they have to make a tableau of tragedy. You will find the energy is mostly inward, heavy and downward: some of the people will be isolated and closed.

- End the group audition by asking for any questions they might have.

An Invaluable Ally

In order that you might work in a creative and exciting way, I suggest you find an 'ally'. This ally needs to have a good knowledge of Shakespeare and perhaps an academic bent towards it. It cannot be your stage manager who will be in rehearsals with you; it needs to be someone else. When I direct at the university, I generally find a willing PhD student. If you are working in a youth theatre or even a school you might be able to find someone on placement from a local college to perform this task as part of their coursework.

Their task is to go through the text line by line with young actors and make sure everyone understands it. The way I set this up is that the ally meets up with the actors who are speaking in a scene before it is rehearsed for the first time. She goes through the text with them. Whilst this meeting is based on *understanding the text*, she might also look at emphasis; in other words, how to make the text clear. Another area she might explore might be particular to the play. *A Midsummer Night's Dream*, for instance, is absolutely littered with tales of mythical heroes and gods. For me it is important that the young actors know and understand these stories. For *Twelfth Night*, she might focus more on the meaning of Elizabethan jokes and slang. It depends on the play. As a teacher/director you are working on the prerequisites for them to learn and perform as well as they can.

The ally will not be able to reveal *everything* with regards to understanding, but they can make a start. For me, this ally should not go too much into character or motivation; that shouldn't be their focus. I also suggest that they do not start until the end of the foundation week.

The Director's Hunch

Peter Brook talks about 'the director's hunch' and, especially when you are working with young people, this is exactly what it ought to be; some kind of feeling about where you need to be going. I have touched earlier on the dangers of going into rehearsal with a too highly developed 'concept'.

What is a concept? Well, at worst it can be a straitjacket that you put on the minute you say, 'We will set it in this or that period,' or 'We will do this play to make this particular point.' For you as a director it can be reassuring; it makes you feel you have a plan. Indeed, it is the way many professional directors work (which is why there are so many unsatisfying productions out there). A concept can shut you off and, worse, can slam creative doors into your young actors' faces. You might have a concept which they cannot embody for some reason, or is simply too challenging for them. You will have some ideas from editing the text (I deal with that in the next chapter) but that's what they should be: ideas, feelings and images. Eventually, with your whole team, you will settle upon a concrete direction for the production. It will be like a symphony, but one you compose with your cast, and not on your own.

For some people this might sound like chaos, particularly when organising a Shakespeare production where the language can be a challenge, but believe me, your group will get a feeling of ownership and wholeness from working this way which is far less likely to emerge from a fully realised concept.

Brook discusses the role of the director in *The Empty Space*, one of the most impressive books on modern theatre; see bibliography. The production of theatre, he says, is an ensemble project. And it really is: it doesn't mean you do not have the final say, but your cast and production team can and must influence the project enormously. Let me give an example from my production of *Twelfth Night*.

As an older person, I initially had a view of *Twelfth Night* as a rather whimsical piece, with charming scenes and a bittersweet aftertaste. I felt, rather cynically, that it showed up romantic love as a fraud, that it said much about identity, gender and self-worth. I did not see the anarchic struggle between chaos and order, and between grief and joy, that we as a group discovered together. I also did not see the tremendous force with which my young actors' belief in romantic love would pour into the production and out to the audience. Despite all the cruelty, confusion and unpleasantness that exists within the play, this force of romantic love shone through and empowered the young actors through the piece. If there had ever been an example of going with a hunch and letting the ensemble guide, albeit with my help, then this was it.

We are now going to look at editing the text. By the audition stage, you will probably have done this already. Editing is something about which Peter Brook and Michael Chekhov (and I!) have a lot to say.

Chapter Twelve
Editing and Transposing the Text

For the modern theatre, all Shakespearean plays should
be shortened, and scenes even transposed, in order to
give them their proper tempo and increase their driving
force.

Michael Chekhov, *To the Actor*

This chapter looks at editing, which is not simply how to make
the play shorter. It is a big subject and crucial when doing a
production of Shakespeare with young actors, because they are
unlikely to be able to do the whole play uncut, and in reality
cutting the text to some extent is always essential. I am going to
examine what will govern your decisions about editing the text
to suit your group, yourself and your time constraints. It will
look at the results of those decisions. How do you make those
decisions? We will look at some particular examples of editing
scenes within *Twelfth Night* and *A Midsummer Night's Dream*. We
will also look at the wisdom of transposing scenes and what
you gain and potentially lose from this practice.

Why Edit?

Editing Shakespeare can raise hackles in some people who feel
every word is sacrosanct; others are very cavalier and hack a
play to pieces, destroying much of its richness. You need to

tread a fine line. This editing is not merely to deal with the inexperience of your performers, but often to clarify and even, dare I say it, shape the play for the audience.

Michael Chekhov had strong views on editing and shaping a Shakespearean text. He was a firm believer in the rules of composition; the beginning, middle and end of a piece. At one time I would have abhorred Chekhov's ideas about reordering and editing expressed at the start of this chapter, but now I embrace them fully.

You want to release something from the play and your company with your editing and shaping. That is an alchemical task, influential and creative. Those plays with a strong focus and narrative, *Macbeth* and *A Midsummer Night's Dream* for instance, both have a strong trajectory. That means you can use the *story* as your guide as a rule towards editing scenes. (The Hecate scene in *Macbeth*, Act Three, Scene Five, for instance, is often cut out as it just embroiders the role of the Witches and does not advance the story.) *Twelfth Night* is less reliant on this kind of narrative thrust, with a whole series of different plots which come together at the end, so it can be much harder to decide what to cut.

Obeying a sense of composition, as Chekhov explains it, can give a stronger focus, supply you with a raft of choices, and allow more accessibility. You might look at Chapter Eight of his book *To the Actor*, which discusses composition in depth.

Things to Consider

- You need to consider how much rehearsal time you have, as to how full you can leave the text. I would suggest 60 to 70 hours' rehearsal time at least for a full-length Shakespeare play, and this excludes your introductory workshops or foundation week. There is no point throwing a young person onto the stage just for an experience with little skills support. You need to factor in warm-ups and voice work when you consider how much rehearsal time you have.

- You need to balance the demands of the play and your own 'director's hunch' with the skill level of your performers. If your performers are vocally strong then you can trust more in their ability to deliver large speeches. That means your need to cut is going to be less pronounced. Be flexible; someone who might be ideal for a particular role in many ways might not be at their best handling big chunks of text and you may need to cut down their text for that reason alone.

- You want to edit the play into something manageable which will harness their enthusiasm and focus, rather than overfacing them. Consider *your skills* as well as *theirs*; how much you will be able to help them.

- You might need to adjust your edits once rehearsals begin.

- One of the goals of editing is to clarify the play for audience, cast and team. Ask yourself: What is this play primarily *about* and is the narrative clear?

- However, I now sound a loud word of caution. Transposing scenes and editing invariably has an impact on the whole piece. Most obviously, you could omit an element of the plot which is vital to the development of the characters; or if you strip the language and wordplay down, then you have to ask what you are losing. Is it changing the focus and trajectory of the story? Is it confusing the plot or clarifying it? Is it having the effect you want?

What Am I Looking For?

Editing Shakespeare simultaneously requires, on the one hand, a love for the author's work and, on the other, a healthy disrespect for it.

Start off by looking at the play as a whole and consider what, in its deepest sense, it is about. Look especially at the first scene and the last scene. This is a consideration you will return to with the actors. But consider it for yourself now. Every first scene may not give you that key, but many do. If I imagine the first scene of *Macbeth*, it seems to me to be about the nature of evil that seeps in like a thick tar into an already brutal world. If I look at *Twelfth Night*, I would say it was about romantic love in a confusing, lovesick, languorous place. If I look at *A Midsummer Night's Dream*, I might say it was about forbidden love; *Henry V*, the heroics of war; *Julius Caesar*, honour and rebellion. All these plays are about many more things than these, but it gives us something to consider.

Repetition

First of all, various scholars attest that Shakespeare was not the sole author of many of his plays (see Hutchings and Bromham, 2008). Sometimes this is noticeable, with a radical change of style. Collaboration might well have encouraged repetition, as co-authors working separately may cover ground already covered by the main author, Shakespeare.

In addition, many of the plays, especially the comedies, have multiple teams of characters, mechanicals or fairies for example, who disappear for large chunks of the play. That means, like a TV series, the audience needs to be continually reminded of the 'story-so-far' of any particular character group every time they reappear. *Twelfth Night* is full of this kind of repetition. If you edit or transpose the scenes effectively, you may not need to remind the audience of the story of a returning group of characters so often.

For instance, in *Twelfth Night*, the build-up to the scene in which Malvolio is tricked into dressing up in yellow stockings to woo Olivia has many interlacing scenes featuring the more romantic plot of Viola, Orsino, Sebastian and Olivia. Shakespeare's juxtaposition of these scenes is effective, however, by putting more of Malvolio's scenes together you can cut several preambles by the 'Malvolio team' which recap what has gone before. This has the added bonus of simplifying the playing of it for the performers.

The Opening of Scenes

A second area for consideration is the opening of many (though not all) scenes which have very long introductions. This was necessary in the Elizabethan theatre, which had little scenery and no lighting, to assist with creating the atmosphere of the forthcoming scene: the potent words had to do it all. So, as beautiful as these openings often are, you do not always need them. A classic example is the opening of Act Two, Scene Four of *Twelfth Night*, which has fifteen lines or so settling us back into Orsino's house before the meat of the scene begins when he talks intimately to Cesario (Viola in disguise).

Elizabethan Jokes and Wordplay

The Elizabethan jokes and wordplay are obvious contenders for editing. The first thing to consider is whether there is any chance at all of the modern audience grasping the meaning of a particular joke or line. There is nothing more tiresome to me than seeing actors making suggestive gestures, grabbing various parts of their anatomy, in order to make sure we in the audience get the point. Professional actors are always doing this. It drives me mad! We have to accept that Shakespeare, however magical many of his plays might be, was still writing in the sixteenth/seventeenth century. Some of the jokes work well still; but some do not. You need to judge both for yourself and your team as to what is worth keeping in.

However, if you edit too strongly you have to be aware that this is going to radically alter the whole timbre of the play. I had this issue with *Twelfth Night* in particular, which has scenes that delight primarily in nifty wordplay but do not move the story on a jot. I discovered that I needed to restore some of my hefty cuts because they denuded the play of what I felt was a kind of confusing Alice-in-Wonderland quality, which explores shifts in our imagination. By editing the scene but retaining enough to keep the flavour, the two young actors were well able to make it both lively and fun.

Transposing Scenes and Speeches: Two Beginnings and a Speech Reassignment

If your audience knows the play, then transposing speeches or even reassigning them can be jarring. On the other hand, it can also jolt them out of their complacency. Transposing speeches and scenes can really help you shape the play for a modern audience. The great thing about young actors is they do not question this transposing too much.

When we do not have sufficient actors we transpose speeches to make two characters into one. That is transposing from necessity. Sometimes, though, we want to give a young actor more to do because he might be talented, and in any case, you want to give him more of a stake in the production. In *Twelfth Night* I made Valentine and Curio into one character, partly because the young actor was very good and also because the character then became a very definite presence. It enhanced the feeling that Orsino was alone apart from his sad, loving servant.

An Example from A Midsummer Night's Dream

It is crucial that the play starts well. When working with Galway Youth Theatre on *A Midsummer Night's Dream*, I made a strong transposing choice. I had been involved in several productions of this play and never been content with the opening. It seems a bit lame and slow. Theseus and Hippolyta, who open the play, get very little stage time, we never get to know them, yet they are the rulers of Athens. Unless the two actors playing them double as Oberon and Titania, King and Queen of the Fairies (something fairly challenging for young actors) I feel they have little significance.

I therefore decided to transpose Puck's speech from Act Five, Scene One to the top of the play.

> PUCK. Now the hungry lion roars
> And the wolf behowls the moon,
> Whilst the heavy ploughman snores,
> All with weary task fordone.
> Now the wasted brands do glow,

Whilst the screech-owl, screeching loud,
Puts the wretch that lies in woe
In remembrance of a shroud.
Now it is the time of night
That the graves, all gaping wide,
Every one lets forth his sprite
In the churchway paths to glide.
And we fairies, that do run
By the triple Hecate's team
From the presence of the sun,
Following darkness like a dream,
Now are frolic.

This transposing began the play particularly well because we had a very strong Puck, but it also acknowledged something about the production. My reasons were several: it overcame the difficult opening sequence discussed earlier; it allowed a way of introducing the supernatural mischief from the very beginning; it allowed us to begin the play with a joyous and ferocious stamping and awakening, and it suggested that Puck was the Master of the Revels, which I thought was central to the play. The madness that Puck and the fairies represent is everywhere, even in the most ordered worlds! As the speech is quite dark, it also gave the play a slightly menacing edge.

It also meant that Puck began and ended the play, which gave the piece a 'Feeling of the Whole': a Chekhov principle we will be discussing in Chapter Fourteen (The Foundation Week).

Polarities and Another Transposed Speech

Another aspect of Chekhov's work is the question of 'Polarities' (see his *To the Actor*, Chapter Eight) where he suggests that, as we are in constant movement, the story and its characters take us on a journey through opposing forces: life/death, love/hate, chaos/order. It is the tension between polarities that can create much of the dynamic of the play. In your editing it is useful to look for these polarities, particularly between characters. We will be exploring exercises using polarities within our foundation week. Transposing speeches can really enhance this sense of the polarities within the story.

If I were to consider *A Midsummer Night's Dream*, I might ask: what are the polarities or struggles within it? True love and illusion? Jealousy and love? Order and chaos?

In *A Midsummer Night's Dream*, I asked myself who it was who really represented repressive order: who was, if you like, the *opposite* of Puck. The answer has to be Egeus, Hermia's father, who demands her life because she will not marry the man to whom she has been betrothed. Even when they find her in the forest towards the end of the play, Egeus still demands 'justice'. It seems to me that he is the absolute opponent of any kind of love or joy.

I felt his story faded away in the play and was not completed. It could be that Shakespeare was no longer concerned with him and the character had served his purpose. Who knows? Alternatively, he might have been cross-cast with another character and not available: a practice common in Shakespeare, and one we might meet ourselves when we are working with a limited number of actors.

I took Theseus's wonderful speech from the opening of Act Five, which berates the stories of the lovers in the forest, indeed Love itself. It has a sneering, dismissive quality to love and imagination. I gave the speech instead to Egeus, sitting alone after the marriage celebrations:

> I never may believe
> These antique fables, nor these fairy toys.
> Lovers and madmen have such seething brains,
> Such shaping fantasies, that apprehend
> More than cool reason ever comprehends.
> The lunatic, the lover, and the poet
> Are of imagination all compact:
> One sees more devils than vast hell can hold:
> That is the madman. The lover, all as frantic,
> Sees Helen's beauty in a brow of Egypt.
> The poet's eye, in a fine frenzy rolling,

Doth glance from heaven to earth, from earth
   to heaven;
And as imagination bodies forth
The forms of things unknown, the poet's pen
Turns them to shapes, and gives to airy nothing
A local habitation and a name.
Such tricks hath strong imagination
That if it would but apprehend some joy,
It comprehends some bringer of that joy;
Or in the night, imagining some fear,
How easy is a bush supposed a bear!

In our production, the fairies arrived and tormented him after he had spoken this, really seeing him off the stage like the Lords of Misrule before the customary blessing of the house. This again reminded the audience of the anarchy of the fairies, and the madness and danger they embody, in addition to their benevolent and magical aspects. It was something I developed in our riotous transposed opening and was now appearing again towards the end.

A Problem with Transposing: Twelfth Night

There can be problems, though, with transposing. We might call them unforeseen consequences. In a number of productions I have seen of *Twelfth Night*, the first two scenes have been transposed.

Scene One concerns the lovesick Duke Orsino, lonely, yearning and desperate with his helpless courtiers. It begins with the beautiful, 'If music be the food of love, play on'. Scene Two shows Viola, who has just been shipwrecked, on a beach with the Captain who has rescued her. She believes her twin brother to be drowned. She is in despair and resolves to disguise herself as a man.

So here we have two scenes: one about love and one about tragedy. They are two themes to which the Elizabethans were attached: Love (Life) and Death. So what does it matter if you turn these first two scenes around? Well, quite a bit. On the surface, it looks incredibly sensible. Starting with the shipwreck is a very dramatic beginning: Viola struggling from the ocean, washed up on the beach, or sailing in a boat from the wreck in the darkness. Despite *Twelfth Night* being a real ensemble play, Viola has the most stage time of the characters, and putting her scene first seems a good idea.

However:

- *Twelfth Night* is not solely about Viola: putting Scene Two first suggests the play is about her.

- The play is a comedy and so perhaps the audience's first encounter needs to be lighter than a poor young woman dragged from the water dealing with her brother's death.

- The play is *primarily* about romantic love and longing. So whilst Orsino is largely absent for the middle of the play, his unrequited love for Olivia is the spur that sets the story in motion. Having his scene play first tells the audience what the play is about and sets the atmosphere and mood: to start with the shipwreck scene disturbs this.

However, it does depend on the group. I was lucky enough to have a strong and confident Orsino, but what would have happened had he been less good? I would have wanted the play to have a strong beginning and a shipwreck is a powerful opening. In that situation I just might have transposed the scenes, even though artistically it does not seem quite right.

Some Thoughts on Editing

Take any film version of a Shakespeare play: it will inevitably have been cut. Really consider what effect this editing, transposing or reassignment of lines has brought about in the way we respond to the film.

Consider Franco Zeffirelli's 1990 film version of *Hamlet*. He cuts the first scene, where Horatio and the soldiers see the Ghost on the ramparts. In his version the Ghost is not made manifest to us until Act One, Scene Four, when Hamlet himself sees it. What effect does this have on the audience?

On the one hand, if you do not know the story, the edit gives a powerful energy to the first few scenes, which makes the opening section climax with the Ghost's appearance. So far, so good. However, I would suggest that it makes the Ghost a figment of Hamlet's imagination, rather than signifying the corruption of the state and therefore witnessed by all on the battlements.

Try looking at other film versions of Shakespeare and consider the edits. Often these are made for the particular strengths and weaknesses of the film medium, yet even if they are, ask yourself what effect such editing/transposing has.

After Editing

Here is a final checklist to consult after editing your script:

- Make sure you feel confident that your edit will be as accessible as possible and, as much as you can gauge, that your edit is going to suit your group.

- When you re-read your edit, can you follow the story? Is anything about the plot unclear? Perhaps give it to a colleague to read and check this out.

- Does your edit make sense in terms of the characters' emotional development?

- Make sure that you have understood the ramifications of your edit and how it might affect the production. Remember the reasons *why* you edited and the effect you wanted to achieve. Always read aloud when you have made an edit, to make sure it flows well.

- I would suggest that, when you present the edited script to your group, you tell them that this is the script you are working from. If they want to check out the full script they can, but not to get engaged in restoring any missing text. This will only be an issue in older, more experienced groups.

Chapter Thirteen
A Few General Notes on Directing

A director is not free of responsibility, he is totally responsible, but he is not free of the process either. At best a director enables an actor to reveal his own performance, that he might otherwise have clouded for himself.

Peter Brook, *The Empty Space*

What is the Director's Role?

It should be stated at the outset that directing young actors is quite similar to directing professional actors, more similar than professional actors might like to think. When you are working with young people there is a stronger element of teaching but, to some extent, less ego than with many professionals.

You are the leader but not the dictator. Whilst you will have a lot of your own ideas, you need to listen to the group and work with their ideas as well as your own.

Working on a play is very intense, and whilst it is important to make the project as enjoyable as possible, you need also to be very much the team captain. You need to be disciplined, kind and artistic; to teach well, and be fair and firm when there are disputes and difficulties; to be well prepared but always open and do it all with as much humour as you can manage.

You will have a lot more contact time with your group than usual, and a production is a great time to really develop the group skills and team spirit that doing a play always creates. More time together, however, also creates tensions (this also happens in professional productions) and you need to be constantly mindful. Use your stage manager to check out if there are any tensions within the team. Do not let these tensions fester under the surface if you discover them.

The Goal of Your Production

What is the goal of your project and your expectation of the team? Is it to make the play accessible to your actors? Is it to explore the wonder of the language? Is it to give your group a stronger sense of the play? Is it a bonding exercise for the group? Is it simply to make a good piece of work? Of course, ideally, it needs to be all of these things, but try and be clear about your own priorities.

Here is an extract from my book, *Teaching Voice* (page 211), which sets out some of my priorities for a particular project.

> Be selective with what you are trying to achieve. For instance, once when directing a youth theatre production of *A Midsummer Night's Dream*, I decided that a full expression of the language was the most important exploration we could do – not so much an *academic* one but an *emotional* one. This sometimes meant that the group over-projected slightly, but this was a very conscious trade-off in terms of the learning goals of the production. The confidence with the language affected their performances strongly and this in turn developed their physicality and released their general energy.

Rules of Engagement

You and your production team need to create a very safe space with a strong work ethic. That means:

• No absences unless something serious has occurred.

- Good timekeeping. Tell them always to contact the stage manager if they are going to be late.

- Given that the group have already had a text exploration with my 'invaluable ally' (see Chapter Eleven), I usually allow one rehearsal on the scene *with* the script, and then they need to know the scene when it is next rehearsed. Tell them that until they lose the scripts they cannot be truly creative. (For many young people I have worked with, this is a massive lesson.) I would say that it is better they *know* it, rather than *understand* every word. You can always iron out some of the issues of meaning and emphasis as you work through rehearsal.

- This early learning of the text cannot always be achieved, especially with Shakespeare, but it is something to be aimed for. You can always be more lenient if there are extenuating circumstances: if the actor finds learning hard, or if she has a big part and a lot of text to learn.

- If you are not fairly firm, no one will be able to be creative. You will end up having to tell everyone what to do, in order to make the production presentable. You want to make the play with *their* talents and emotions in order that they can own it fully.

- It is always important to remind people that doing a play well is a serious business, though it can also be fun. Unless your group is experienced, they will be used to doing things quickly and achieving a 'make-do' result, rather than something which really improves their work. You will have mentioned all about the seriousness of the project when your actors filled in the rehearsal sheets during the audition process, but if they have never experienced a substantial rehearsal period some may find it hard. 'Why are we wasting so much time on this?' is a complaint you might hear. They may get bored and irritated and start missing rehearsals. Whilst you need to be firm, it is vital to reinforce and encourage the work of the group. I remind them that I want this production to be as professional as it can be, so that the audience can be blown away by their skill and commitment, rather than there simply being good-natured applause from family and friends.

- Do not work on a scene when any of the actors are missing if you can possibly avoid it. It impedes everyone's creativity.

- Many young actors (and sadly, professional actors too) will ask you what you want them to do, as if they were merely your puppets. 'You're the director, aren't you?' 'Isn't that what a director does?' When this happens, I laugh, and say something along the lines of, 'Who's playing the part, you or me? What do *you* feel? What do *you* think?' So many times people have looked at me open-mouthed when I have said this, realising suddenly that the area of creating the character has to come from them. When they start this voyage of discovery, they may sometimes make decisions which do not fit with the play or the production, but then it has to be negotiated, just like a professional production. You must work with them. It is important they realise it is a *team* effort from the start. Part of the job of the 'foundation week' (explored in the following chapter) is to reinforce this group ensemble approach.

- Remember when you give your acting notes after rehearsing a scene that they are as succinct as possible. Do not give them too much information and keep the goals clear when you want them to improve something. Make sure they write the notes down. Never accept, 'Yeah, sure, I'll remember that', as an excuse to not record stuff.

- Because it is a Shakespeare play with big speeches, make sure you make time for solo rehearsals once you have a general shape for the piece. This will enable you to explore these long speeches without having to worry about the other cast members in the scene, and really help the young actor who is speaking. Try not to do this too much until rehearsals are underway and everyone gets a general feel of the piece. If you feel the young actor is having difficulty, assure them early on that you will take time to help them later in the process.

Preparing Scenes Before Rehearsal

If you have done a serious edit, you may already have started to consider some of the points we will touch on here. Every scene you look at is going to have a beginning, a middle and an end. The characters will not be the same at the end of the scene as they were at the start, and some piece of information or action by at least one of the characters is going to move the story along. Try and decide which lines suggest this to you. This is so obvious you might feel it does not need to be stated. Believe me, it is often forgotten in major production houses with Shakespeare, because of their world-weary attitude and assumption that everyone has seen the play before.

Nowadays, I would really make 'hunches' and mark them into the text: atmosphere, images, actions, plot and content, depending on how the scene plays out in my imagination. However, some of these decisions may not suit the actors, and hopefully they are going to find at least some of their own solutions. You have to be open to try things, especially when working with young actors.

On the other hand, do not be seduced into accepting an idea simply because it comes from the actor. They are not always right. Do try the idea out, though, because often they would find out it was wrong simply by trying it. Always make time to try things out. Experience is the best way to learn.

I am going to give an example of working on a scene in Chapter Fifteen (Starting on Scenes) below. However, I want to spend a moment talking about *long* scenes, which are often very difficult in Shakespeare, and how you can make them simpler.

You have to split the scene into sections at home. You cannot leave this to rehearsal because it's a big job. I am going to split up a scene from *Twelfth Night*: Act One, Scene Five. You will need to read it, and have some sense of it, to get the full benefit of the advice below. It is a long scene so I have not reproduced it here.

Splitting Up a Scene

Act One, Scene Five of *Twelfth Night* is the second scene set in Olivia's house – and is quite a marathon, though not as much of a marathon as Act Five! It's important to realise that the scene is about Olivia. She is the *spine* of the scene, though Viola, Feste and Malvolio are, of course, important. (Line numbers below are from the 2008 Arden edition.)

After reading the scene, let's start to split it into sections. These sections will depend not only on groups of characters (which will make it easier to organise for rehearsal) but upon moods, plot, direction and substance.

Section One (lines 1–27) is the short exchange between Maria and Feste, before Olivia and Malvolio enter. This important opening section tells the audience the location (Olivia's house) and prepares us for the arrival of Olivia. Feste is also new to the audience, and he sets his teeth against the austere world of Olivia's mourning.

Section Two (28–94) begins with the arrival of Olivia and Malvolio, her steward. It continues with a verbal duel between Malvolio and Feste: they are fighting for her heart. Feste wins as Olivia sides with him, so we already feel the forces of fun and lightness are succeeding against the dark order over which Malvolio seems to rule.

Section Three (95–160) begins when Maria enters and announces the arrival of Cesario (Viola in disguise), the Duke's messenger. This whole section has an air of confusion and excitement. It ends as Cesario enters.

Section Four (161–213) involves the playful banter between Olivia, Maria, Cesario and ends when Olivia decides to send the servants away. She is obviously interested in Cesario romantically and starts to open and follow her heart.

Section Five (214–304) takes us to the end of the interview, includes the instructions to Malvolio, and Olivia's love-struck confession to the audience and herself.

We gave the whole scene a title, 'The Awakening of Olivia', which culminates in her yearning declaration of love at the end of the scene ('Methinks I feel this youth's perfections...'). The title was very useful to the cast as to where this scene was going. The scene begins with a sense of death and worn-out despair, and moves to ecstatic, uncontrollable love and excitement.

We also 'baptised' each *section* with a title to focus us and looked at what the prevailing atmosphere was in each section.

Section One: Title: *Meet Feste the Fool*. Maria chides Feste for his absence and tells him that Olivia is missing him. Feste is immediately seen as important to Olivia's well-being. The atmosphere was dour and dry, though Feste tried not to be.

Section Two: Title: *The Duel for Olivia*. The atmosphere was a battle between dark and light, a struggle, a matter of life and death.

Section Three: Title: *Cesario is Coming!* The atmosphere was one of excitement and fizz (champagne bubbles).

Section Four: Title: *The Approach of Love*. An atmosphere of fizz and mischief continues, as slowly, for Olivia, it starts to turn into something else. There is an atmosphere of dissolving as she is left alone with Cesario.

Section Five: Title: *A Woman Reborn!* An atmosphere of passion, almost like the power of the tide, prevails. It is almost, you might say, an atmosphere of *love*: Olivia succumbs.

An Exercise for Splitting Up Scenes

I would suggest you pick the longest scene you are doing in your production, or if you are not as yet doing one, to take any long scene from a Shakespeare play and experiment with this process with your group. Don't worry too much about motive. Look at story first, then try looking for titles and atmospheres.

Chapter Fourteen
The Foundation Week

Is all our company here?
A Midsummer Night's Dream: Act One, Scene Two

When I start any production, I have a foundation week or a series of weekend workshops to get my young actors up to speed and to fully involve them in the project's creation. With Shakespeare, this preparation is even more important because you also have to awaken the voice, in addition to preparing the group for the world of the play.

The objective of this foundation week is twofold. The first is to get the group ready for the task by developing individual skills: voice, body and character. If they do this work *together*, they will start to get a sense of *all* the characters at once. They are not working in a box, nor looking exclusively at performances on YouTube and starting their exploration by imitation.

Remember that many young actors will have little or no sense of acting technique. This makes developing character challenging, though it can also make them freer to experiment. This first week will give you the chance to help them in that development and hopefully in learning to sustain their performances.

The second strand of the week is to develop a score (as if the play were a symphony) *together*, encouraging the group to work on the story, developing a beginning, middle and end of the production – or, as Michael Chekhov would call it, a Feeling of the Whole. Chekhov believed that we all, as a team, should have a view as to what the play is saying and how the audience *might* feel at the end. This is a joint responsibility, not just yours. It might change radically as the rehearsals progress, but at least it is something to aim for. You need to find a hunch for this ending within this foundation week. This sounds impossible, I know. It isn't. Some people might imagine that making these decisions closes down too many possibilities early on; it doesn't do that because you can always change the ending you have found. Also, this ending might not be something literal; it might just be a feeling. For instance, I had to consider in *Twelfth Night*, whether at the end of the play we focused on the romantically thwarted characters (Sir Andrew, Antonio and Malvolio) or the fulfilled ones, or both? How bittersweet *is* this play? Did I want the audience to consider the madness, the pain and inconsistency of love, or to focus on the joy of it?

An important point is that we find this mostly by *doing*, not by talking.

At this stage we do very little reading of the text, though I do expect them to have read the play and know the story before they arrive. You might wonder why initially I do not spend too much time on the text when I speak so often about language being the key. I find with young people that read-throughs are not really very successful, especially with Shakespeare. The last thing you want is to make them feel that this is going to be an uphill task. This week has to enthuse them and build bridges to the play.

Having said that, I ask them all to learn a speech from their character (between eight and ten lines) that we can use to explore imagery and breathing, much as I have suggested earlier in this book. Working with short speeches, as with short scenes, gives the young actor confidence and prepares them for the bigger challenge once rehearsals start.

In this week we must also imagine and experience many of the *atmospheres* of the play. The group will also find the themes and polarities within the play, and how they affect the characters as the story progresses.

Unless you are working on a full-time performance course, the young actors will be unused to working at this level. One of the pluses to working so intensely is that people understand quickly that making a good piece of work is within their grasp but takes commitment. By working hard, they can take their skills and performance to a new level.

I always ask the production/design team to attend the last two days and get involved with some of the work, most particularly atmosphere.

The Foundation Week Plan

Rather than give a blow-by-blow account, I am going to give an overview of each day and focus on one or two specific aspects we explored in my first exploratory week of *Twelfth Night*. This way, you can use this loose template for any play you do. I will also focus on new exercises/areas not yet covered in this book.

Please Note: I have *not* included a description of breathing practice on the floor in this plan because I feel if you want to do it (and I would advise you to include it) you need to work with my book *Teaching Voice*, or any other book that focuses on that aspect of the work.

Day One: Morning

Ensemble and Voice

My goals for the morning: to set out the goals for the week; to warm up and then work on a series of ensemble and voice exercises; and introduction to feeling through the body and Ideal Centre.

I cannot stress enough how important it is to work in ensemble, especially with young people, because it has all the additional benefits of working as a team, as well as strengthening the work. Shakespeare may not look as if it is too well suited to ensemble work, but it is if you work imaginatively. In Chapter Sixteen, we'll be looking at a few ways in which you can use the ensemble group with Shakespeare to strengthen individual performers, clarify scenes and enhance your production.

My other initial priority in this week was voice work. (Some of my group had done voice work; some had not.) I introduced diaphragmatic breathing, we did about 15 minutes of floor work every day during this week and I incorporated as much of this as I could throughout the entire rehearsal period. We used the *Verbing the Body/Speaking the Text* and *Consonant Characters* exercises, as well as other exercises from the voice workshops in this book (Chapters Four and Five).

I used *Ideal Centre* and *Open the Hand/Close the Hand*, using different qualities on their learned text to start to get the group to find the connection to the body and their acting. Another priority was to develop radiating and receiving.

Let Rehearsals Begin!

Here are the main points I made in my introduction to the company on Day One, taken from my notes.

1. What are we doing? Giving a shape and finding a score. Developing ensemble skills/movement/voice tools for the acting.

2. Some things you find out in this week about the play and the character may well be in the final performance. Keep a look out for those things and make notes. IMPORTANT: keep a journal of your discoveries.

3. You will meet with my 'ally' next week to go through the text, scene by scene.

4. Things I hope you will have discovered as possibilities for your character by the end of the week: the physicality of

the character, the rhythm, the voice, the journey. These things may change, but they may change less than you think. Use your instinct and inspiration from reading the play and working with your cast members to find these things.

5. Work with the voice sheet I gave you. (This is at the back of *Teaching Voice*, and available to download from www.nickhernbooks.co.uk/teachingvoice, and is a short voice warm-up/relaxation programme to keep everyone mindful of the importance of voice on this production.)

6. Remember that you have to come to the group with ideas, feelings and sensations about the characters. Everything we do this week, more or less, is to *find out*.

7. You will work with the composer on some of the music this week.

8. In the end we have to remember that we are doing this play as if it has never been done before. This is challenging with Shakespeare – but essential. The show needs to surprise.

9. I will establish teams for line-learning, of characters who appear together in the same scenes, to help you keep up with the learning deadlines.

Some New Exercises on Ensemble and Voice

Find the Sound

- Ask them to close their eyes. Maybe ask them for a second to listen to the sounds outside, then the sounds in the room, and finally the sound of their own breathing.

- Explain that every person in the room is going to sing a '*mmmaaaahhhh*' sound. They can breathe whenever they like but they need to keep the sound going and keep their eyes closed.

- Make sure everyone keeps their eyes closed. This can be hard for some, so suggest they put a hand over their eyes if they have any trouble. While you are talking, you walk around the room. You explain that you are going to touch someone on the shoulder. When every person starts to make the '*mmmaaaahhhh*' sound, the person you have touched will instead sing a '*mmmeeeeeeee*' sound. So everyone but one person will be saying '*mmmmaaaah*' and one person will be saying '*mmmeeeeeeee*'.

- The job of the '*maaaaah*'s is to find the '*meeeee*' with their eyes closed. Once the '*meeeee*' person is found (the '*meeeee*' can also move around as well), anyone who finds her then needs to stay with her and change their own sound to '*mmmeeeeeeee*'. Eventually the whole room is full of people hanging on to each other singing '*mmmeeeeeeee*'.

- Once all are together, tell them you are going to clap your hands and then everyone must open their eyes and keep the sound going. When they open their eyes, they will want to relax and giggle. Try and control that because it destroys the energy.

- If it does work okay, call out a name and that actor must now, with their eyes open, lead and change the sound adding a repetitive movement that goes *with* the sound; then all must follow. Then call another who must change the sound and movement, and then all follow. Then another and so on. To end the exercise ask the leader to bring the movement and sound to a close. All stop together.

- Now ask them to start again and be aware that if one leader makes a smooth vowel sound, then the next might change the rhythm totally and make a '*k-k-k-k-k*' sound for everyone to follow. Tell them to feel free to travel around the room.

Follow My Eyes 1

This is a great ensemble exercise which I learned from my friend Jonathan Gunning, a Lecoq-trained actor and teacher. It is one of my favourite team-building exercises.

- Everyone goes into pairs. Tell them that one of the partners is in charge: let's call them the Leader (they decide who). The Leader and Follower look at each other.

- When the Leader moves their eyes, the Follower, maintaining eye contact, has to go to where the Leader is looking, as quickly as possible. The Leader then moves their eyes somewhere else; the Follower moves again.

- Let this go on for a couple of minutes ,and then swap over, so the Follower can get their revenge!

Teaching Tip: Tell them not to make it too fast and difficult for the Follower despite any desire they might have to do so! Tell them they are playing and need to make it just difficult *enough*.

Follow My Eyes 2

This is a continuation. You will need to show them how to do this first.

- Ask everyone to stand against the walls of the room. An actor comes into the centre and rules the space, radiating out to the people watching. He is the Leader.

- When someone new is ready, she leaves the wall and enters the space. Now *she* is the Leader. The new Leader looks at the first actor and moves her eyes. The first actor becomes the Follower, maintaining eye contact with the Leader, as in the earlier exercise.

- After a minute or two, a third person enters the space. She now becomes the Leader. The other two, now acting as a team, move together to where the new Leader is looking. The new Leader changes her gaze and the Followers follow.

- After a minute, a fourth person enters the space and they become the Leader. The third person joins the following group. Keep going until the whole group is working.

Teaching Tip: You will notice big drops in energy, and confusion when a new person enters the space and the leadership changes.

Everyone needs to be aware when a new Leader has entered the space and to make these changeovers smooth. Run the exercise again and ask them to heed those moments. This time, get the people who became Leaders towards the end of the exercise to be the first people to enter the space, as they will be less tired from the running around. Also, check that when the Followers become a big group they try to stick together.

Blue Voice, Green Voice

This is a really useful exercise from *Teaching Voice* to get young actors to explore what their voices can do, and how a different use or timbre to the voice is easily within their grasp.

- Get everyone to find their own space and to close their eyes. Get them to be present in the moment: ask them to feel the earth beneath their feet and their body full of golden energy. Tell them to breathe in through the nose and out through the mouth.

- Now ask them to imagine they have a centre in their belly which is *dark blue* and that their whole body is full of dark-blue energy. As they breathe out through their mouth, dark blue comes out. Ask them to really feel that: feel what it is like to have dark-blue breath, and get them to make their breath audible.

- Then ask them to voice that blue sound. Ask them to keep the sound open rather than growling. Ask them to try saying one of their own lines, or if they cannot think of one to use at that moment, suggest 'If music be the food of love, play on'. Have them repeat the line a few times with their blue voice.

- Then get them to take a breath in and shake out the whole body. Really make them shake for about twenty seconds, making a low sound as they do. This helps them to shed whatever the imagination brought up for them when they were working. It helps them to let it go.

- Now try the same process with *orange*: the sound will be different. Let them try the line again. Breathe in/shake out.

- Now with *silver*. Ask them to try the lines. Breathe in/shake out.

- *Flyback*. Ask them what they noticed. Many will notice that not only did their voices sound different, but they *felt* differently saying the line.

Day One: Afternoon
Archetypes and the Theme of Love

My goals for the afternoon: I set out to work a little on the theme of *love* in its widest meaning: romantic, family, devotional, gregarious, intoxicating, making a Museum of Love with actors making statues of love. We had a quick fun session working with the *In On It* exercise in Chapter Three, which explored talking to the audience. We also explored archetypes, an element of the Chekhov work. These are extremely useful for Shakespeare where the roles and types of character are often way beyond the young actor's life experience. For more information on the use of archetypes, I would strongly recommend Lenard Petit's book, *The Michael Chekhov Handbook for The Actor* (pages 149–163).

Archetypes

Archetypes are like creative templates that bear a certain potent energy, either by dint of what they do in the story ('The Coward' or 'The Hero', for instance) or what the character's actual role, job or status is in the play ('The Princess' or 'The Servant', say). For instance, Feste in *Twelfth Night* is not only a 'Fool', just as Macbeth is not merely a 'Warrior', but there is something of The Fool and The Warrior about these two characters respectively; it is something that fills them. Considering archetypes can be a great way to make some initial explorations because most of the characters in Shakespeare have very powerful archetypal energy. As Chekhov puts it, in *Lessons for the Professional Actor*:

There is another thing in our actor's nature which might be called the archetype… for instance there are different types of lions running around in the desert – each is a lion, one bigger, one smaller, but there is a lion as an archetype. There is an idea of a lion which is the source of all lions.

Archetypes Exercise 1

- Ask each person to stand in a circle and face outwards. Ask them to imagine that in front of them there is an atmosphere: it is the energy of 'The Thief'.

- Ask them what it looks like. Does it have a colour? Is it thick? Can you see through it? Does it smell of anything ? Tell them not to think whether they can or cannot do this, just tell them to open the imagination. Does the atmosphere have a movement, like a wind or a pressing-down?

- Ask them to step into the atmosphere and breathe it in. Ask them to experience it on their skin. Is it hot or cold? Dry or wet?

- Ask them to breathe the atmosphere in, really deeply, and let the atmosphere mould them into a gesture/statue of 'The Thief'. Tell them not to think about it.

- When they have all settled on a gesture/statue, tell them to remember the form, but to then step back.

- Ask them to turn around so they are facing inwards, then ask them to make their gesture/statue again into the circle, so that everyone can see each other. You will find that many of them are similar: low, grasping, mean-looking, appearing to move forward but pulling back.

- Ask everyone to have a quick look round at them all, and to note the many similarities between them.

- Try a few different archetypes: 'The King', 'The Mother', 'The Servant', 'The Politician'.

Teaching Tip: Tell your actors that these archetypes are not *all* the character is, but that the energy of these archetypes is a force which helps power the character.

Archetypes Exercise 2: Exploring the Characters

Following on from the core exercise above, we moved on to develop the characters, and to find something deep inside that made them tick.

- I told the actors we were now going to explore archetypes with regards to the actual play. I asked one of the actors to stand out: Olivia, the woman in mourning for her brother who Orsino is pursuing. I asked the actor to suggest an archetype that might suit her character. She chose 'The Princess'. (She could equally have chosen something completely different like 'The Mourner' or 'The Spoiled Child'.) I told her she was going to watch whilst the rest of the cast embodied various moving versions of this archetype. She would then step into the space and 'try on' the 'Princess' archetypes the others had created for her, like a coat. Whilst she was doing this, she would speak some of her lines.

- I asked each member of the group (except the actor playing Olivia) to stand in a circle, face outwards, and to imagine in front of them the energy of the archetype: 'The Princess'. As before, I asked them what it looked like. Did it have a colour? Was it heavy or light? Could you see through it? Did it smell of anything? I told them them not to think about whether they could or couldn't do this; I just wanted them to open the imagination.

- Then I asked them to step into the energy and breathe it in, to experience it on their skin. I then asked them to breathe the atmosphere in, really deeply, and let the energy mould them into a gesture/statue.

- Working this way made it less likely that the intellect 'got in the way' of something deeper, because they were responding more instinctively and thinking less about the end-result. Then I asked them to make a sound and start to explore movement on the spot: then to move around the room. Everyone gave their own version of 'The Princess'. I told them to make sure that the physicality was strong.

- As everyone was moving round the room, I now asked the actor playing Olivia to walk amongst the group and find one of the archetypes that she liked. I told her to follow the actor playing the archetype and imitate their sound and movement. Once our Olivia was moving and making sound as this archetype, I asked her to start her text.

- When she was ready, I suggested she look around the room and find another archetype that appealed to her. (The first person she had copied could now stand back and watch.) She copied and inhabited the new version and tried her text whilst she was moving as before.

- I let her try a few versions of the archetype, then got everyone to shake out thoroughly. I asked her to fly back. Did she find any she liked? If so, what did it tell her about the character of Olivia?

- Every actor explored one archetype for their character with the whole group.

Teaching Tip: This is a very tiring exercise if you go through each character but it is extremely useful because you are immediately getting some character choices into the body without too much discussion. The actors got a glimpse into the myriad possibilities of the characters. The exercise also allowed all the actors to have an input into every character. It was very encouraging to watch the whole group help each other to 'find out'. I made sure they got time to note down any thoughts or discoveries they had made.

Here is a list of archetypes we came up with for *Twelfth Night*:

Orsino	Hero. Lover.
Viola	Orphan. Seeker. Actor.

Olivia	Princess. Mourner. Lover.
Feste	Fool. Entertainer. Magician.
Sir Toby	Drunk. Tramp. Joker.
Sir Andrew	Dunce. Innocent. Coward. Failure.
Maria	Smart-ass. Avenger. Trickster. Lover. Servant.
Sebastian	Bewitched Hero. Lost Boy.
Fabian	Servant. Prisoner. Avenger.
Malvolio	Snob. Judge. Prefect.
Antonio	Lover. Outlaw.
Curio	Servant. Protector.

Day Two: Morning

Ensemble, Voice and Story

My goals for the morning: As before, I found it essential to continue with the voice work and to sensitise the young people to the power of the language. We worked with imagination, breathing, diction and resonance. Many of today's exercises were working to further develop a sense of ensemble. We also continued to develop the Chekhov work and encouraged listening to the body. I introduced two of the qualities: *floating* and *moulding*.

The focus for today was going to be on the story and the shape of it. I expected the whole group to know the story by this stage. If this seems unlikely or impossible, you need to send out a synopsis with your preparatory email but *only do this as a last resort* because it will stop some of them reading the play.

To prepare us for the storytelling, I wanted us firstly to explore the Feeling of Form. This is one of the four guiding principles of Chekhov Technique and it was something we needed to get into the body before we began our story work.

It is back to our old tenet of things having a beginning, middle and end. Every movement, every small piece of scene (like the short scenes we looked at in Chapter Nine) has a sense of completion: not so that we can just relax but so that we can spring off into the next movement.

When doing *Radiating and Receiving* (*Throwing the Ball*) today, I asked the group to focus very much on the *form* of the throwing and catching, in particular to focus on ending the movement and sustaining it out to the person to whom they were throwing the imaginary ball.

In using the *Breath Dance* exercises, I asked people to focus on the opening and end of the movement, and the sustaining, when you are neither breathing in or out. How did those different things *feel*?

Feeling of Form

The Feeling of Form is an absolutely crucial element in making any strong performance. To understand this feeling of initiating movement in the body, following it through, ending and sustaining it, gives every moment of a performance a focus and sense of meaning.

Here is an early form exercise I learned from David Zinder, the Chekhov teacher and author of *Body, Voice, Imagination* (2009). The exercise seems simple, though it is not as simple as it appears.

- Everyone stands still somewhere in the room, working on their own. Tell the group to ask their body where it wants to go. Does it want to raise an arm, bend over, stride or point? Ask them to make a movement from the body's impulse.

- When the movement reaches its end, tell them to sense in the body again where it wants to move. Tell them to try not to think or panic, just to move instinctively and try and engage the whole body. Then ask them to move again. And so on.

- The movements need not be fancy or balletic. Tell them they can simply put a hand in their pocket if that is what the impulse is.

- Tell them that the main goal is not to think or to judge themselves; tell them to listen to the body and find an ending for each movement.

- Let this go on for a few minutes. You may need to 'side-coach' and help some individuals to really finish their movement. ('Side-coaching' means helping people individually whilst the whole group is working.)

- Ask them to consider what it felt like to finish the movement. Some might say they felt a sense of satisfaction. Simply stress that you are trying to teach them to *complete* their movements, just as we have to *complete* our scenes and, ultimately, the play.

- Try this exercise a few times. Ask them to notice that, when they finish a movement, there is a moment of suspension like in the *Breath Dance* exercises, where the energy is travelling in one direction before it gives the body a new impulse to travel somewhere else. Suggest they consider that, when a dog jumps to catch a ball, there is a moment of suspension, before it drops back down to earth with the ball in its mouth.

Ensemble Tableaux

As we were going to use a good deal of tableau work on this second day, I decided to simply ask them to stand by the walls of the studio and make a tableau all together following my suggestions. I did not choose specific locations, but concepts, atmospheres and emotions I felt were in the play. One of these tableaux, or a version of it, appeared in the final moments of the play.

- Tell the group they are all going to make an instant tableau, all together, without discussion. You will say the title and they will move at once. Tell them they need to make connections with the other actors.

- Tell them you might take a picture of it. Don't forget to ask permission for this!

- With each tableau ask them one question: where is the energy of it going? For instance, in the case of Joy, it may be going *up* and *forward*.

- Here are some suggestions for *Twelfth Night*: Love, Loss, Obsession, Comedy, Joy, Lust and Longing. (For *Romeo and Juliet*, they might be: Youth, Hatred, Love, Fire, Pressure, Tragedy and Death.)

- All of these tableaux will offer definite directions of energy. If some are conflicting, don't worry. Generally, the whole group will be in one accord.

Teaching Tip: Many young actors are quite fascinated by this feeling that emotion has direction. Doing these sorts of exercises starts to create a flow in energy which makes acting a lot easier. Furthermore, this is a great ensemble exercise because everyone is acting intuitively, together.

Story Exercise 1

Before lunch we embarked on this first telling of the story together. We had a similar exercise, *Telling the Story*, in Chapter Eight. Here is the process:

- Get everyone to stand in a circle. Ask someone to start to tell the story to everyone else in their own words. Tell them to speak to the group directly, not into some vague space, nor as if trying to tell the story like a test or a memory exercise. (This is very hard to maintain, especially the first time.)

- Encourage anyone else to jump in and continue at any point. Don't let anyone go on for too long. It is a group telling, their first group telling of the story of the play. If someone wants to contradict or add something, let them do it, but keep the energy going. Stay in the circle yourself. You might need to add part of the story.

- When they get to the end, try and note for yourself who they seem to think is the main character by the way they tell the story; what attitudes they might express about a character's behaviour and what they believe the play is saying. All this will be incredibly useful. You are not only trying to get the group to find a shared idea of the story, but also to explore their feelings about it.

What we discovered with *Twelfth Night* was that the plot became more and more complex as we went on, like a farce. We realised that as a group there was 'a knot to untie' and that this released the energy of the play as it progressed. Issues for the characters got tighter and tighter, and then they unravelled before getting resolved. This gave us a lot of clues as to how to act the second part of the play. We realised that the characters become more wound up, more disorientated and more confused in the later scenes. *Please Note*: We learned this very important aspect about the story through working on our feet. This was much more successful for us than too much intellectual discussion.

Day Two: Afternoon

Story and Tableaux

My goals for the afternoon: To continue with the storytelling element. We also started to look at the beginning and the end of the play so we might find some idea of what the broad emotional journey for the characters might be.

Story Exercise 2

After this process of active discovery before lunch, I asked the group to stand in a circle. They would tell the story again with various narrators, but this time, while the narrator was speaking, the others would act out what the narrator was saying in the middle of the circle. They could play any characters they wanted or swap characters. For example, many people could play Viola or any of the characters as narrators were switched. This was all very scrappy as no one got to discuss it beforehand. That didn't matter. What mattered was that they were having fun acting out the story and discovering details. Meanwhile, I was finding out what they thought important.

Here is a rough idea of the sort of thing we did:

The whole group is in a circle. Someone says:

ACTOR 1. Once upon a time there was a rich guy called Orsino who was sulking because this woman was not paying him any attention. He was making all his friends miserable and worried about him.

At the same time, in the centre, someone enters the space as ORSINO and others come in mopping his brow, trying to show him pictures of other possible lovers, giving him food to eat. Someone might be miming playing a guitar, etc.

ACTOR 2. Outside there's a storm and a young girl is shipwrecked on the coast.

Storm acting. Everyone floating about. VIOLA appears from the sea. Other actors act as if they are drowning.

ACTOR 3. She has a strange idea to keep her identity a secret; she decides to wear men's clothes and go to the court.

In the centre, VIOLA starts pulling herself together and looking at herself in a mirror and practising bowing, as the court come in to look at her.

And so on.

Teaching Tip: I made it fun, but tried to get them to be precise with the whole story. I didn't worry about great acting, just got them to enjoy it and really have fun with it. They were engaging immediately with the tale and with their whole being; if their knowledge of the whole story was scrappy, then this exercise only improved it. (You might need to do this exercise in two chunks, depending on how much detail they get into when telling the story.)

Tableaux: Beginning and End

This exercise was a useful way into the atmosphere and energy of the play, as well as giving a sense of what the journey of the play might be. It's based on a Chekhov exercise and gives everyone concerned a Feeling of the Whole. We have used a version of this in Chapter Eight (Devising a Group Project on Shakespeare). Here is something of what we did.

I split the group into manageable numbers (6 to 8 in each group). I told them they all had to make a tableau, a still photo, a painting (however you want to put it) of the opening of the play. Even if there were only two characters in the scene, everyone in the group had to be used: as architecture, furniture or other characters. With *Twelfth Night*, for instance, in our opening scene, those not playing the named characters played courtiers and musicians. I told them this tableau as a whole had to express the start of the play. How did it feel? What was the atmosphere? Who was the focus of the scene? What was it about? I asked them to make sure that when they made their tableaux every gesture had an ending and a flow of energy. They needed to be fully focused.

I didn't let them sit too long, discussing. As they were working out their tableaux, I sometimes suggested they 'turned the tableaux up', sent their energy out more strongly, made bigger gestures. They usually noticed the difference and the tableaux had a stronger impact.

They showed the two tableaux they had prepared to the rest of the group and we then used them as a talking point to discuss the start of the play. We wondered together what the feel of it was. Was it heavy or light? Sad or hopeful? Grim or joyous? We discussed whether we thought Orsino had a chance with Olivia. In the first tableau he looked hopeful, his energy pouring forward. Was he a vain and supercilious character or was he sincere? This choice alone had massive ramifications for the whole production. If he was sincere, then the audience knew we were going to take this theme of love at least partially seriously; if not, then the production may have made a more cynical statement. I told them this was not a value judgement here; it was a choice.

We later tried a tableau in which Orsino was in despair. In discussion later, we decided that whilst the character could travel from despair to happiness through the play, and that was a good choice, Orsino needed to be more of a champion for love and be somewhat more positive and confident at the start, as the actors found in the first tableau. That was also the instinct of the young actor, John, who played Orsino, and I went with his decision: it was much more upbeat. After all, if the play began gloomily it created a tragic atmosphere for the audience, particularly as the second scene was about bereavement, grief and rescue.

I then asked them to make tableaux of the ending of the play in their groups. We discussed them as before. I asked them how they thought the play ended. What was the feeling audiences might experience when they leave? This kind of question gave them a sense of responsibility and an ownership of the creative process; it also made for the promise of an impactful production.

Finally, I asked them to move from their beginning tableau to their end tableau, *very slowly*. I told them to try this a few times. It started to give them a sense of the emotional movement of the play in its entirety. It gave a space for discussion, enabled the group to start relating to each other on the play and helped to get the play into their bodies.

Turning Points

This dynamic exercise is for the group to find the turning points within a scene. Later on, it would become an important aspect of our rehearsals and, whilst we started with a short scene to introduce the idea, it is a fantastic exercise to use for longer scenes. Initially, though, don't pick a marathon scene, especially for the first attempt. Again, here is what we did.

I put everyone into groups and I chose the scene in which Sebastian goes from being completely confused and stressed to agreeing to marry Olivia, and a priest arrives to lead them to the church: all in thirty-five lines! (You need to look at this; it is Act Four Scene Three). I told them this time to focus less on the atmosphere and more on the story.

I asked them first to make a tableau of the beginning and the end of the scene and then two more *within* the scene where something changes: this change could be psychological or actually physical. We might pick the arrival of Olivia and the Priest for one, and then the moment Sebastian agrees to the marriage for the other.

Having established their four tableaux, I asked them to move slowly from one tableau to the next. We started asking questions like, 'I wonder how desperate Olivia is?' 'Is Sebastian clear about what he is doing or is he just swept away?' 'How does the Priest feel?'

I am sure from this example you understand the process. You might explore Act One, Scene Four of *Macbeth*, for example; Act Five, Scene Two of *Romeo and Juliet*; or Act Four, Scene One of *King Lear*.

Day Three: Morning

Character and Character Journey

My goals for the morning: I began the session with a warm-up, then ensemble and further voice work using imagery with words and phrases from the text. I continued to work on more technical aspects of voice: diction, resonance and projection. I had to keep up this aspect of the training or they may not have continued to practise these technical elements once our regular rehearsals began.

For the bulk of this third day I wanted to work primarily on character and possible character journeys using Psychological Gesture and Centres, as explored below.

Three Centres: Head, Heart and Will

Remember the *Ideal Centre* exercise I introduced in our first Chekhov Acting Workshop? Well, Michael Chekhov used centres as a basis for character: characters operating from a centre. These centres could be anywhere, even outside the body, but for our exercise here we are going to stick to the three core centres of head (Intellect), heart (Ideal Centre) and pelvis (Will). By placing the centre for our character in a different place we can create different types of character.

Here is a basic exercise: it takes a bit of time, so don't rush it with them.

- Begin by working with the *Ideal Centre* exercise, as mentioned in the Chekhov Acting Workshop above (Chapter Six), where you ask the group to imagine a sun in the centre of the chest. If you have not done this exercise with them before, then refer back and take it very slowly.

- Once the Ideal Centre (heart) is being experienced by the group, then get them to walk around the room, picking things up, putting them down, looking at people and greeting them with a line or two of their texts, all powered from the Ideal Centre.

- Once you have done this, then get them to close their eyes. Now ask them to move their centre from the chest into the head.

- Tell them their bodies are still full of energy, but the energy is now focused in the head. All their thought, feelings, movements and impulses come from that place.

- Ask them to imagine a path going up through their feet, up their legs, into the pelvis, into the torso, the chest, the neck and up into the head.

- Ask them to focus on the tips of their fingers and make a path through the hands, wrists, lower arm, elbow, upper arm, shoulder, into the neck and into the head centre.

- Now ask them to feel that energy in their head. It is the power for their whole body. Ask them to try moving an arm from that place. Tell them that if they lose the connection, just use the imagination to connect up again. You will notice that several people move quite differently when they have placed the centre in the head.

- Tell people they are going to open their eyes in a moment, and that they need to remember that their eyes and voices are connecting to that centre too, and that head energy will be streaming from their eyes. Now get them to open their eyes and look around.

- Ask them to move their bodies from that head centre and try moving around the room. Ask them to notice how it makes them feel. Suggest they try to use one of their lines. You will notice that for many of them the text will sound very different.

- Now ask them to close their eyes. The body is full of energy, but now you ask them to move the centre down into the pelvis (what Chekhov calls the 'Will centre').

- Ask them to connect their whole body to this centre, as they have already done with the heart and head. Take your time. Get them to move from that place. You will notice particularly that they will walk with a different intention, usually strongly, and more grounded and forceful. Ask them to walk around the room and pick up a chair, sit down, and so on, all operating from that centre. Ask them to try a line or two and shake hands with people, sharing their lines.

- Ask them to close their eyes and have a thorough shake-out.

- *Flyback.* Not everyone may get this exercise at once, but those that do will notice that they felt very differently with every centre, that their rhythm changed, as well as the way they spoke their lines and how they felt when they said them. The heart centre allows us to feel open and giving and, often, vulnerable; the head centre makes some feel tense, focused and not in touch with the body; the will centre (in the pelvis) makes us feel strong and focused and determined. You will, of course, get variations on these qualities (and that's fine), but there will probably be some consensus.

- Now ask them about where their *character's* centre might be. It doesn't matter at this stage if you don't agree. Ask them to write it down in their journal/notebook. We might say, for example, that Olivia's centre is the heart; Viola's is the will and that Malvolio's is the head. Ask them how the character would change for them if they had a different centre.

Working with Image Centres

This process of looking at centres will give the actors a short cut to an essence of the character without too much initial analysis. This time, instead of placing a ball of energy or a sun where the character's centre might be, the actor has to come up with an *image* to place in the body, and this image is the inspiration for the character herself. Take the example of Juliet in *Romeo and Juliet*, whose centre might be a lighted candle in her heart centre. All her impulses, movements, sensations, thoughts and feelings would come from that lighted candle in her heart centre. This would make for a light, fiery but delicate Juliet.

Let's try exploring some *images* for a character's centre. This is quite a jump on, but it is an exercise that has an immediate impact and, if you are doing a production with young actors, you have to explore some tools quickly. *Working with Image Centres* was something I returned to a few times through rehearsal.

- Ask them to imagine that they're using the will centre and that they have a large block of ice there. Ask the group to imagine that their whole body is connected to this block of ice in their pelvis.

- Ask them to start moving around, being really free with the body, connecting the body to this centre: *always* connected. For instance, with this cold ice in my belly I might feel ruthless, determined and stiff. (That's just me: other people might feel differently.) Now ask them to make a sound and remind them that this sound too is coming from this block of ice in their pelvis. While still moving around, ask them to start speaking their lines. *Please Note*: It doesn't matter at this point whether what the centre gives them is appropriate for the particular lines: they are just exploring. If people are not opening and connecting fully, ask them to 'turn it up'.

- Now ask them to calm down the physical movement and feel that centre strongly *inside*. Ask them to keep the feeling of the centre strongly in the *voice* as they speak their lines. Get them to say their lines a couple of times.

- If you do feel they have let the centre go, get them to put back the physical movement, speak their lines, then ask them to take out the physical movement again.

- Get them to close their eyes, then shake it out thoroughly.

- *Flyback*. See what they say. Many will be surprised at how they spoke the text and how it made them feel.

- Ask them to focus now on the head centre; all their thoughts, feelings and impulses are now coming from there. Take a bit of time to 'connect up'. This time ask them to take the image of a *bubble*. They have a head centre which is a *bubble*.

- Follow the same procedure as before, ending with getting them to use their text with movement, then finally taking out the big physical movement. You will notice a completely different feel, rhythm and character emerging from the text.

- Shake out. Finally, try the image of a *beast in a cage* in the heart centre. Follow the same procedure as before.

- Have a really good shake-out.

- *Flyback.* Ask the group how it felt to work with these images. Some people will say they never expected to speak the lines that way. Point out to the young actors that they can always find a different image for their character centre, which will produce different results. They can find the character powered by these image centres. Some will work; some might not. Tell them if they want to use this technique, it will take practice.

Teaching Tip: The only rule they *have* to follow is to be as faithful and open to the image as they can be. The image may not give them what they need but that does not mean that the technique doesn't work. They can always change the image or the place they put it to make a profound impact, both on how the character feels and on the way they speak.

Finding an Image Centre for Your Character

On this third day of *Twelfth Night*, having done some of the preparatory centre exercises, I asked the actors to take this one step further. They were going to find a centre for the character they were going to play. The whole of this exercise took 25 minutes. I explained the exercise straight through at the start so that I did not have to break the flow with too many details.

I gave them about 10 minutes for the initial exploration to find an 'Image Centre' for their character and was on hand to help. If they weren't sure when they suggested an image, I might ask them why they picked it and see if it matched up with a plausible vision of the character. I might suggest an alternative.

I suggested they tried using one of the three centres we had explored in the body already: heart, head and pelvis. For some that was still too complicated, so I asked them to put the image in the heart centre.

Maria in *Twelfth Night*, for example, is a servant who begins by being on the side of the status quo, but who ultimately throws her hat in with Sir Toby and ends up marrying him. Let us suppose that she picks a teacup as her image and all her thoughts, feelings and impulses come from that image. She might say it is a round, serviceable thing for everyday nourishment, but perhaps the actor playing Maria sees the teacup as having very fancy patterns on it, maybe fine china. Let's say she sees this as being a centre in her head. This might give her certain feelings; feelings of being a very ordinary servant, but with notions of grace and social climbing. She seems warm, but is not as warm as she seems. This centre might give her a way of moving. Alternatively, the same actor might pick an image of a feather duster and put it at her heart centre. This might make her voice lighter, flightier, it might make her giggly, sillier and give her a completely different physical rhythm. So you see with these images we can already build up psychological complexity.

When the 10 minutes of exploration were up, I asked everyone to come to the middle of the room, generating and radiating their character's centre. As they did so, it was obvious that something unusual was going on. The actors were not the people I knew and something about them had fundamentally changed.

One by one, each person took a turn in the centre of the circle radiating their character's energy, and very slowly looking at every other character in the circle, each of whom was also radiating *their* centre towards the character in the middle. I told them to take their time and feel what was happening between certain characters. What were they picking up from this character they were looking at?

Having radiated and received with all in the circle, the character spoke a few of her lines and walked back to the outside of the circle. Then someone else went in and went through the same procedure.

The intensity of this exercise is always powerful: whilst not everyone could keep their centre going throughout, I felt that the characters, and sometimes the relationship between them, entered the room for the first time. It was an incredible exercise for the discovery of relationships.

After it was over and I had got everyone to shake out thoroughly, I asked the actors to write things down about their characters that they felt they had discovered. Once you start this experiential process, ideas will flood in. I asked them to share some with the group. Several of them carried these discoveries through to performance.

Teaching Tip: I am well aware, and this is a very important point, that simply doing a few exercises will not give the actors a full grasp of centres. As with all acting techniques, Chekhov Technique needs study and practice. But even if this has merely stimulated ideas for the character, it is of great value. For those who experience it more fully, it will give them a transformational way to generate the character.

Day Three: Afternoon

Character Journey

My goals for the afternoon: To continue with the initial exploration of character and to explore a possible journey for the character.

Gesture: Character Beginning, Middle and End

This exercise is a combination of the work we did with tableaux and *Psychological Gesture* (see Chapter Six). This is my exercise (though there is nothing new under the sun!), but it is based on Chekhov principles. It gives the actors a feeling of the journey the character might be on. When I use the word 'journey', I am talking about the individual story of the character through the narrative: most characters have them.

What was interesting when we did this for *Twelfth Night* was that it revealed character journeys which pretty much everyone stuck to. In Week Four of rehearsal, I showed the pictures I had taken of their gesture/statues in this exercise, and many of them were astonished at how true they were to the final performance.

- Tell everyone to consider their character: perhaps by using the character centre, the archetype they chose earlier, or maybe just by thinking about how the character feels at the beginning of the play: she is standing there just before she enters the play.

- Now ask them to create a gesture/statue for the character at that moment. Be clear that it is not a realistic portrayal of them. It portrays how they feel, what they want and something of their quality. For instance, let's take Sir Andrew Aguecheek, a lonely, dim young man with a title, who cannot make connection with anyone, doomed to be exploited. He is looking for something: companionship, friendship, love. His confidence is only intermittent. Our young actor reached out sadly and hopefully, out into the world.

- Look at all the gesture/statues. Get the actors to talk about them. Then ask them to create another gesture/statue for the final moments of the character in the play. (Sir Andrew ended up crushed and closed.)

- Ask them now to slowly move from one gesture to the other. Tell them each actor has just told their character's story.

- Let everyone look at each other's statues, again giving them a glimpse into all the actors' creative process.

- Now ask everyone to consider the middle of the play and find a moment where things change forever for the character; stepping out of *Twelfth Night*, it might be when Macbeth kills the King; when Romeo kills Tybalt; when Juliet decides to take the poison, etc.

- Ask them to make a gesture/statue of that moment for the character.

- Now ask them to move through the sequence: beginning, middle and end.

- Ask them to make notes in their notebooks. What did they find out?

House of Beauty

Finally, I used a Chekhov exercise called the *House of Beauty*. It is another imaginative character exercise of incomparable depth, but happens without too much talking or discussion. It allows the actor free rein to create their character and opens the door to an imaginative response to the character herself.

- Ask them to find their own space and tell them they are going to work alone.

- Tell them to work with their eyes open. Ask them to imagine they are the character right now, whatever that means to them. Maybe they will use the centre, maybe an image of what the character looks like, the archetype, or something from the last exercise we did.

- Tell them that in front of them is the character's ideal house, the house that expresses who they are, how they feel and what they want. It does not have to be a 'period' house. It is just a place that expresses the character as you understand them now. Everyone is going to do a tour of their house, moving around the rehearsal room, but working on their own.

- Ask them to imagine they are at the front door. Ask them what it is like: What colour is it? What it is made of? Are there keys? Is the door open? How big is the door? What shape is it? Ask more questions like this, often directing their focus to minor details, to help them visualise the house and front door.

- Ask them to open the door and step into the hallway. Tell them there are several doors. Check out the stairs, but we are not going up there as some people will not have an upstairs. Ask them what they can see. How big is the hall? What colour is it painted? Are there pictures on the walls? What are these pictures? Ask questions along these lines. Then you tell them they are going to walk to a door. Tell them it is the door to the kitchen.

- Ask them to open the door and step in. Ask them questions about it: How is it decorated? Is there food in the fridge or cupboards? Is there anything to sit on? Are there windows? Do you, the character, like the room? Is it one you would like to spend time in? After a few questions, ask them to have one last look round, go back into the hallway and shut the door.

- Ask them to go to another door. This is the door to the bedroom. Go through the same procedure. After a few minutes of questions ask them to come back into the hall.

- Ask them to go to another door. This time we are in the bathroom. Ask questions about the bathroom. Maybe ask if the character spends much time in here. Eventually, after a few minutes, get them to go into the hallway and shut the door.

- Ask them to stand before another door. This is their study/hobby room. How is it decorated? What does it look like? Is it large or small? After a few more questions, get them to step out into the hall.

- Now to the final door. This is the door to their secret room, where no one else is ever admitted. Maybe they have a key. Ask them to step into the room and explore everything they find there. How do they feel to be in there? Is it light or dark? Do you get the feeling you spend much time in here? How is this room decorated? What is the atmosphere like in here? And so on. Now ask them to step back into the hall and shut the door to the secret room.

- Ask them to spend a moment looking round the hallway. See if they have overlooked anything. Then they go to the house's front door and go through it, back to the outside world.

- Ask them to take a deep breath and shake out thoroughly.

- Send them off to their notebooks to write down some of the things that stuck out for them.

- *Flyback*. Ask them to share anything with the group they feel might be useful for the character. Only ask them to share information on the secret room if they want.

Teaching Tip: Spend a good deal of time in each 'room'. Don't rush.

This is a rich exercise. Explain to your cast that they will find some things that are incredibly useful and some things that are not. This is fine. Some things can be junked instantly and some may stay for a time. Some discoveries might continue through to the performance. A lot of it is going to depend not just on how well they explore the exercise but how well they know the play.

Day Four

General Atmosphere

My goals for the day: Having focused thus far on story, character and ensemble, it was time to add atmosphere.

I did several of the early atmosphere exercises (see Chapter Seven for more details) with the actors to awaken their skills. Afterwards, we started to consider what the General Atmospheres might be within the play. We put a line of tape on the studio floor. On one side of the line they were in the studio, and on the other side, they were engulfed by our chosen atmosphere.

We first tried an atmosphere of *Love*. As they stepped over the line of tape into the atmosphere, everyone made open, floating movements, bright eyes, many sighs and much excitement. We also tried a *Maze*, which caused fast frenetic movements and confusion which, whilst it did bring out something of the play, seemed more appropriate to *Hamlet*. We then tried *Longing*, which isolated the characters and made their bodies and eyes reach forwards. We realised that Longing caused a very personal response, which made the characters rather ruthless because they all longed for different things. It had a cruelty and sadness in it, which was very much in the story. It caused them to make a lot of floating-type movements, which again brought us back to the sea and drowning. In the end this feeling helped us create our opening and closing pieces for the production, and supplied the quality of movement for many of our scene changes.

We also explored atmospheres for particular environments in the play using the same method. We tried colour atmospheres for Orsino's house: brown and dark blue. The dark blue seemed most appropriate because, although it was sad, it was also rich and indulgent. For Olivia's house, a place almost compelled into mourning, there was a sense of Miss Haversham's house in *Great Expectations*, where the audience is simply waiting for the musty curtains to be pulled down! We tried a heavy treacle-like atmosphere and afterwards one of suffocating stale air. The latter proved the most successful. The tension between this enforced atmosphere and the characters' attempts to break free of it made a strong dynamic for the early scenes in Olivia's house.

I cannot stress enough how radical and exciting working with atmosphere can be for a production. Plays you know well can be transformed into new work and you can find a sense of truth within them that had never revealed itself before. However, a word of caution: there cannot be two equally strong General Atmospheres going on at once in a scene or it can get confusing. So, for instance, in Act One, Scene One of *Twelfth Night*, I encouraged the actors to go for the atmosphere of dark blue, rather than of Longing. The latter atmosphere would have made the scene much too tortured and was not something neither I nor the actors felt was right for the opening. At the very least, this element of the work encourages everyone to consider the play from a feeling perspective.

Day Five

Structure and Polarities

My goals for the day: In addition to all our regular training, I wanted to make some firmer decisions about one or two areas of our script, however tentative they might be, as well as reminding people about the rules of our work. There was a lot more talk on this day than others, though we still did our basic training work on voice, body and imagination in the morning. We also did a lot of revision on character centres, atmosphere and gesture. I told them that some of this work would continue throughout the rehearsal period.

The Feeling of the Whole

I wanted to go back to the score of our text, which we had explored on the second day when we worked on the story, and make it more specific. I wanted us to decide on our beginning, middle and end, as that would affect our performance. From our earlier explorations, we had a beginning full of yearning, loneliness and grief, and a tentative ending filled with a kind of confused, frenetic happiness.

Our decision was:

> *The Beginning*: This went from the opening right up to the end of the scene in Olivia's house, where the oppressive

atmosphere of yearning and loss starts to dissipate as Olivia falls in love with Cesario (Act One, Scene Five). Even though there was humour in this early section, it had to contend with this darker, heavier atmosphere. At this point, nearly all the main characters have been introduced.

The Middle: From Viola's realisation that she is loved by Olivia to the scene with Malvolio humiliated in the prison (Act Four, Scene Two), this section marks how the anarchy begins to break forth and, in the prison scene, reaches its height of cruelty.

The End: From the scene in which Sebastian and Olivia decide to marry to the end of the play, in which all the characters are involved in an unravelling, the truth is revealed and love, for some at least, is triumphant.

What difference would it have made if we had chosen another structure? Actually, quite a lot. Imagine a novel you have read, and in your mind change where the chapters end; or imagine the *Mona Lisa* as if you could only see her mouth. The Feeling of Form and the Feeling of the Whole are crucial to making a play, and so it is really important that everyone knows this form and agrees with it. It could be changed, of course, as rehearsals progress, but it gave us a vessel into which all our creativity could be poured.

This structure did not only come from the morning's discussion, but from much of the practical experiential work we had done on story, character, character journey and atmosphere. As we moved forward the young actors started to realise the value of the work done earlier in the week.

Who or What is the 'Spine' of Our Play?

Continuing with the Feeling of the Whole, Chekhov defines a play's *spine* as its 'guiding idea'. Again, the group's answer to this question was enhanced by the practical exploration we had done earlier. We had decided that the play said something about love and yearning, but it was not a ringing endorsement of romantic love. It did not end happily for everyone. I asked them what they felt the play was saying, 'the guiding idea', and how we wanted the audience to feel at the end. We ultimately settled on 'Whatever happens, you have to follow your heart.' By finding this 'guiding idea', we all found a sense of where we might be going.

Does any character in *Twelfth Night* follow this 'guiding idea' through the play? Is there a character who could be seen as the *spine*? If we were doing *Macbeth*, *Hamlet*, *King Lear* or *Romeo and Juliet* for instance, this would be easy because there are core protagonists. In *Twelfth Night*, we could perhaps say it was Viola or Olivia, but they have long stretches offstage, and no one is really the core. The theme of 'following your heart' was for everyone. In the end it was Feste who opened and closed the production, acting as a commentator on the 'follies' of those who *do* 'follow their heart'.

If you feel you want to examine these ideas on composition in greater depth, I would refer you again to the chapter on composition in Michael Chekhov's *To the Actor*.

Polarities and Character Polarities

Polarities are opposites, conflicting energies (Hot and Cold, Grief and Joy, Love and Hate), which exist within a play and within the characters. We have touched on polarities already in Chapter Twelve. I would like to refer to an exercise we did which can be very useful. It works *only* if everyone has a character centre (or at least a way of 'checking in' with the character) and knows the play well enough.

Here is an extract from my blogpost on the production:

> In *Twelfth Night* one of the polarities I see is *Riot and Order*. Feste represents the former and Malvolio the latter. These two characters are diametrically opposed and it is their battle, culminating in the highly ambiguous prison scene, which for me is one of the big polarities of this play. The other is *Love and Death*, not exactly opposites, but in the Elizabethan world view, they are. In the beautiful Act Two, Scene Four, Orsino and the disguised Viola speak intimately and lovingly in a conversation interrupted by the

arrival of Feste who sings the haunting song 'Come Away, Death'. Orsino's mood is transformed and he becomes violent and desperate, whilst Viola refers to her brother (supposedly dead). In that moment the two young people are forced to face the dark side of their souls.

www.maxhafler.wordpress.com

By finding and experiencing these polarities within the play, the group will start to understand how the characters think, feel and act.

Polarities: An Exercise

They might need a couple of attempts at this. Do not worry. If you have time, it might also be a useful exercise to try again later in rehearsal when they are more familiar with the play.

- Tell them you are going to consider a polarity, or set of opposites, which is important in the play. Ask them to suggest some: Love and Hate, Life and Death, Riot and Order, Fun and Solemnity. Suggest to them that the more pronounced these opposing polarities are, the more we can explore them in the play. Tell them it will help us find out what the play is *about* and how the characters respond and relate to the polarities.

- Let's choose Fun and Solemnity. One wall of your studio represents Total Fun, and the opposite wall, Deep Solemnity.

- Ask your actors to use their centre, archetype, beginning gesture/statue or whatever else might help them to focus on the character. Tell them to use that to anchor the character.

- Ask them, using what they know of their characters, to stand in the studio between the two polarities in the place where they feel instinctively the character begins their journey in the play. For instance, Malvolio, Viola and Olivia would probably be very near the Solemnity wall. Malvolio might even be hugging it as something delicious and glorious. Sir Toby reaches towards the Total Fun wall but feels he is being pulled in the opposite direction.

271

- You then ask everyone, all at once, to go through the play considering what happens to their characters. How does what happens to them change where they are standing? Tell them they must move accordingly.

- Let's follow Malvolio through the play. He stays pretty attached to meanness and solemnity until he gets the forged love letter, which unleashes an abandon within him. When he appears in the yellow stockings, you might say he completely surrenders to the Fun wall. At some point in the story, when he is in prison, he might not be at either wall but wandering between the two. At the end of the play, he is assuredly back at the Wall of Solemnity – or perhaps he is still in the middle, completely enraged and confused.

- We noted down some of the polarities which were important for us. This process was extremely useful and reminded us of important themes for the play and for the characters.

Polarities can also help us when working with the text, as so many of Shakespeare's lines contain polarities within them. To take just two examples: 'My only love sprung from my only hate' from *Romeo and Juliet* (Act One, Scene Five); and Macbeth's 'that his virtues / Will plead like angels trumpet-tongued against / The deep damnation of his taking off' (Act One, Scene Seven). The Macbeth example is less obvious, but polarises a high-angelic Heaven with a damnable Hell. This will affect the way the actor speaks the line if he is aware of it.

Polarities for Other Plays

Let's consider some polarities for a few other plays:

A Midsummer Night's Dream: Heart/Head, Illusion/Reality, Forest/City, Love/Hate, Anarchy/Society, Comedy/Tragedy.

Macbeth: Trust/Betrayal, Truth/Deceit, Life/Death, Hope/Despair, Good/Evil, Power/Weakness.

Romeo and Juliet: Danger/Safety, Love/Hate, War/Peace, Fate/Free Will, Age/Youth, Ecstasy/Pain.

King Lear: Kindness/Cruelty, Truth/Deceit, Trust/Betrayal, Folly/Wisdom, Youth/Age, Power/Powerlessness, Wealth/Poverty.

In Conclusion

This has been an attempt to take you through some of our process when we worked on *Twelfth Night*, but also to give you suggestions for tackling any Shakespeare play. We have covered a lot of ground.

Some or all of this may be useful for your individual groups. Note that we have been mostly on our feet, that we have explored through *doing*. All being well, you will be surprised by the depth of exploration you can do this way. As one young actor said to me after a week like this, 'I feel like we have done the play already.'

Always make sure you make plenty of notes on the process and record through photos (provided you have permission), because you will need to remind the actors of their discoveries. The problem with a week like this is that you get great work and the group make real discoveries, but they can subsequently become imprisoned by the text and the expectations of 'proper' rehearsal. In the next chapter I am going to give you a short precis of how I might tackle a scene, and negotiate this jump from workshop exploration to rehearsing for the play.

Chapter Fifteen
Starting on Scenes

I am sure care's an enemy to life…
> *Twelfth Night*: Act One, Scene Three

You have finished your foundation week/weekend workshops and much exciting preparatory work has been done. Your group has often surprised you with their engagement, their response to the play and each other. All is going well.

Then you come to the first week of rehearsals and the shutters come down. Suddenly it is as if everyone has been put into straitjackets. They are stumbling over the text and have not done much preparation for the scene. Instead of being imaginative, they are hamstrung. Some of them are waiting for you to tell them what to do.

This happens as much in professional situations as it does with young actors in youth theatres, but for different reasons. For our young people, they are probably daunted by the task and slightly bewildered; perhaps questioning why their foundation week could have been such fun and that now it feels like they are back in a classroom. In order to help deal with this insecurity, you need to have a firm schedule for the rehearsal through the whole week, and everyone must be clear when they are required. In the first rehearsal you need to focus on the speaking characters. My rule is, if they speak, even if it is only, 'I will, my lord,' they have to be there.

Remind and reassure them about the discoveries of the foundation week. What did they find out about the character? Tell them they need to approach the scenes in the same spirit and develop their discoveries. You need to be constantly reminding them. Refer back to various moments of *specific* revelation: 'Do you remember when you discovered Sir Andrew was really lonely?'

Your Goals for the First Rehearsal of a Scene

Given the average rehearsal time available, it will vary on your situation, at best you will only have four rehearsals on any given scene: which is quite a daunting thought for a start! The less experienced you are as a director, the more you will want to have everything settled after the first rehearsal. Resist that urge because, aside from everything else, it is impossible. Don't worry. Any run-through of the scene will not be brilliant. If you get a few good moments it will be positive; something to build on.

I do not focus too much on diction to begin with, or whether they drop the ends of their sentences (usually a breath problem). It is very tempting with Shakespeare to zone in on this type of issue but it will make the whole rehearsal over-academic at a time when you want to remind them of the fun, creative aspects of the foundation week. Don't neglect the voice and language aspects but leave it until next time.

Whenever I ask the actors a question, I always keep them on task and get them to give direct and straightforward answers. At the start, they will tend to intellectualise and make long, complicated statements: these statements are impossible to act. Try to ask questions like, 'What is the character *doing?*' '*How* do you think he is doing it?' or 'How did you *feel* when Sir Toby said that to you?' Such questions encourage a focused response and guide them to look at the text in an expansive way.

In any first rehearsal, I aim for these goals. They are not always achievable:

1. To let them experience radiating/receiving with their partners and the text.

2. To know the story of the scene.

3. To have some understanding of what they are saying and broadly how the characters behave and act, both individually and with each other.

4. To instil in the actors the most important aspect of the scene. Depending on the scene, this might be developing the character action/relationship, the atmosphere, the plot or the imagery.

5. To give the actors a sense, by the end of the rehearsal, of where they need to go next.

Blocking

Do not feel you have to do anything other than the most rudimentary blocking (simply where they come in and where they go out) in this first rehearsal. If you get the actors to be creative, the scene will eventually block itself. Indeed, if you try to block it in detail immediately, the verb 'block' will do just what it says: it will block creativity for everyone. If you are working with a less-experienced group, your time is extremely limited or you are working on a scene which has a lot of people in it, you may have to block more, but otherwise just give their entrances and exits. If something works well, then by all means get your stage manager to record it for the time being, but do not make blocking the goal of this first rehearsal.

First Rehearsal

You probably have about 45 minutes to an hour on each scene. As this is the first rehearsal, I do not expect the actors to be off the book, though I hope they have a familiarity with the scene. If it is possible, they should have already gone through the scene with the 'ally' for meaning. (See above, page 212.)

I would almost never start with a bare read-through of the scene. With young actors, and with Shakespeare, even a read-through of a scene may simply drain everyone's energy. However, if you read the scene very slowly standing up, and add radiating and receiving, then reading the scene through aloud can be helpful, as you are not only getting used to the words but getting something of a sense of what is going on between the characters. The actors must do this standing up. If they are seated, they close the body off (and reading from the text is already pushing them in that direction). Remember the process of 'ghosting' which we introduced in Chapter Nine? That can be especially useful in the first rehearsal.

Have a look at the rest of Chapter Nine (Working on Short Scenes) for a whole raft of suggestions on where to start with your actors. Each scene will be a bit different, depending on the type of scene it is, the performers and how much they have prepared. Below is an example of how I started rehearsals on a particular scene in *Twelfth Night*:

Twelfth Night: *Act One, Scene Three*

This scene concerns Sir Toby Belch, the penniless, drunken knight, Olivia's uncle, who lives in her house; Maria, Olivia's housekeeper, who is trying to keep order; and Sir Andrew Aguecheek, the silly, rich, lonely friend who has been encouraged by Sir Toby to woo Olivia. I suggest you read this scene and have it in front of you.

This is the first scene in which the comic characters appear (so for these three actors it was their first scene rehearsal). It takes place in a house of mourning, which is Olivia's house, and Sir Toby is bridling against the fact that they have to be quiet and solemn there. Sir Andrew arrives to tell him he is leaving but Sir Toby persuades him to stay.

After a short physical and vocal warm-up, I spent some time on archetypes for this scene to get the actors to play strongly and find that broad comic energy. I would not necessarily choose archetypes as a first tool to use for *every* scene, but for them it was paramount as a means of comic release. Once the actors became confident, we could start to tone it down a bit. It also challenged their post-foundation-week blues!

I asked them to think what archetype each character might be, and got them to explore it with a couple of lines: Sir Toby: 'The Show-Off', Sir Andrew: 'The Hanger-On', and Maria: 'The Schoolmistress'. Archetypes are great in that they do get people to play with energy straight away. It was vital to assert from the start that a strong relationship with the audience needed to be established. I asked them to bow to the audience and introduce themselves saying, for example, 'My name is Sir Toby Belch and I am a show-off!' Then I asked them to add their line.

I then asked them to read the scene standing up, leaving long pauses between lines and being aware of what their scene partners were giving them. I asked them what they felt from the other actors in the scene, especially in the moments of silence between lines. This avoided making it a 'read-through': it encouraged them to focus on the energy of the other actors/characters and experience what they might find out about them. I asked them how the characters might *feel*. Sir Toby is miserable, harassed by Maria and the gloomy atmosphere, and is upset to discover Sir Andrew may leave town, but is then cheered up when Sir Andrew says he will stay. *How* Sir Toby gets him to stay would be something I would address next time.

I also asked them about atmosphere and we tried a couple out, using a few lines of the scene. It was a sombre, stifling atmosphere, where no one can have fun. An actor said it was 'suffocating'. This was useful, but did not really take root until, at a later rehearsal, we used mournful introductory music for the scene, which really helped the actors.

I asked them to suggest a title for the scene: 'Clowns in the Funeral Home' or 'Meet the Mischief-Makers' were two very good suggestions. I remarked how those two titles would shift the emphasis as to how they might play the scene. I got them to run the scene with one of the titles we had come up with, 'Meet the Mischief-Makers', using the script, to get a feel of what was going on. I had to work to keep them on task with this as they kept forgetting the title as they performed, but it had some success, particularly towards the end of the scene. We got a few good moments and a useful sense of the scene and characters.

Then I gave them some homework. I told them the next time we came to this scene (in addition to them knowing the lines) we would want to look at what the characters were *doing* in the scene. (Again, nothing too complicated was allowed!) Maria might be *protecting* her job and her mistress. Sir Andrew, though he may have come to say goodbye, might be trying to hang on to someone, anyone, who will stop him being lonely; he might be *reaching*. Sir Toby might be *pushing behind* the gloomy atmosphere which is suffocating him. I would also ask them to review the character journeys they created from their gesture-statues in the foundation week.

At the end of this rehearsal I asked if they could share something they found out about the scene and their characters that they did not know before, and how they felt about what we had done. I told them that next time, having got something of a *feel* for the scene, we would focus more on the story of it. I also told them that everything would not slot into place straight away, that we were making something together which would develop and grow; this was only the beginning.

Chapter Sixteen
Ensemble Work with Shakespeare

We hear the wind tearing round the turrets. It is the breath of the actors. They make the wind. They act as orchestra, both physically and psychically.
Steven Berkoff, *I Am Hamlet*

Everything that matters in the theatre is a collective act.
Peter Brook, *Platform Papers*

What is Ensemble?

There is nothing like the power of the group onstage, invoking a feeling or performing a movement together, magnifying or creating a visual image or atmosphere. It creates a holistic experience for audience and performer. Ensemble, young actors and Shakespeare are an exciting combination. In what follows I am going to illustrate a few ways I have used ensemble in some of the productions I have done.

Working in ensemble, especially with young people, is my desired mode of travel. There are so many definitions of what 'ensemble' means, but for me it is principally two things. Ensemble exists as an *ethos* and a *style*.

As an *ethos*, I am absolutely committed to the idea that we are creating our production *together* and the group's influence is going to change my view of the play, often in very profound ways. However, especially with young people, creating a Shakespeare production still requires the director to take a fairly strong role. I have talked a lot about this approach already.

Ensemble *style*, which is really what this chapter is about, can enhance your youth theatre production and empower the performance of your young people. It involves having actors onstage for much of the time, and creating dynamics, environments or atmospheres for the main characters to work in. Other than the play itself, the performers are the most valuable resource we have. We need to use them, not waste them in the dressing room! Besides, for many young people, having them leave the space means they also have to re-enter with commitment. This is often difficult for those with limited performance experience. The more they are involved in the performance, the more committed they will be to the production. For instance, when I explained to the young actors playing the fairies in *A Midsummer Night's Dream* that they were going to be a kind of strange alien 'girl gang' who hung out in the forest – that we needed to find a whole way of being for them that was different to human characters; that they would create 'fairy-time' with sound and magical effects – they were completely committed.

For me, the art of ensemble is shown no more powerfully than in the classical orchestra, where the individual players unite, with all their artistry and skill, to produce a wonderful performance without denying the individual sounds of their instruments (or the role of the conductor!). At different times, different players are leading it: those who are 'in major' (a term I first heard from the famous teacher Philippe Gaulier) are being served and supported by the rest.

What ensemble requires is a realisation from everyone that you are only as powerful as the group. When audience and actors experience this group work in operation, it can be spectacularly powerful.

Enhancing Your Production Artistically with Ensemble Work

Here are some creative possibilities to this kind of ensemble work:

- Ensemble allows you to create an environment and atmosphere in which the main players can perform.

- It allows you to create magical and powerful effects.

- By using the ensemble you can *illustrate* some of the longer narrative speeches as they are spoken, assisting both the actor and the audience to understand what is going on. For me this is usually preferable to editing them to a few lines.

- Ensemble work amplifies the emotional content of the main characters. For instance, in the scene discussed in Example 3 below, Titania and Oberon each had a tribe of supporters. These supporters mirrored and magnified the Fairy King and Queen's rage in a way that lit up the space and supported the speaking actors. This in turn created an energy which enabled the main actors to play more fully.

Empowering Young Actors Through Ensemble

Below are a few immediate advantages of ensemble work for young people.

- Ensemble gives you the opportunity to use a chorus of actors, not necessarily included within the original text, to express the main character's thoughts or feelings. An example might be that someone enacts Hamlet whilst a chorus speaks his soliloquy. This kind of idea might take some pressure off an inexperienced actor, thereby making the role feasible for them to perform, and also give the others opportunities.

- An ensemble production also allows you, with impunity, to cast one actor in a number of roles. (Shakespeare's theatre must have encompassed this too.) Whilst some young actors are happy and fulfilled in one small role, many are not, and the opportunity to be versatile and more involved is a great challenge. It means you can be very flexible in casting, giving each person the right level of opportunity.

- Creating work with the ensemble can enable and include young actors who might want to perform but are uneasy with the text. This is of huge value to a mixed-ability group.

This gives you just a flavour of what you can do. I want to cite now a few further examples from my own work. These are ways I chose to use ensemble to illuminate the text, the production, and to engage the cast. Sometimes I have included the speech I am talking about, but if it is a whole scene, I have left it to you to take it down from your shelf or look online.

Examples of Ensemble

Example 1: Making the Boat: creating magic, power and atmosphere (Macbeth: *Act One, Scene Three*)

FIRST WITCH. A sailor's wife had chestnuts in her lap
    And munched, and munched, and munched.
    'Give me,' quoth I.
    'Aroint thee, witch,' the rump-fed ronyon cries.
    Her husband's to Aleppo gone, Master o'th' Tiger:
    But in a sieve I'll thither sail,
    And like a rat without a tail,
    I'll do, I'll do, and I'll do.

SECOND WITCH. I'll give thee a wind.

FIRST WITCH. Th'art kind.

THIRD WITCH. And I another.

FIRST WITCH. I myself have all the other,
    And the very ports they blow,
    All the quarters that they know
    I'th' shipman's card.
    I will drain him dry as hay:
    Sleep shall neither night nor day
    Hang upon his penthouse lid:

He shall live a man forbid.
Weary sev'nights nine times nine
Shall he dwindle, peak, and pine:
Though his bark cannot be lost,
Yet it shall be tempest-tossed.
Look what I have.

SECOND WITCH. Show me, show me.

FIRST WITCH. Here I have a pilot's thumb,
Wrecked as homeward he did come.

As the First Witch tells the story, she raises one of the corpses that are strewn around the space from the previous battle, like a puppet. The corpse moves her lips but the First Witch speaks. As the Witch speaks of the ship, she conjures it, and the corpses take their places on the phantom, imaginary ship: rowing, drumming, standing on the rigging and steering. The sea gets rougher and the sailors sway violently. The Captain starts to be sick, and then when the Witch has finished speaking at the end of this section, she extends her arms and the corpses fall to the floor. The ship has vanished.

This piece of ensemble work emphasises and amplifies the evil power of the Witches, pulling the audience into another reality, in this case that of the storm-tossed sailing ship. By utilising the ensemble, we made that power manifest for the audience.

Example 2: Macbeth's Hall: expanding the play, creating a world
(Macbeth: *Act One, Scene Seven*)

Ensemble work gives a fantastic opportunity to expand the play and really create a world. In Act One, Scene Seven of my youth theatre production of *Macbeth* (which begins, 'If it were done when 'tis done'), Macbeth leaves the banqueting hall to consider the morality of King Duncan's assassination. In the production, the King and his soldiers sat in a long line eating in slow motion behind the main actors, whilst Macbeth confronted the audience with his dilemma. The victims were devouring their feast. When Lady Macbeth came to chide her husband, the eaters froze, creating a ghoulish tableau behind them. When the scene finished and the Macbeths reunited round the murder of the King, drumming and raucous singing began. The Porter began to dance in a devil mask and everyone began drunkenly singing a fiendish but simple jig as they went to sleep in various parts of the stage.

This achieved so much. It created atmosphere, enhanced the themes, and gave a feeling that the whole world of this play was about to take a step into hell. It included the entire group, and gave the actor playing the Porter a moment which both mirrored the later speech about Hell's Gate and developed her role.

Example 3: Illuminating the Story: telling the story, creating magic and helping the speaking actor (A Midsummer Night's Dream: Act Two, Scene One)

> TITANIA. These are the forgeries of jealousy;
>   And never, since the middle summer's spring,
>   Met we on hill, in dale, forest or mead,
>   By pavèd fountain or by rushy brook,
>   Or in the beachèd margent of the sea
>   To dance our ringlets to the whistling wind,
>   But with thy brawls thou hast disturbed our sport.
>   Therefore the winds, piping to us in vain,
>   As in revenge have sucked up from the sea
>   Contagious fogs, which, falling in the land,
>   Have every pelting river made so proud
>   That they have overborne their continents.
>   The ox hath therefore stretched his yoke in vain,
>   The ploughman lost his sweat, and the green corn
>   Hath rotted ere his youth attained a beard.
>   The fold stands empty in the drownèd field,
>   And crows are fatted with the murrion flock.
>   The nine men's morris is filled up with mud,
>   And the quaint mazes in the wanton green,
>   For lack of tread, are undistinguishable.
>   The human mortals want their winter here;
>   No night is now with hymn or carol blest.
>   Therefore the moon, the governess of floods,

Pale in her anger, washes all the air
That rheumatic diseases do abound.
And thorough this distemperature, we see
The seasons alter: hoary-headed frosts
Far in the fresh lap of the crimson rose,
And on old Hiems' thin and icy crown
An odorous chaplet of sweet summer buds
Is, as in mockery, set. The spring, the summer,
The childing autumn, angry winter, change
Their wonted liveries; and the mazèd world,
By their increase, now knows not which is which.
And this same progeny of evils comes
From our debate, from our dissension:
We are their parents and original.

OBERON. Do you amend it then; it lies in you.
Why should Titania cross her Oberon?
I do but beg a little changeling boy
To be my henchman.

TITANIA.   Set your heart at rest.
The fairy land buys not the child of me.
His mother was a votaress of my order;
And in the spicèd Indian air by night,
Full often hath she gossiped by my side,
And sat with me on Neptune's yellow sands
Marking th'embarkèd traders on the flood,
When we have laugh'd to see the sails conceive
And grow big-bellied with the wanton wind,
Which she with pretty and with swimming gait
Following (her womb then rich with my young squire)
Would imitate, and sail upon the land
To fetch me trifles and return again
As from a voyage, rich with merchandise.
But she, being mortal, of that boy did die,
And for her sake do I rear up her boy;
And for her sake, I will not part with him.

This is part of the argument between the King and Queen of the Fairies in *A Midsummer Night's Dream*. It is mainly Titania who speaks, and the speech is a real tour de force. It is very daunting and hard to maintain the audience's attention, whatever your level of experience. This ensemble work took us into a magical world (not unlike the Witches earlier) where the fairies have power to create and change the realities we, the audience, see. The ensemble changed our perspective.

As Titania spoke of the winds, the lighting began to fade and the fairies en masse started to blow and create something like those blowing cherubs you might see on an old-fashioned map; when 'contagious fogs' were mentioned, the wind was changed to a hiss. Puck appeared carrying the globe on his back like Atlas, and knelt before the audience, as Titania and Oberon looked on.

When she spoke of 'the moon, the governess of floods', all the fairies had small torches and started to move gently around the space as if they were stars. It was as if they and the audience were looking down at the earth. When the argument resumed, the lights returned to normal, but only for a moment: for when Titania described her servant-friend, the mother of the changeling child, the mother appeared dancing and someone played a flute.

The effect of this enhanced the fairies' powers and clarified the effects of their dissension, thereby making it more accessible for everyone to understand. It also retained the audience's attention, whilst not detracting from Titania's speech, because the ensemble work was directly linked to the text. It also supported the actor delivering the text, helping her deal with its operatic nature and the narrative. Not a line of this famous speech needed to be cut.

Example 4: 'Come Away, Death': enhancing the theme, creating the image (Twelfth Night: *Act Two, Scene Four*)

In this beautiful scene from *Twelfth Night*, Viola/Cesario and Duke Orsino begin with an intimate conversation. When Feste arrives to sing the song 'Come Away, Death', which has at its core the struggle between Love (or Life) and Death, their conversation is cut short. When the song is finished and Feste dispatched, it is clear the conversation cannot go on as before. Orsino and Viola/Cesario become more intense; Orsino becomes enraged that Olivia will not accept his offer of marriage and Viola remembers her brother who she believes is dead (though she refers to a 'sister'). It was at this point in our production that Sebastian, her brother, appeared for the first time onstage, as if in her imagination (his first scene with Antonio, having been transposed so it followed this one).

The song is pivotal to the scene. Normally when I've seen this play we hear the mournful song and Viola looks soulfully at Orsino. In reality, though, what the song is saying is that death is round the corner. It is not soothing; it has a movement and an underlying impatience and anger. It is essential to see it this way, otherwise the scene just droops.

Our song was mournful, and our Feste had a beautiful voice. I felt we needed a hard, suffering image to go with this to create a polarity, the reality of death and decay. I took in a copy of *The Blind Leading the Blind*, a painting by Hieronymus Bosch, and asked the group to use this as inspiration to create a funeral procession, across the stage. A Death figure led this procession, holding a skull. I asked them to find a way to move so only their legs moved while their upper bodies remained rigid, so that the tableau, though moving, had the feel of a static painting. Using this piece of movement stopped the audience relaxing into the song, and highlighted the stark reality of it. As this procession passed over the stage, Orsino and Viola/Cesario watched it, using it to contemplate the fleetingness of life and, in Viola's case, the misery of her unrequited love and the loss of her brother. It was powerful and gave the second half of the scene an emotional impact it may not otherwise have had.

Example 5: Creating the Library (*Marlowe's* Doctor Faustus: *Act One, Scene One*)

I am citing this 1992 production in which I played Faustus (Commonweal Theatre Company at the Lyric Hammersmith, directed by Tony Hegarty) because it shows another use of ensemble. Even though it is not a Shakespeare play, it is from the same period and it illustrates how exciting ensemble work can be if you are daring with the possibilities.

In the opening scene of this play, we follow Faustus into the bowels of his library, seeking out wisdom, before he is tempted to sell his soul to the Devil for supreme knowledge. Each time Faustus consulted a learned book, the other actors one-by-one created first the authors in gesture/statues, and then opened their arms to become their books so Faustus could read them. This gave the scene an arcane and sinister feel, created a library, and made it very clear to the audience what kind of book Faustus was exploring: Galen the doctor, St Jerome, Aristotle, Justinian the lawmaker. The actors helped to create atmosphere, environment and props all at once, as well as usefully illuminating the text.

Ensemble Scene Changes

Scene changes are not just there to move furniture! In Shakespeare's plays there are a lot of different scenes, so keep the scene change simple if you are less experienced. Shakespeare often handles these changes of location through the arrival of a new group of characters and verbal description, so, for example, as one group of Romans is leaving, a group of Egyptians are coming on from the other side. It can be as fast as a cut in cinema!

However, ensemble scene changes can be exciting and really enhance a production. See them as an opportunity rather than a nuisance. They should always be done by the actors. Scene changes by stage managers in black stage gear always makes the audience relax and 'zone out'. Blackouts can also produce a similarly negative effect. Shakespeare did not write for blackouts as his plays were mostly presented in daylight.

A good scene change can be a bridge from one scene to the next, a way to change the atmosphere. They can also highlight the storytelling. In one of the productions I did of *A Midsummer Night's Dream*, I remember a rather beautiful moment where the very young actors playing Lysander and Hermia, who have not been seen for some time, appeared during the scene change with their suitcase and moved off, hand in hand, like fairytale characters towards the forest, as trees were lowered from the ceiling and we moved into the scene with Puck and the Fairy. This enhanced the narrative at the same time as reminding the audience of the journey of these two characters.

The scene change can also keep the audience connected to the themes. In *Twelfth Night* we came up with an image of drowning. In our opening, the whole group, bathed in blue light, *floated* onto the stage and, at a given moment, reached up desperately and gasped for air then went back into *floating*. This opening movement piece was repeated more briefly at the end. By returning to this drowning motif we emphasised the transitory nature of love and life as expounded in 'Come Away, Death', and indeed the whole play. Only Feste, immune, looked on. We continued this *floating* quality through many of the scene changes.

Some Practical Considerations

- Ensemble work grows like an energy in the group and helps them to tackle the emotional and linguistic issues of the play. It does, however, require more availability for rehearsals, so that can be challenging to organise.

- Whilst you do need to train people up in ensemble work, something simple can often work best. Ensemble work does not have to be complicated, but it needs to be full of feeling and commitment. Even some actors walking slowly across the space in a group with a certain quality can create an atmosphere.

- To my mind, the more you can keep the young actors on the stage, the better. One of the biggest problems for young actors is lack of energy when they return to the stage after they have been off for a few scenes. Ensemble keeps the less-experienced actor committed and prevents them from 'hanging out' in the dressing room. However, you have to be cautious and not push their limits too far or their energy in performance will be unfocused. There is almost nothing worse for an audience than to be drawn to an ensemble member 'zoning out' onstage whilst those around him are still engaged.

- One way to help their focus is to tell them they must always know onstage *what* they are doing and *how* they are doing it. They have to be active all the time. If they become unclear as to what they are doing, they will lose focus. What unifies the group might be a quality of movement, on the other hand they might be archetypes, ghosts, spirits or drunken lords. As suggested earlier, they may even speak the 'thoughts' of the principal character. They may be a chorus.

- Something to understand is when you need to use ensemble work and when you don't. Sometimes this is down to the level of ability in your group; sometimes it is important to think about the power of having one or two people onstage without the ensemble.

- If you are using ensemble work, take as much care of it as the text. It has to be intrinsic to the scene (even if it is providing a counterpoint) and support the speaking actors or the trajectory of the play itself.

- It should always *support* the text rather than *distract* from it.

- When you are creating an ensemble moment, if you pull a couple of people from the group to watch and make suggestions as to how things might be improved, you will find that the group will get more and more involved in the process – and the creative direction can be owned not just by you but by the whole group.

We have used ensemble techniques in many of our exercises up to now: archetypes, tableaux, gesture and General Atmosphere. An incredibly useful book for ensemble exercises is Dymphna Callery's *Through the Body: A Practical Guide to Physical Theatre*. I also suggest you have a look at *I Am Hamlet* by Steven Berkoff to give you more ideas on how the ensemble may be used in a Shakespeare play: though Berkoff's level of total ensemble involvement in the production, as he describes it, might be challenging for a group of relatively inexperienced youth theatre actors. However, there are many elements within his book that you might use.

If you really embrace the possibilities of using your group's potential in this way, you will involve your whole group, clarify the language, the story – and make something really magical.

Chapter Seventeen
Sustaining Performance

Gentles, perchance you wonder at this show;
But wonder on, till truth makes all things plain.
A Midsummer Night's Dream:
Act Five, Scene One

The chances are your group will not be giving more than five or, at the most, six performances. Nonetheless, there is a challenge you need to consider and that is the consistency of their performance.

All actors vary from performance to performance, but young actors can be very erratic indeed and make you wonder why you bothered with all that rehearsal when you see someone who was previously good now acting without energy or focus. This is not, for me, a question of them giving *exactly* the same performance every night. It will change and grow as they get more confident. What's essential is that they remain fully engaged.

Having said that, once performances begin, young actors are very prone to being 'advised' by those not in the production, and may change things quite radically without discussion. This is not just a youth theatre phenomenon. Sadly, I have been involved in productions where professional actors acted independently of the group to radically change their performance and then called it 'development', ruining the feeling of the whole aimed for in rehearsal.

Always warn your group about this. Remind them that the production is not about the solo performer but about everyone. Making radical changes can upset a production. Tell them that if they are unhappy about something fundamental, they need to discuss it with you.

Technique is what makes for some level of consistency, though that alone does not always create an authentic performance. In fact, it may actually stifle young people if they are pushed too far in a technical direction because then they will become overly concerned with 'doing it right'. It is a fine balance.

If you are working with a less-experienced group, they may need stronger performance parameters; by which I simply mean that they may need more help. You may need to block them and go through the text more methodically. That approach will not be as creative or enjoyable for you or for them. Try and encourage them to make their own decisions. One of my favourite responses is, 'Well, what do *you* feel/think?' when they ask me a question on blocking or what something might mean.

The Line-run

Towards the end of the rehearsal period, I usually get the stage manager, provided they have a level of competence and authority, to organise a speed line-run of the whole play with the cast. This is useful because it gives them time to 'own' the play without you. I also insist on a speed line-run if there are a few days' break between performances (if you are performing over two weekends, for instance). Here are the rules:

- Have the seats arranged in a circle. The stage manager has a script. No one else is allowed one. The stage manager says they are going to start from the beginning and go as fast as possible through the text without losing the clarity of the words (there needs to be leeway with this but it is an aim!). If there are songs don't miss them out but sing them quickly.

- Tell them they have to radiate and receive with the actors they are working with, and to be as entertaining as possible. Anyone not acting in the scene is their audience. Tell them they do not need to keep to the same emotional discoveries, they can be free, as long as the text is clear; they can have fun.

- Tell them the only time they will stop is when someone makes a text mistake. The stage manager corrects it and notes it to give to the actor at the end: the line-run goes on. On no account is anyone to leave the circle or use their phones while the line-run is happening. Take a break at the interval.

- If they can keep going at speed they should be through it in an hour or so. The problem is keeping everyone on track and going quickly. Also, if you do have someone with line issues, it will slow things down.

Where in the Play

This is especially useful if you have really committed to an ensemble production with everyone onstage much of the time. I learned this exercise when I was an actor and it has been a staple ever since. It keeps everyone alert and fresh and is usually incredibly popular.

- Tell everyone to walk around the space. At a given moment someone will start their text and everyone has to run to the position they are in when that line is spoken. This includes being offstage, getting ready to come on, wherever they are.

- The scene continues until someone else interrupts, beginning another piece of text from a completely different part of the play; everyone abandons the first scene and runs to the position they are in for the new scene. The scene goes on.

- Then someone else starts another piece from a different scene and everyone goes to their positions for that scene, acts the scene and so on.

A Last Word on Group and Personal Warm-ups

Prior to every performance, you have to insist on a warm-up, both physical and vocal. The vocal component is absolutely vital when doing Shakespeare: connecting the sound, breath, diction and emotional energy. You simply cannot miss it out. The aim is to unite the team of performers together, so make sure you do several ensemble exercises and practise any singing or any other piece of group work the whole team does in the show. Tell them this warm-up is not a matter of pleasing you, but about making sure they are ready to perform to the best of their ability. It is always good to cite sport in this regard, because most people would not run a race if they had not warmed up. Acting is the same.

The warm-up needs a focus. You need to let them know it's not only to loosen them up but also to get into the zone of the play. I would suggest you work with the General Atmosphere of the play you discovered together in your workshops, exercises and rehearsals. Another useful exercise would be *Crossing the Threshold* (page 193) to help the young actor prepare for their entrance. If you are not going to lead these warm-up sessions yourself and your group is mature enough, you might look for a warm-up leader in the cast, or let your assistant do it, if you are lucky enough to have one.

After they have done the group warm-up, you might give them some time to work on their own to warm up. Individual warm-up can calm the nerves and prepares the young actor for their performance. However, very often the young actor does not really know what to do with this time, so you might prepare people for individual warm-up by seeing them individually towards the end of rehearsal, just for 10 minutes or so. Tell them the goal of the warm-up is *what they need* to settle into the character and the world of the play. It is also for them to focus on technical issues they have problems with: diction within a certain passage or the body of the character, for instance. Find out what they have built on through rehearsal: character journey, gesture, centre, archetype or Personal Atmosphere. They want to focus on something in this individual warm-up which just summons up the character for them. Tell them to find an ending to their personal warm-up.

Chapter Eighteen
A Final Word

Our revels now are ended
The Tempest: Act Four, Scene One

Directing a play with a group of young people requires a spectacular number of skills: director; acting teacher; voice coach; administrator; limit-setter; counsellor; manager. All of these roles exist for a director at all levels, it is simply that with professional actors there are different emphases. This myriad skill set needs to be taught to would-be directors if they are considering directing as a career. A stint at performing is vital too. (If you have not performed yourself, then consider it. You will be much more help to your young actors.)

In the educational setting, a production allows the teacher/director increased contact time. An intensive period for a production, working with students every day for a few weeks, bears out the reality that contact time counts; that the amount of time you spend on the show gives the work depth and rapid individual progress can be made. Working intensively and for more time produces a powerful learning experience.

I have tried to show in this book that Shakespeare is nowhere near as difficult as you might think. His plays can be very accessible if you follow the right paths for your group. Remember that Shakespeare wrote his plays for all walks of life, and his work is direct and involving. I hope you have found some useful suggestions and approaches to exploring his work, whether you are working with youth theatre or undergraduate actors, doing workshops, furthering an understanding of the text, exploring themes and characters, devising performances, or creating a full production.

'Be not afeard'

'Be not afeard,' says Caliban to his team in Act Three of *The Tempest*. This is good advice for all of us working on Shakespeare with young people: do not be afraid of Shakespeare; do not be afraid of the language; do not intellectualise but explore the language for the most part viscerally and in the body. If you are doing a production, play the drama for all it is worth; respect the views of your young actors but have a view yourself and always give them as much help as you can. Build bridges between the text and your group effectively, and together you can share these discoveries with the audience; that way you will create an accessible and exciting experience for everyone.

Appendices

Bibliography

Shakespeare's Plays

All quotations and line numbers have been taken from the 'Arden 3' Shakespeare series.

A Midsummer Night's Dream, ed. Sukanta Chaudhuri (2017)

Hamlet, ed. Ann Thompson and Neil Taylor (2006)

Henry V, ed. T. W. Craik (1995)

Macbeth, ed. Sandra Clark and Pamela Mason (2015)

Romeo and Juliet, ed. René Weis (2012)

The Tempest, ed. Virginia Mason Vaughan and Alden T. Vaughan (1999)

Twelfth Night, ed. Keir Elam (2008)

Other Works Cited and Further Reading

Berkoff, Steven, *I Am Hamlet* (Faber, 1989)

Brook, Peter, *The Empty Space* (Penguin Books, 1968)

Brook, Peter, *Evoking (and Forgetting!) Shakespeare* (Nick Hern Books, 1998)

Callery, Dymphna, *Through the Body: A Practical Guide to Physical Theatre* (Nick Hern Books, 2001)

Chamberlain, Franc, *Michael Chekhov* (Routledge, 2004: revised edition 2018)

Chekhov, Michael, *Lessons for the Professional Actor* (PAJ Publications, 1985)

Chekhov, Michael, *On the Technique of Acting* (Harper Collins, 1991)

Chekhov, Michael, *To the Actor: On the Technique of Acting* (Routledge, 2002)

Hafler, Max, *Teaching Voice: Workshops for Young Performers* (Nick Hern Books, 2016)

Hutchings, Mark and Bromham, A.A., *Middleton and his Collaborators* (Northcote House Publishers, 2008)

Knight, G. Wilson, *The Imperial Theme* (1931; Methuen, 2002)

Petit, Lenard, *The Michael Chekhov Handbook* (Routledge, 2009; second edition 2019)

Zinder, David, *Body Voice Imagination ImageWork Training and the Chekhov Technique* (Routledge, 2009)

See also my blog, www.maxhafler.wordpress.com, which includes my thoughts on Michael Chekhov training, applied drama, directing and acting.

Glossary of Terms
from Michael Chekhov Technique

Below is a list and definitions of the Chekhov terms which appear in this book. They are my take on these terms, so may differ slightly from those of others.

Archetypes

An archetype is an essence, an energy which permeates the character. It is not a stereotype, nor is it the whole story of the character. The archetype might be something the character does in the play, for instance how they behave. Lucio, for instance, in *Measure for Measure* might be considered as someone who behaves in a cowardly manner, so an actor playing him might explore the archetype of 'The Coward'. On the other hand, an archetype can be used for exploring something the character *is* that we have not experienced: a 'Soldier', a 'King', a 'Wizard', a 'Murderer' or a 'Princess'. This is very relevant in Shakespeare, where we are exploring characters in a world that is so different from ours.

Centres

The centre may be the soul or the engine of the character. It powers everything they do, what they do and how they do it. It is the source of their quest. The centre can be anything: an image, a colour, a shape; it can have any texture, any size and can be placed anywhere in the body, or even beyond it. An example of this might be Juliet who might have a lighted candle as a centre: something that is fiery but also pure and clear. This idea of character centre is an incredibly powerful tool to transform the actor.

Feeling of Ease

Chekhov never liked the term 'relax'. And, if you think about it, the first thing that happens when we hear that instruction is that we tense up, and then start to ask ourselves whether we are relaxed... which makes us more tense! Instead, he suggested that we move with a Feeling of Ease. He said that all performance should come with this ease.

Feeling of Form

The Feeling of Form respects the idea that everything we do is 'a little piece of art' which has its own completeness. Every movement, every exercise and every scene has a beginning, middle and an end, or you might call it an impulse, a sustaining and a completion. Notice how much better a young actor's work is when he respects this simple concept.

Feeling of the Whole

This applies more to the whole play or to entire scenes; basically we are following the beginning/middle/end concept, but now in its entirety. It considers how things transform in a play from one thing to the other, that there is always a movement, and that, as artists, we understand what that movement is, can experience it, and let our character experience and act within it. This concept encourages us to treat a play like a piece of music, flowing and developing from one movement to another. It is incredibly useful when devising a piece.

General Atmosphere

Chekhov believed the General Atmosphere of a play or scene was the oxygen of the theatrical experience. He believed that every place and situation has an atmosphere, every scene, every play; that every person in a scene is responding to that atmosphere in one way or another. It is one of the most powerful things the cast has to generate and transmit. It is palpable but cannot be easily put into words or discussed around a table. It is where the characters find themselves, and what influences their actions and feelings. For instance, there might be a General Atmosphere of *darkness*, or of *mist*, or of a *tunnel* or *electricity*, or of *grief*. The choice you make provokes radical change.

Personal Atmosphere

We all carry our own Personal Atmosphere around with us. It might be what we use to protect ourselves from harm. It might be a mood, an assumption of what we are, or a response by other people. It might be a shell: a way to retain our prejudices. It might be the smell of cheap perfume, or the smell of the sea. Where the Personal and General Atmosphere interact is always an interesting place.

Polarities

As part of the Feeling of the Whole (see above), we need to experience polarities. Chekhov said that, in a play, we journeyed from one state into its opposite; from Life to Death, for example. As a broad sweep this idea contains a deep truth. It means the play involves transformation. In *Twelfth Night*, for instance, the play begins with an atmosphere of longing and bereavement; it ends to some degree with the joyful resolution of love. It has that trajectory. This does not mean that Antonio, Sir Andrew and Malvolio (whose romantic dreams are not fulfilled) need to be happy at the end, but their sadness and concerns are swept away. If we choose to focus on the unhappy characters we are making a statement which changes the play's trajectory. With regard to the characters, each needs to be on a journey which embraces polarity. Olivia, in *Twelfth Night* changes from a woman embracing death to someone ready to embrace life. You might say she moves from Death to Life.

Anchoring these polarities within the character's journey can be incredibly useful.

Psychological Gesture

This is where we ask the question, 'What is the character doing and how are they doing it?' Psychological Gesture is the physicalising of intention, the use of the body to seek sensation in order to provoke emotion and action. For example: are they *reaching*, *pulling*, *piercing* or *embracing* the other character or characters, and if so *how* are they making that Psychological Gesture? We use gestures like these to explore what the character is doing in a scene, the whole play or in a moment. In something as highly poetic as Shakespeare we might use a gesture to explore a single image or even a word.

Psycho-Physical Training

Michael Chekhov's training is *psycho-physical*. This means more or less what it says: that through the body we can access a whole range of psychology, sensations and emotions for the character. He says, 'Our primary aim is to penetrate all parts of the body with psychological vibrations.' In other words, if you move sadly, you feel sad; if you move angrily, you feel angry. It is instant: magical.

Qualities of Movement

There are four basic qualities of movement, all of which we have used in exercises in this book: *floating* (water), *flying* (air), *radiating* (fire) and *moulding* (earth). Learning to open your body to these qualities offers the actor a wide range of sensations, enabling discovery of the character.

Radiating and Receiving

Radiating is a term for the energy that radiates from the performer to the other actors and the audience; receiving is when you allow that energy to influence and move you. It is not 'listening', though it includes it; nor is it only 'being in the moment'. It is taking in a scene partner holistically and becoming sensitive to the energy they are sending you when they are speaking or simply standing still. It allows you to truly respond to what they are giving you. Developing a sensitivity towards this reciprocal movement of energy between people improves not only our acting but all the communications we have in everyday life.

Some Useful Websites and Organisations

Michael Chekhov Technique

There are many organisations teaching Michael Chekhov Technique all over the world. Here are the ones of which I have direct knowledge:

Chekhov Training and Performance Ireland
www.chekhovtrainingandperformanceireland.com

The Michael Chekhov Association
www.michaelchekhov.org

Michael Chekhov Europe
www.michaelchekhoveurope.eu

Chekhov Collective UK
www.chekhovcollectiveuk.co.uk

Further Learning and Organisational Support

National Association of Youth Theatres
www.nayt.org.uk

National Youth Council of Ireland
www.youth.ie

National Youth Theatre
www.nyt.org.uk

Scottish Youth Theatre
www.scottishyouththeatre.org

Ulster Association for Youth Drama
www.uayd.co.uk

Youth Theatre Arts Scotland
www.ytas.org.uk

Youth Theatre Ireland
www.youththeatre.ie

Index of Exercises

www.nickhernbooks.co.uk

facebook.com/nickhernbooks

twitter.com/nickhernbooks